I0150342

What God Meant This World to Be

Our Spiritual and Human Rights

Copyright©2007 Anita DeMeulenaere – All Rights Reserved

Preface

All through history there has been conflict that has governed our country and the world from the beginning of time. Ever since sin came into the world there has been a good vs. evil concept which has driven mankind. There has to be order and rules of conduct to make it possible for man to live along side of his brother. We need to stick together for the greater good.

This country as we know it now was founded on the principles handed down from our fore fathers in The Constitution of the United States. Included in the document is the Bill of Rights and our Declaration of Independence as we broke free from the government and kingship rule of England. We formed our own United States (Colonies) which originated with thirteen.

Our fore fathers also founded this country on the beliefs in the Bible. They made all their decisions praying for God's guidance in the decision making process. I was thinking that we have strayed far left from the original Constitution and the Bible. Today sin is not as clear or are the rights imposed on mankind fair and/or equal. There is something very wrong when it is legal to have an abortion or we can burn the American flag in the name of freedom of speech or freedom to choose. I would never had believed that these issues would even be considered as rights because I believe they are both wrong.

I am going to draw a comparison between the rights of our country and the spiritual rights laid down in the Bible. As I was researching my material I got excited to realize how much they compare. This analogy I will try to bring into comparison as we explore both pieces of history. Both are founded on God and meant to be God inspired. If that were the case, there would not be laws that protect the criminal and not the victim. As we explore this issue, I pray that possibly you will get back to your roots that your country and family were raised on if you were born in the United States. Even the slaves had deep spiritual beliefs even though they could not read or write.

-Anita DeMeulenaere

Contact Information:

Email: mad63@comcast.net

Storefront: www.lulu.com/mad63

Table of Contents

PART 1: OUR SPIRITUAL RIGHTS

CHAPTER 1: **Our Roots as a Christian– Our Fore Fathers**

Our Christian beginning goes back to the beginning of the Bible. It speaks of the creation of the world by God and the beginning of mankind. The world is older than the recordings of the Bible which we calculate to be about six thousand years ago. The Garden of Eden, is where spiritual man and woman was created who are our spiritual heritage. Christianity begins with God and ends with God. The journey can be different for everyone but it is important to know our beginning and how did we come to believe as we do. The Bible is our reference book and we believe it was written under the inspiration of the Holy Spirit. This is why we take so much value in it because it was written by the "Hand of God" through the men and women God choose to bring salvation to mankind.

Our spiritual fore fathers are many. I have listed some who are easily recognized and known. There are many more, as there are many more in the human rights segment. I chose some to the great men in American History. In this segment, I have chosen the great men of our Christian History.

Profile of Adam

We can hardly imagine what it must have been like to be the first and only person on earth. It's one thing for us to be lonely; it was another for Adam, who had never known another human being. He missed much that makes us who we r – he had no childhood, no parents, no family or friends. He had to learn to be human on his own. Fortunately, God didn't let him struggle too long before presenting him with an ideal companion and mate, Eve. Theirs was a complete, innocent, and open oneness, without a hint of shame.

One of Adam's first conversations with his delightful new companion must have been about the rules of the garden. Before God made Eve he had already given Adam complete freedom in the garden, with the responsibility to tend and care for it. But one tree was off limits, the tree of the knowledge of good and evil. Adam did not pause to consider the consequences. He went ahead and ate.

In that moment of small rebellion something large, beautiful, and free was shattered…God's perfect creation. Man was separated fro God by his desire to act on his own. The effect on a plate glass window is the same whether a pebble or a boulder is hurled at it – the thousands of fragments can never be regathered.

In the case of man's sin, however, God already had a plan in motion to overcome the effects of the rebellion. The entire Bible is the story of how that plan unfolds, ultimately leading to God's own visit to earth through his Son, Jesus. His sinless life and death make it possible for God to offer forgiveness to all who want it. Our small and large acts of rebellion prove that we are descendants of Adam. Only by asking forgiveness of Jesus Christ can we become children of God.

Strengths and accomplishments:
- The first zoologist – namer of the animals
- The first landscape architect, placed in the garden to care for it
- Father of the human race
- The first person made in the image of God, and the first human to share an intimate personal relationship with God

Weakness and mistakes:

- Avoided responsibility and blamed others; chose to hide rather than to confront; made excuses rather than admitting the truth
- Greatest mistake; teamed up with Eve to bring sin into the world

Lessons from his life:

- As Adam's descendants, we all reflect to some degree the image of God
- God wants people who, though free to do wrong, choose instead to love him
- We should not blame others for our faults
- We cannot hide from God

Vital statistics:

- Where: Garden of Eden
- Occupation: Caretaker, gardener, farmer
- Relatives: Wife: Eve, Sons: Cain, Abel, Seth, Numerous other children. The only man who never had and earthly mother or father.

Profile of Noah

The story of Noah's life involves not one, but two great and tragic floods. The world in Noah's day was flooded with evil. The number of those who remembered the God of creation, perfection, and love had dwindled to one. Of God's people, only Noah was left. God's response to the severe situation was a 120-year-long last chance, during which he had Noah build a graphic illustration of the message of his life. Nothing like a huge boat on dry land to make a point! For Noah, obedience meant a long-term commitment to a project.

Many of us have trouble sticking to any project, whether or not it is directed by God. It is interesting that the length of Noah's obedience was greater than the lifespan of people today. The only comparable long-term project is our very lives. But perhaps this is one great challenge Noah's life gives us – to live, in acceptance of God's grace, an entire lifetime of obedience and gratitude.

Strengths and accomplishments:

- Only follower of God left in his generation
- Second father of the human race
- Man of patience, consistency, and obedience
- First major shipbuilder

Weakness and mistake:

- Got drunk and embarrassed himself in front of his sons

Lessons from his life:

- God is faithful to those who obey him
- God does not always protect us from trouble, but cares for us in spite of trouble
- Obedience is a long-term commitment
- A man may be faithful, but his sinful nature always travels with him

Vital statistics:

- Where: We're not told how far from the Garden of Eden people had settled
- Occupation: Farmer, shipbuilder, preacher
- Relatives: Grandfather: Methuselah. Father: Lamech. Sons: Ham, Shem, and Japheth.

Profile of Abraham

We all know that there are consequences to any action we take. What we do can set into motion a series of events that may continue long after we're gone. Unfortunately, when we are making a decision most of us think only of the immediate consequences. These are often misleading because they are short-lived.

Abraham had a choice to make. His decision was between setting out with his family and belongings for parts unknown or staying right where he was. He had to decide between the security of what he already had and the uncertainty of traveling under God's direction. All he had to go on was God's promise to guide and bless him. Abraham could hardly have been expected to visualize how much of the future was resting on his decision of whether to go or stay, but his obedience affected the history of the world. His decision to follow God set into motion the development of the nation that God would eventually use as his own when he visited earth himself. When Jesus Christ came to earth, God's promise was fulfilled; through Abraham the entire world was blessed.

You probably don't know the long-term effects of most decisions you make. But shouldn't the fact that there will be long-term results cause you to think carefully and seek God's guidance as you make choices and take action today?

Strengths and accomplishments:
- His faith pleased God
- Became the founder of the Jewish nation
- Was respected by others and was courageous in defending his family at any cost
- Was not only a caring father to his own family, but practiced hospitality to others
- Was a successful and wealthy rancher.
- Usually avoided conflicts, but when they were unavoidable, he allowed his opponent to set the rules for settling the dispute.

Weakness and mistake:

- Under direct pressure, he distorted the truth

Lessons from his life:

- God desires dependence, trust, and faith in him – not faith in our ability to please him
- God's plan from the beginning has been to make himself known to all people

Vital Statistics:

- Where: Born in Ur of the Chaldeans; spent most of his life in the land of Canaan
- Occupation: Wealthy livestock owner
- Relatives: Brothers: Nahor and Haran. Father: Terah. Wife: Sarah. Nephew: Lot. Sons: Ishmael and Isaac
- Contemporaries: Abimelech, Melchizedez

Profile of Isaac

A name carries great authority. It sets you apart. It triggers memories. The sound of it calls you to attention anywhere.

Many Bible names accomplished even more. They were often descriptions of important facts about one's past and hopes for the future. The choice of the name *Isaac,* "he laughs," for Abraham and Sarah's son must have created a variety of feelings in them each time it was spoken. At times it must have recalled their shocked laughter at God's announcement that they would be parents in their old age. At other times, it must have brought back the joyful feelings of receiving their long-awaited answer to prayer for a child. Most important, it was a testimony to God's power in making his promise a reality.

In a family of forceful initiators, Isaac as the quiet, "mind-my-own-business" type unless he was specifically called on to take action. He was the protected only child from the time Sarah got rid of Ishmael until Abraham arranged his marriage to Rebekah

In his own family, Isaac had the patriarchal position, but Rebekah had the power. Rather than stand his ground, Isaac found it easier to compromise or lie to avoid confrontations.

In spite of these shortcomings, Isaac was part of God's plan. The model his father gave him included a great gift of faith in the one true God. God's promise to create a great nation through which he would bless the world was passed on by Isaac to his twin sons.

It is usually not hard to identify with Isaac in his weaknesses. But consider for a moment that God works through people in spite of their short comings and, often, through them. As you pray, put into words your desire to be available to God. You will discover that his willingness to use you is even greater than your desire to be used.

Strengths and accomplishments:

- He was the miracle child born to Sarah and Abraham when she was 90 years old and he was 100
- He was the first descendant in fulfillment of God's promise to Abraham
- He seems to have been a caring and consistent husband, at least until his sons are born
- He demonstrated great patience

Weaknesses and mistakes:

- Under pressure he tended to lie
- In conflict he sought to avoid confrontation
- He played favorites between his sons and alienated his wife

Lessons from his life:

- Patience often brings rewards
- Both God's plans and his promises are larger than people
- God keeps his promises! He remains faithful though we are often faithless
- Playing favorites is sure to bring family conflict.

Vital statistics:

- Where: The area called the Negev, in the southern part of Palestine, between Kadesh and Shur (Genesis 20:1
- Occupation: Wealthy livestock owner
- Relatives: Parents: Abraham and Sarah. Half brother: Ishmael. Wife: Rebekah. Sons: Jacob and Esau

Profile of Jacob

Abraham, Isaac, and Jacob are among the most significant people in the Old Testament. It is important to realize that this significance is not based upon their personal characters, but upon the character of God. They were all men who earned the grudging respect and even fear of their peers; they were wealthy and powerful, and yet each was capable of lying, deceit, and selfishness. They were not the perfect heroes we might have expected; instead, they were just like us, trying to please God, but often falling short.

Jacob was the third link in God's plan to start a nation from Abraham. The success of the plan was more often in spite of than because of Jacob's life. Before Jacob was born, God promised that his plan would be worked out through Jacob and not his twin brother, Esau. Although Jacob's methods were not always respectable, his skill, determination, and patience have to be admired. As we follow him from birth to death, we are able to see God's work.

Jacob's life had four stages, each marked by a personal encounter with God. In the first stage, Jacob lived up to his name, which means "he grasps the heel" (figuratively, "he deceives"). He grabbed Esau's heel at birth, and by the time he fled from home, he had also grabbed his brother's birthright and blessing. During his flight, God first appeared to him. Not only did God confirm to Jacob his blessing, but he awakened in Jacob a personal knowledge of himself. In the second stage, Jacob experienced life from the other side, being manipulated and deceived by Laban. But there is a curious change; the Jacob of stage one would simply have left Laban, were as the Jacob of stage two, after deciding to leave, waited six years for God's permission. In the third stage, Jacob was in a new role as grabber. This time, by the Jordan River, he grabbed on to God and wouldn't let go. He realized his dependence on the God who had continued to bless him. His relationship to God became essential to his life, and his name was changed to Israel, "he struggles with God." Jacob's last stage of life was to be grabbed – God achieved a firm hold on him. In responding to Joseph's invitation to come to Egypt, Jacob was clearly unwilling to make a move without God's approval.

Can you think of times when God has made himself known to you? Do you allow yourself to meet him as you study his Word? What difference have these experiences made in your life? Are you more like the young Jacob, forcing God to track you down in the desert of your own plans and mistakes? Or are you more like the Jacob who placed his desires and plans before God for his approval before taking any action?

Strengths and accomplishments:
- Father of the 12 tribes of Israel
- Third in the Abrahamic line of God's plan

- Determined, willing to work long and hard for what he wanted
- Good businessman

Weaknesses and mistakes:

- When faced with conflict, relied on his own resources rather than going to God for help
- Tended to accumulate wealth for its own sake

Lessons from his life:

- Security does not lie in the accumulation of goods
- All human intentions and actions – for good or evil – are woven by God into his ongoing plan.

Vital statistics:

- Where: Canaan
- Occupation: Shepherd, livestock owner
- Relatives: Parents; Isaac and Rebekah. Brother: Esau. Father-in-law: Laban. Wives: Rachel and Leah. Twelve sons and one daughter are mentioned in the Bible

Profile of Moses

Some people can't stay out of trouble. When conflict breaks out, they always manage to be nearby. Reaction is their favorite action. This was Moses. He seemed drawn to what needed to be righted. Throughout his life, he was at his finest and his worst responding to the conflicts around him. Even the burning bush experience was an illustration of his character. Having spotted the fire and seen that the bush did not burn, he had to investigate. Whether jumping into a fight to defend a Hebrew slave or trying to referee a struggle between two kinsmen, when Moses saw conflict, he reacted.

Over the years, however, an amazing thing happened to Moses' character. He didn't stop reacting, but rather learned to react correctly. The kaleidoscopic action of each day of leading two million people in the desert was more than enough challenge for Moses' reacting ability. Much of the time he served as a buffer between God and the people. At one moment he had to respond to God's anger at the people's stubbornness and forgetfulness. At another moment he had to react to the people's bickering and forgetfulness. At another moment he had to react to the people's bickering and complaining. At still another moment he had to react to their unjustified attacks on his character.

Leadership often involves reaction. If we want to react with instincts consistent with God's will, we must develop habits of obedience to God. Consistent obedience to God is best developed in times of less stress. Then when stress comes, our natural reaction will be to obey God.

In our age of lowering moral standards, we find it almost impossible to believe that God would punish Moses for the one time he disobeyed outright. What we fail to see, however, is that God did not reject Moses; Moses simply disqualified himself to enter the Promised Land. Personal greatness does not make a person immune to error or its consequences.

In Moses we see an outstanding personality shaped by God. But we must not misunderstand what God did. He did not change who or what Moses was; he did not give Moses new abilities and strengths. Instead, he took Moses' characteristics and molded them until they were suited to his purposes. Does knowing this make a difference in your understanding of God's purpose in your life? He is trying to take what he created in the first place and use it for its intended purposes. The next time you talk with God, don't ask, "What should I change into?" but "How should I use my own abilities and strengths to do your will?"

Strengths and accomplishments:

- Egyptian education; desert training
- Greatest Jewish leader; set the exodus in motion
- Prophet and lawgiver; recorder of the Ten Commandment
- Author of the Pentateuch

Weaknesses and mistakes:

- Failed to enter the promised land because of disobedience to God
- Did not always recognize and use he talents of others

Lessons from his life:

- God prepares, then uses. His timetable is life-sized
- God does his greatest work through frail people

Vital statistics:

- Where: Egypt, Midian, Desert of Sinai
- Occupations: Prince, Shepherd, leader of the Israelites
- Relatives: Sister: Miriam. Brother: Aaron, Wife: Zipporah. Sons: Gershom and Eliezer.

Profile of David

When we think of David, we think: shepherd, poet, giant-killer, king, and ancestor of Jesus – in short, one of the greatest men in the Old Testament. But alongside that list stands another betrayer, liar, adulterer, and murderer. The first list gives qualities we all might like to have; the second, qualities that might be true of any one of us. The Bible makes no effort to hide David's failures. Yet he is remembered and respected for his heart for God. Knowing how much more we share in David's failures that in his greatness, we should be curious to find out what make God refer to David as "a man after my own heart: (Acts 13:22).

David, more than anything else, has an unchangeable belief in the faithful and forgiving nature of God. He was a man who lived with great zest. He sinned many times but he was quick to confess his sins. His confessions were from the heart, and his repentance was genuine. David never took God's forgiveness lightly or his blessing for granted. In return, God never held back from David either his forgiveness or the consequences of his actions. David experienced the joy of forgiveness even when he had to suffer the consequences of his sins.

We tend to get these two reversed. Too often we would rather avoid the consequences than experience forgiveness. Another big difference between us and David is that while he sinned greatly, he did not sin repeatedly. He learned from his mistakes because he accepted the suffering they brought. Often we don't seem to learn from our mistakes or the consequences that result from those mistakes. What changes would it take for God to find this kind of obedience in you?

Strengths and accomplishments:

- Greatest king of Israel
- Ancestor of Jesus Christ
- Listed in the Hall of Faith in Hebrews 11
- A man described by God himself as a man after his own heart

Weaknesses and mistakes:

- Committed adultery with Bathsheba
- Arranged the murder of Uriah, Bathsheba's husband
- Directly disobeyed God in taking a census of the people
- Did not deal decisively with the sins of his children

Lessons from his life:

- Willingness to honestly admit our mistakes is the first step in dealing with them

- Forgiveness does not remove the consequences of sin
- God greatly desires our complete trust and worship

Vital statistics:

- Where: Bethlehem, Jerusalem
- Occupation: Shepherd, musician, poet, soldier, king
- Relatives: Father: Jesse. Wives; included Michal, Ahinoam, Bathsheba, Abigail. Sons: included Absalom, Amnon, Solomon, Adonijah. Daughters: included Tamar. Seven brothers
- Contemporaries: Saul, Jonathan, Samuel, Nathan

Profile of Mary

Motherhood is a painful privilege. Young Mary of Nazareth had the unique privilege of being mother to the very Son of God. Yet the pains and pleasures of her motherhood can be understood by mothers everywhere. Mary was the only human present at Jesus' birth who also witnessed his death. She saw him arrive as her baby son, and she watched him die as her Savior.

Until Gabriel's unexpected visit, Mary's life was quite satisfactory. She had recently become engaged to a carpenter, Joseph, and was anticipating married life. But her life was about to change forever.

Angels don't usually make appointments before visiting. As if she were being congratulated for winning the grand prize in a contest she had never entered. Mary found the angel's greeting puzzling and his presence frightening. What she heard next was the news almost every woman in Israel hoped to hear – that her child would be the Messiah, God's promised Savior. Mary did not doubt the message, but rather asked how pregnancy would be possible. Gabriel told her the baby would be God's Son. Her answer was the one God waits in vain to hear from so many other people: "I am the Lord's servant…May

it be to me as you have said" (Luke 1:38). Later, her song of joy shows us how well she knew God, for her thoughts were filled with his words from the Old Testament.

Within eight days of his birth, Jesus was taken to the temple to be dedicated to God. There Joseph and Mary were met by two devout people, Simeon and Anna, who recognized the child as the Messiah and praised God. Simeon directed some words to Mary that must have come to her mind many times in the years that followed. "A sword will pierce your own soul" (Luke 2:35). A big part of her painful privilege of motherhood would be to see her son rejected and crucified by the people he came to save.

We can imagine that even if she had known all she would suffer as Jesus' mother, Mary would still have given the same response. Are you, like Mary, available to be used by God?

Strengths and accomplishments:

- The mother of Jesus, the Messiah
- The one human who was with Jesus from birth to death
- Willing to be available to God
- Knew and applied Old Testament Scriptures

Lessons from her life:

- God's best servants are often ordinary people available to him
- God's plans involve extraordinary events in ordinary people's lives
- A person's character is revealed by his or her response to the unexpected

Vital statistics:

- Where: Nazareth, Bethlehem
- Occupation: Homemaker
- Relatives: Husband: Joseph. Relatives: Zechariah and Elizabeth. Children: Jesus, James, Joseph, Judas, Simon, and daughters

Profile of Joseph

The strength of what we believe is measured by how much we are willing to suffer for those beliefs. Joseph was a man with strong beliefs. He was prepared to do what was right, despite the pain he knew it would cause. But Joseph had another trait – he not only tried to do what was right, he also tried to do it in the right way.

When Mary told Joseph about her pregnancy, Joseph knew the child was not his. His respect for Mary's character and the explanation she gave him, as well as her attitude toward the expected child, must have made it hard to think his bride had done something wrong. Still, someone else was the child's father – and it was mind-boggling to accept that the "someone else" was God.

Joseph decided he had to break the engagement, but he was determined to do it in a way that would not cause public shame to Mary. He intended to act with justice and love.

At this point, God sent a messenger to Joseph to confirm Mary's story and open another way of obedience for Joseph – to take Mary as his wife. Joseph obeyed God, married Mary and honored her virginity until the baby was born.

We do not know how long Joseph lived his role as Jesus' earthly father – he is last mentioned when Jesus was 12 years old. But Joseph trained his son in the trade of carpentry, make sure he had good spiritual training in Nazareth, and took the whole family on the yearly trip to Jerusalem for the

Passover, which Jesus continued to observe during his adult years.

Joseph knew Jesus was someone special from the moment he heard the angel's words. His strong belief in that fact, and his willingness to follow God's leading, empowered him to be Jesus' chosen earthly father.

Strengths and accomplishments:

- A man of integrity
- A descendant of King David
- Jesus' legal and earthly father
- A person sensitive to God's guidance and willing to do God's will not matter what the consequence.

Lessons from his life:

- God honors integrity
- Social position is of little importance when God chooses to use us
- Being obedient to the guidance we have from God leads to more guidance from him
- Feelings are not accurate measures of the rightness or wrongness of an action

Vital statistics:

- Where: Nazareth, Bethlehem
- Occupation: Carpenter
- Relatives: wife: Mary. Children, James, Joses, Judas, Simon, and daughters
- Contemporaries: Herod the Great. John the Baptist. Simeon, Anna

Profile of John the Baptist

There's no getting around it – John the Baptist was unique. He wore odd clothes and ate strange food and preached an unusual message to the Judeans who went out to the wastelands to see him.

But John did not aim at uniqueness for its own sake. Instead, he aimed at obedience. He knew he had a specific role to play in the world – announcing the coming of the Savior – and he put all his energies into this task. Luke tells us that John was in the desert when God's word of direction came to him. John was ready and waiting. The angel who had announced John's birth to Zechariah had make it clear this child was to be a Nazirite – one set apart for God's service John remained faithful to tat calling.

This wild-looking man had no power or position in the Jewish political system, but he spoke with almost irresistible authority. People were moved by his words because he spoke the truth, challenging them to turn from their sins and baptizing them as a symbol of their repentance. They responded by the hundreds. But even as people crowded to him, he pointed beyond himself; never forgetting that his main role was to announce the coming of the Savior.

The words of truth that moved many to repentance goaded others to resistance and resentment. John even challenged Herod to admit his sin. Herodias, the woman Herod had married illegally, decided to get rid of this desert preacher. Although she was able to have him killed, she was not able to stop his message. The One John had announced was already on the move. John had accomplished his mission.

God has given each of us a purpose for living, and we can trust him to guide us. John did not have the complete Bible as we know it today, but he focused his life on the truth he knew from the available Old Testament Scriptures. Likewise we can discover in God's Word the truths he wants us to know. And as these truths work in us, others will be drawn to him. God can use you in a way he can use no one else. Let him know your willingness to follow him today.

Strengths and accomplishments:

- The God-appointed messenger to announce the arrival of Jesus
- A preacher whose theme was repentance
- A fearless confronter
- Known for his remarkable life-style

Lessons from his life:

- God does not guarantee and easy or safe life to those who serve him
- Doing what God desires is the greatest possible life investment
- Standing for the truth is more important than life itself

Vital statistics:

- Where: Judea
- Occupation: prophet
- Relatives: Father; Zechariah. Mother: Elizabeth. Distant relative: Jesus.
- Contemporaries: Herod, Herodias

Profile of the Some of the Twelve Apostles

The twelve apostles were hand picked by Jesus. I believe He chose each one because they represent character traits in all of us. This is why we can identify with them. Both their strengths and weakness we can see in us so we can relate to the twelve chosen. Jesus loved them in spite of their faults and used their strengths to Glorify God. It was not until Pentecost that the apostles could truly commit to Jesus with the Baptism of the Holy Spirit. This is the only way we can rise above our flesh.

The twelve are as follows:

- Simon called Peter
- Andrew, his brother
- James, the son of Zebedee
- John, his brother
- Phillip
- Bartholomew
- Thomas
- Matthew, the Publican
- James the son of Alphaeus
- Thaddaeus
- Simon, the Caanite
- Judas Iscariot, betrayer of Jesus

I am going to profile only Simon called Peter, Judas Iscariot and Thomas, the doubter of the apostles right now.

Profile of Simon Peter

Jesus' first words to Simon Peter were "Come, follow me: (Mark 1:17). His last words to him were "You must follow me" (John 21:22). Every step of the way between those two challenges, Peter never failed to follow – even though the often stumbled.

When Jesus entered Peter's life, this plain fisherman became a new person with new goals and new priorities. He did not become a perfect person, however, and he never stopped being Simon Peter. We may wonder what Jesus saw in Simon that made him greet this potential disciple with a new name, Peter – the rock." Impulsive peter certainly didn't act like a rock much of the time. But when Jesus chose his followers, he wasn't looking for models; he was looking for real people. He chose people who could be changed by his love, and then he sent them out to communicate that his acceptance was available to anyone – even to those who often fail.

We may wonder what Jesus sees in us when he calls us to follow him. But we know Jesus accepted Peter, and, in spite of his failures, Peter went on to do great tings for God. Are you willing to keep following Jesus, ever when you fail?

Strengths and accomplishments:

- Became the recognized leader among Jesus' disciples – one of the inner group of three
- Was the first great voice of the gospel during and after Pentecost
- Probably knew Mark and gave him information for the Gospel of Mark
- Wrote 1 and 2 Peter

Weaknesses and mistakes:

- Often spoke without thinking; was brash and impulsive
- During Jesus' trial, denied three times that he even knew Jesus
- Later found it hard to treat Gentile Christians as equals

Lessons from his life:

- Enthusiasm has to be backed up by faith and understanding, or it fails
- God's faithfulness can compensate for our greatest unfaithfulness
- It is better to be a follower who fails than one who fails to follow

Vital statistics:

- Occupations: Fisherman, disciple
- Relatives: Father: John. Brother: Andrew
- Contemporaries: Jesus, Pilate, Hero

Profile of Judas Iscariot

It is easy to over look the fact that Jesus chose Judas to be his disciple. We may also forget that while Judas betrayed Jesus, all the disciples abandoned him. With the other disciples, Judas shared a persistent misunderstanding of Jesus' mission. They all expected Jesus to make the right political moves. When he kept talking about dying they all felt varying degrees of anger, fear, and disappointment. They didn't understand why they had been chosen if Jesus' mission was doomed to fail.

We don not know the exact motivation behind Judas's betrayal. What is clear is that Judas allowed his desires to place him in a position where Satan could manipulate him. Judas accepted payment to set Jesus up for the religious leaders. He identified Jesus for the guards in the dimly lit Garden of Gethsemane. It is possible that he was trying to force Jesus' hand – would Jesus or would Jesus not rebel against Rome and set us a new political government?

Whatever his plan, though, at some point Judas realized he didn't like the way things were turning out. He tried to undo the evil he had done by returning the money to the priests, but it was too late. The wheels of God's sovereign plan has been set into motion. How sad that Judas ended his life in despair without ever experiencing the gift of reconciliation God could give even to him through Jesus Christ.

Human feelings toward Judas have always been mixed. Some have fervently hated him for his betrayal. Others have pitied him for not realizing what he was doing. A few have tried to make him a hero for his part in ending Jesus' earthy mission. Some have questioned God's fairness in allowing one man to bear such quilt. While there are many feelings about Judas, there are some facts to consider as well. He, by his own choice, betrayed God's Son into the hands of soldiers (Luke 22:48). He was a thief (John 12:6). Jesus knew that Judas's life of evil would not change (John 6:70). Judas's betrayal of Jesus a part of God's sovereign plan (Psalm 41:9; Zechariah 11; 12, 13; Matthew 20:18; 26:20-25; Acts 1:16, 20).

In betraying Jesus, Judas made the greatest mistake in history. But the fact that Jesus knew Judas would betray him doesn't mean that Judas was a puppet of God's will. Judas made the choice. God knew what that choice would be and confirmed it. Judas didn't lose his relationship with Jesus; rather, he never found Jesus in the first place. He is called "doomed to destruction" (John 17:12) because he was never saved.

Judas does us a favor if he makes us think a second time about our commitment to God and the presence of God's Spirit within us. Are we true disciples and followers, or uncommitted pretenders? We can choose despair and death, or we can choose repentance, forgiveness, hope, and eternal life. Judas's betrayal sent Jesus to the cross to guarantee that second choice, our only chance. Will we accept Jesus' free gift, or, like Judas, betray him?

Strengths and accomplishments:

- He was chosen as one of the 12 disciples; the only non-Galilean
- He kept the money bag for the group
- He was able to recognize the evil in his betrayal of Jesus

Weaknesses and mistakes:

- He was greedy (John 12;6)
- He betrayed Jesus

- He committed suicide instead of seeking forgiveness

Lessons from his life:

- Evil plans and motives leave us open to being used by Satan for even greater evil
- The consequences of evil are so devastating that even small lies and little wrongdoings have serious results
- God's plan and his purposes are worked out even in the worst possible events

Vital statistics:

- Where: Possibly from the town of Kerioth
- Occupation: Disciple of Jesus
- Relative: Father: Simon
- Contemporaries: Jesus, Pilate, Herod, the other 11 disciples

Profile of Thomas

Thomas, so often remembered as "Doubting Thomas," deserves to be respected for his faith. He was a doubter, but his doubts had a purpose – he wanted to know the truth. Thomas did not idolize his doubts; he gladly believed when given reasons to do so. He expressed his doubts fully and had them answered completely. Doubting was only his way of responding, not his way of life.

Although our glimpses of Thomas are brief, his character comes through with consistency. He struggled to be faithful to what he knew, despite what he felt. At one point, when it was plain to everyone that Jesus' life was in danger, only Thomas put into words what most were feeling, "Let us also go, that we may die with him" (John 11:16). He did not hesitate to follow Jesus.

We don't know why Thomas was absent the first time Jesus appeared to the disciples after the resurrection, but he was reluctant to believe their witness of Christ's resurrection. Not even ten friends could change his mind!

We can doubt without having to live a doubting way of life. Doubt encourages rethinking. Its purpose is more to sharpen the mind than to change it. Doubt can be used to pose the question, get an answer and push for a decision. But doubt was never meant to be a permanent condition. Doubt is one foot lifted, poised to step forward or backward. There is no motion until the foot comes down.

When you experience doubt, take encouragement from Thomas. He didn't stay in his doubt, but allowed Jesus to bring him to belief. Take encouragement also from the fact that countless other followers of Christ have struggled with doubts. The answers God gave them may help you too. Don't settle into doubts, but move on from them to decision and belief. Find another believer with whom you can share your doubts. Silent doubts rarely find answers.

Strengths and accomplishments:

- One of Jesus' 12 disciples
- Intense both in doubt and belief
- Was a loyal and honest man

Weakness and mistakes:

- Along with the others, abandoned Jesus at his arrest
- Refused to believe the others' claims to have seen Christ and demanded proof
- Struggled with a pessimistic outlook

Lessons from his life:

- Jesus does not reject doubts that are honest and directed toward belief
- Better to doubt out loud than to disbelieve in silence

Vital statistics:

- Where: Galilee, Judea, Samaria
- Occupation: Disciple of Jesus
- Contemporaries: Jesus, other disciples, Herod, Pilate

Profiles of the Authors of the Gospels and Epistles (Letters)

Profile of Matthew

More than any other disciple, Matthew had a clear idea of how much it would cost to follow Jesus, yet he did not hesitate a moment. When he left his tax-collecting booth, he guaranteed himself unemployment. For several of the other disciples, there was always fishing to return to, but for Matthew, there was no turning back.

Two changes happened to Matthew when he decided to follow Jesus. First, Jesus gave him a new life. He not only belonged to a new group; he belonged to the Son of God. He was not just accepting a different way of life; he was now an accepted person. For a despised tax collector, that change must have been wonderful! Second, Jesus gave Matthew a new purpose for his skills. When he followed Jesus, the only tool from his past job that he carried with him was his pen. From the beginning, God had made him a record-keeper. Jesus' call eventually allowed him to put his skills to their fines work. Matthew was a keen observer, and he undoubtedly recorded what he saw going on around him. The Gospel that bears his name came as a result.

Matthew's experience points out that each of us, from the beginning, are one of God's works in progress. Much of what God has for us he gives long before we are able to consciously respond to him. He trusts us with skills and abilities ahead of schedule. He has made us each capable of being his servant. When we trust him with what he has given us, we begin a life of real adventure. Matthew couldn't have known that God would use the very skills he had sharpened as a tax collector to record the greatest story ever recognized Jesus saying to you, "Follow me"? What has been your response?

Strengths and accomplishments:

- Was one of Jesus' 12 disciples
- Responded immediately to Jesus' call
- Invited many friends to his home to meet Jesus
- Compiled the Gospel of Matthew
- Clarified for his Jewish audience Jesus' fulfillment of Old Testament prophecies

Lessons from his life:

- Jesus consistently accepted people from every level of society
- Matthew was given a new life, and his God-given skills of record[keeping and attention to detail were given new purpose
- Having been accepted by Jesus, Matthew immediately tried to bring others into contact with Jesus

Vital statistics:

- Where: Capernaum
- Occupations: Tax collector, disciple of Jesus
- Relative: Father: Alphaeus
- Contemporaries: Jesus, Pilate, Herod, other disciples

Profile of (John) Mark

Mistakes are effective teachers. Their consequences have a way of making lessons painfully clear. But those who learn from their mistakes are likely to develop wisdom. John

Mark was a good learner who just needed some time and encouragement.

Mark was eager to do the right thing, but he had trouble staying with a task. In his Gospel, Mark mentions a young man (probably referring to himself) who fled in such fear during Jesus' arrest that he left his clothes behind. This tendency to run was to reappear later when Paul and Barnabas took him as their assistants on their first missionary journey. At their second stop, Mark left them and returned to Jerusalem. It was a decision Paul did not easily accept. In preparing for their second journey two years later, Barnabas again suggested Mark as a traveling companion, but Paul flatly refused. As a result, the team was divided. Barnabas took Mark with him, and Paul chose Silas. Barnabas was patient with Mark, and the young man repaid his investment. Paul and Mark were later reunited, and the older apostle became a close friend of the young disciple.

Mark was a valuable companion to three early Christian leaders – Barnabas, Paul, and Peter. The material in Mark's Gospel seems to have come mostly from Peter. Mark's role as a serving assistant allowed him to be an observer. He heard Peter's accounts of the years with Jesus over and over, and he was one of the first to put Jesus' life in writing.

Barnabus played a key role in Mark's life. He stood beside the young man despite his failure, giving him patient encouragement. Mark challenges us to learn from our mistakes and appreciate the patience of others. Is there a Barnabas in your life you need to thank for his or her encouragement to you?

Strengths and accomplishments:
- Wrote the Gospel of Mark

- He and his mother provided their home as one of the main meeting places for the Christians in Jerusalem
- Persisted beyond his youthful mistakes
- Was an assistant and traveling companion of three of the greatest early missionaries

Weaknesses and mistakes:

- Probably the nameless young man described in the Gospel of Mark who fled in panic when Jesus was arrested
- Left Paul and Barnabas for unknown reasons during the first missionary journey

Lessons for life:

- Personal maturity usually comes from a combination of time and mistakes
- Mistakes are not usually as important as what can be learned from them
- Effective living is not measured as much by what we accomplish as by what we overcome in order to accomplish it
- Encouragement can change a person's life

Vital statistics:

- Where: Jerusalem
- Occupations: Missionary-in-training, Gospel writer, traveling companion
- Relatives: Mother: Mary. Cousin: Barnabas
- Contemporaries: Paul, Peter, Timothy, Luke, Silas

Profile of Luke

One of the essential qualities of a good doctor is compassion. People need to know that their doctor cares. Even if he or she doesn't know what is wrong or isn't sure what to do, real concern is always a doctor's good medicine. Doctor Luke was a person of compassion.

Although we know few facts of his life, Luke has left us a strong impression of himself by what he wrote. In his Gospel, he emphasizes Jesus Christ's compassion. He vividly recorded both the power demonstrated by Christ's life and the care with which Christ treated people. Luke highlighted the relationships Jesus had with women. His writing in Acts is full of sharp verbal pictures of real people caught up in the greatest events of history.

Luke was also a doctor. He had a traveling medical practice as Paul's companion. Since the gospel was often welcomed with whips and stones, the doctor was undoubtedly seldom without patients. It is even possible that Paul's "thorn in the flesh" was some kind of physical ailment that needed Luke's regular attention. Paul deeply appreciated Luke's skills and faithfulness.

God also made special use of Luke as the historian of the early church. Repeatedly, the details of Luke's descriptions have been proven accurate. The first words in his gospel indicate his interest in the truth.

Luke's compassion reflected his Lord's. Luke skill as a doctor helped Paul. His passion for the facts as he recorded the life of Christ, the spread of the early church, and the lives of Christianity's missionaries gives us dependable sources for the basis of our faith. He accomplished all this while staying out of the spotlight. Perhaps his greatest example is the challenge of greatness even when we are not the center of attention.

Strengths and accomplishments:
- A humble, faithful, and useful companion of Paul

- A well-educated and trained physician
- A careful and exact historian
- Writer of both the Gospel of Luke and the book of Acts

Lessons from his life:

- The words we leave behind will be a lasting picture of who we are
- Even the most successful person needs the personal care of others
- Excellence is shown by how we work when no one is noticing.

Vital statistics:

- Where: Probably met Paul in Troas
- Occupations: Doctor, historian, traveling companion
- Contemporaries: Paul, Timothy, Silas, Peter

Profile of John

Being loved is the most powerful motivation in the world! Our ability to love is often shaped by our experience of love. We usually love others as we have been loved.

Some of the greatest statements about God's loving nature were written by a man who experienced God's love in a unique way. John, Jesus' disciple, expressed his relationship to the Son of God by calling himself "the disciple whom Jesus loved" (John 21:20). Although Jesus' love is clearly communicated in all the Gospels, in John's gospel it is a central theme. Because his own experience of Jesus' love was so strong and personal, John was sensitive to those words and actions of Jesus that illustrated how the One who is love loved others.

Jesus knew John fully and loved him fully. He gave John and his brother James the nickname "Sons of Thunder", perhaps from an occasion when the brothers asked Jesus for permission to "call fire down from heaven" (Luke 9:54) on a village that has refused to welcome Jesus and the disciples. In John's Gospel and letters, we see the great God of love, while the thunder of God's justice bursts from the pages of Revelation.

Jesus confronts each of us as he confronted John. We cannot know the depth of Jesus' love unless we are willing to face the fact that he knows us completely. Otherwise we are fooled into believing he must love the people we pretend to be, not the sinners we actually are. John and all the disciples convince us that God is able and willing to accept us as we are. Being aware of God's love is a great motivation for change. His love is not given in exchange for our efforts: his love frees us to really live. Have your accepted that love?

Strengths and accomplishments:

- Before following Jesus, one of John the Baptist's disciples
- One of the 12 disciples and, with Peter and James, one of the inner three, closest to Jesus
- Wrote five New Testament books: the Gospel of John; 1, 2, and 3 John; and Revelation

Weaknesses and mistakes:

- Along with James, shared a tendency to out bursts of selfishness and anger
- Asked for a special position in Jesus' kingdom

Lessons from his life:

- Those who realize how much they are loved are able to love much
- When God changes a life, he does not take away personality characteristics, but puts them to effective use in his service

Vital statistics:

- Occupations: Fisherman, disciple
- Relatives: Father: Zebedee, Mother: Salome. Brother: James
- Contemporaries: Jesus, Pilate, Herod

Profile of Stephen

Around the world, the gospel has most often taken root in places prepared by the blood of martyrs. Before people can give their lives for the gospel, however, they must first live their lives for the gospel. One way God trains his servants is to place them in insignificant positions. Their desire to serve Christ is translated into the reality of serving others. Stephen was an effective administrator and messenger before becoming a martyr.

Stephen was named among the managers of food distribution in the early church. Long before violent persecution broke out against Christians, there was already social ostracism. Jews who accepted Jesus as Messiah were usually cut off from their families. As a result, the believers depended on each other for support. The sharing of homes, food, and resources was both a practical and necessary mark of the early church. Eventually, the number of believers made it necessary to organize the sharing. People were being overlooked. There were complaints. Those chosen to help manage were chosen for their integrity, wisdom, and sensitivity to God.

Stephen, besides being a good administrator, was also a powerful speaker. When confronted in the temple by various antagonistic groups, Stephen's logic in responding was convincing. This is clear from the defense he made before the council. He presented a summary of the Jews' own history and make powerful applications that stung his listeners. During his defense Stephen must have known he was speaking his own death sentence. Members of the council could not stand to have their evil motives exposed. They stoned him to death while he prayed for their forgiveness. His final words show how much like Jesus he had become in a short time. His death had a lasting impact on young Saul (Paul) of Tarsus, who would move from being a violent persecutor of Christians to being one of the greatest champions of the gospel the church has known.

Stephen's life is a continual challenge to all Christians. Because he was the first to die for the faith, his sacrifice raises questions: How many risks do we take in being Jesus' followers? Would we be willing to die for him? Are we really willing to live for him?

Strengths and accomplishments:
- One of seven leaders chosen to supervise food distribution to the needy in the early church
- Known for his spiritual qualities of faith, wisdom, grace, and power, and for the Spirit's presence in his life
- Outstanding leader, teacher, and debater
- First to give his life for the gospel

Lessons from his life:
- Striving for excellence in small assignments prepares one for greater responsibilities
- Real understanding of God always leads to practical and compassionate actions toward people

Vital statistics:
- Church responsibilities: Deacon – distributing food to the needy
- Contemporaries: Paul, Caiaphas, Gamaliel, the apostles

Profile of Paul

No person, apart from Jesus himself, shaped the history of Christianity like the apostle Paul. Even before he was a believer, his actions were significant. His frenzied persecution of Christians following Stephen's death got the church started in obeying Christ's final command to take the gospel worldwide. Paul's personal encounter with Jesus changed his life. He never lost his fierce intensity, but from then on it was channeled for the gospel.

Paul was very religious. His training under Gamaliel was the finest available. His intentions and efforts were sincere. He was a good Pharisee, who knew the Bible and sincerely believed that this Christian movement was dangerous to Judaism. Thus Paul hated the Christian faith and persecuted Christians without mercy.

Paul got permission to travel to Damascus to capture Christians and bring them back to Jerusalem. But God stopped him in his hurried tracks on the Damascus road. Paul personally met Jesus Christ, and his life was never again the same.

Until Paul's conversion, little has been done about carrying the gospel to non-Jews. Phillip had preached in Samaria and to an Ethiopia man; Cornelius, a Gentile, was converted under Peter; and in Antioch in Syria, some Greeks had joined the believers. When Barnabas was sent from Jerusalem to check on this situation, he went to Tarsus to find Paul and bring him to Antioch, and together they worked among the believers there. They were then sent on a missionary journey, the first of three Paul would take, and that would carry the gospel across the Roman Empire.

The thorny issue of whether Gentile believers had to obey Jewish laws before they could become Christians caused many problems in the early church. Paul worked hard to convince the Jew that Gentiles were acceptable to God. The lives Paul touched were changed and challenged by meeting Christ through him.

God did not waste any part of Paul – his background, his training, his citizenship, his mind, or even his weaknesses. Are you willing to let God do the same for you? You will never know all he can do with you until you allow him to have all that you are!

Strengths and accomplishments:
- Transformed by God from a persecutor of Christians to a preacher for Christ
- Preached for Christ throughout the Roman empire on three missionary journeys
- Wrote letters to various churched, which became part of the New Testament
- Was never afraid to face and issue head-on and deal with it
- Was sensitive to God's leading and, despite his strong personality, always did as God directed
- Is often called the apostle of the Gentiles

Weaknesses and mistakes:
- Witnessed and approved of Stephen's stoning
- Set out to destroy Christianity by persecuting Christians

Lessons for his life:
- The good News is that forgiveness and eternal life are a gift of God's grace received through faith in Christ and available to all people
- Obedience results from a relationship with God, but obedience will never create or earn that relationship
- Real freedom doesn't come until we no longer have to prove our freedom

- God does not waste our time – he will use our past and present so we may serve him with our future

Vital statistics:

- Where: Born in Tarsus, but became a world traveler for Christ
- Occupations: Trained as a Pharisee, learned the tent making trade, served as a missionary
- Contemporaries: Gamaliel, Stephen, the apostles, Luke, Barnabas, Timothy

Profile of Barnabus

Every group needs an "encourager," because everyone needs encouragement at one time or another. However, the value of encouragement is often missed because it tends to be private rather than public. In fact, people most need encouragement when they feel most alone. A man named Joseph was such an encourager that he earned the nickname "Son of Encouragement," or Barnabas, from the Jerusalem Christians.

Barnabas was drawn to people he could encourage, and he as a great help to those around him. It is delightful that wherever Barnabas encouraged Christians, non-Christians flocked to become believers!

Barnabas's actions were crucial to the early church. In a way, we can thank him for most of the New Testament. God used his relationship with Paul at one point and with Mark at another to keep these two men going when either might have failed. Barnabas did wonders with encouragement!

When Paul arrived in Jerusalem for the first time following his conversion, the local Christians were understandably reluctant to welcome him. They thought his story was a trick to capture more Christians. Only Barnabas proved willing to risk his life to meet with Paul and then convince the others that their former enemy was now a vibrant believer in Jesus. We can only wonder what might have happened to Paul without Barnabas.

It was Barnabas who encouraged Mark to go with him and Paul to Antioch. Mark joined them on their first missionary journey, but decided during the trip to return home. Later Barnabas wanted to invite Mark to join them for another journey, but Paul would not agree. As a result, the partners went separate ways, Barnabas with Mark and Paul with Silas. This actually doubled the missionary effort. Barnabas's patient encouragement was confirmed by Mark's eventual effective ministry. Paul and Mark were later reunited in missionary efforts.

As Barnabas's life shows, we are rarely in a situation where there isn't someone we can encourage. Our tendency, however, is to criticize instead. It may be important at times to point out someone's shortcomings, but before we have the right to do this, we must build that person's trust through encouragement. Are you prepared to encourage those with whom you come in contact today?

Strengths and accomplishments:
- One of the first to sell possessions to help the Christians in Jerusalem
- First to travel with Paul as a missionary team
- Was an encourager, as his nickname shows, and thus one of the most quietly influential people in the early days of Christianity
- Called an apostle, although not one of the original 12

Weaknesses and mistake:

- With Peter, temporarily stayed aloof from Gentile believers until Paul corrected him

Lessons from his life:

- Encouragement is one of the most effective ways to help
- Sooner or later, true obedience to God will involve risk
- There is always someone who needs encouragement

Vital statistics:

- Where: Cyprus, Jerusalem, Antioch
- Occupations: Missionary, teacher
- Relatives: aunt: Mary. Cousin: John Mark
- Contemporaries: Peter, Silas, Paul, Herod Agrippa 1

Profile of Timothy

Painful lessons are usually doorways to new opportunities. Even the apostle Paul had much to learn. Shortly after his disappointing experience with John Mark, Paul recruited another eager young man, Timothy, to be his assistant. Paul's intense personality may have been too much for John Mark to handle. It could easily have created the same problem for Timothy. But Paul seems to have learned a lesson in patience from his old friend Barnabas. As a result, Timothy became a son to Paul.

Timothy probably became a Christian after Paul's first missionary visit to Lystra (Acts 16:1-5). Timothy already had solid Jewish training in the Scriptures from his mother and grandmother. By Paul's second visit, Timothy had grown into a respected disciple of Jesus. He did not hesitate to join Paul and Silas on their journey. His willingness to be circumcised as an adult is clearly a mark of his commitment. (Timothy's mixed Greek/Jewish background could have created problems on their missionary journeys, because many of their audiences would be made up of Jews who were concerned about the strict keeping of this tradition. Timothy's submission to the rite of circumcision helped to avoid that potential problem.)

Beyond the tensions created by his mixed racial background, Timothy seemed to struggle with a naturally timid character and sensitivity to his youthfulness. Unfortunately, many who share Timothy's character traits are quickly written off as too great a risk to deserve much responsibility. By God's grace, Paul saw great potential in Timothy, Paul demonstrated his confidence in Timothy by entrusting him with important responsibilities. Paul sent Timothy as his personal representative to Corinth during a particularly tense time (1 Corinthians 4:14-17). Although Timothy was apparently ineffective in that difficult mission, Paul did not give up on him. Timothy continued to travel with Paul.

Our last picture of Timothy comes from the most personal letters in the New Testament: 1 and 2 Timothy. The aging apostle Paul was near the end of his life, but his burning desire to continue his mission had not dimmed. Paul was writing to one of his closest friends – they had traveled, suffered, cried, and laughed together. They shared the intense joy of seeing people respond to the Good News and the agonies of seeing the gospel rejected and distorted. Paul left Timothy in Ephesus to oversee the young church there (1 Timothy 1:3, 4). He wrote to encourage Timothy and give him needed direction. These letters have provided comfort and help to countless other "Timothy's" through the years. When you face a challenge that seems beyond your abilities, read 1 and 2 Timothy, and remember that others have shared your experience.

Strengths and accomplishments:

- Became a believer after Paul's first missionary journey and joined him for his other two journeys
- Was a respected Christian in his hometown
- Was Paul's special representative on several occasions
- Received two personal letters from Paul
- Probably knew Paul better than any other person, becoming like a son to Paul

Weaknesses and mistakes:

- Struggled with a timid and reserved nature
- Allowed others to look down on his youthfulness
- Was apparently unable to correct some of the problems in the church at Corinth when Paul sent him there

Lessons from his life:

- Youthfulness should not be an excuse for ineffectiveness
- Our inadequacies and inabilities should not keep us from being available to God

Vital statistics:

- Where: Lystra
- Occupations: Missionary, pastor
- Relatives: Mother: Eunice. Grandmother: Lois. Greek father
- Contemporaries: Paul, Silas, Luke, Mark, Peter, Barnabas

CHAPTER 2: **Spiritual Government /The Bible**

Every form of truth has to have a basis for its conclusion. We cannot randomly go about saying what we think is right or wrong just because that is how we think and feel. Truth has to have a concrete foundation to be established so that all can build off that foundation to find truth.

As a Christian, our truth comes from the Bible. We believe it is the spoken word of God through His prophets inspired by the Holy Spirit. Whether you agree or not is not the issue. It is the fact the foundation of our faith is based on the Bible. We need a bench mark to decide what to belief in the eyes of God and what man is to do in relationship with each others. Our Human Rights and Our Spiritual Rights have to do with the treatment of each other. Some do it for personal gain and others do it because of spiritually pleasing God. Both have merit to bring peace and harmony, the one will give us earthly reward and the other will give us eternal reward. Either way, God knew man needed rules to follow because if left to his own human nature, he would be self absorbed and do only to please himself.

What is the Bible?

The Bible is the greatest book ever written. In it God Himself speaks to men. It is a book of divine instruction. It offers comfort in sorrow, guidance in perplexity, advice for our problems, rebuke for our sins, and daily inspiration for our every need.

The Bible is not simply one book. It is an entire library of books covering the whole range of literature. It includes history, poetry, drama, biography, prophecy, philosophy, science, and inspirational reading. Little wonder, then, that all or part of the Bible has been translated into more than 1,200 languages, and every year more copies of the Bible are sold than any other single book.

The Bible alone truly answers the greatest questions that men of all ages have asked: "Where have I come from? "Where am I going?" "Why am I here?" "How can I know the truth?" For the Bible reveals the truth about God, explains the origin of man, and explains the age-old problem of sin and suffering.

The great theme of the Bible is the Lord Jesus Christ and His work of redemption for mankind. The person and work of Jesus Christ are promised, prophesied, and pictured in the types and symbols of the Old Testament. In all of His truth and beauty, the Lord Jesus Christ is revealed in the Gospels; and the full meanings of His life, His death, and His resurrection are explained in the Epistles. His glorious coming again to earth in the future is unmistakable foretold in the Book of Revelation. The great purpose of the written Word of God, the Bible, is to reveal the living Word of God, the Lord Jesus Christ (read John1:1-18).

Dr. Wilbur M. smith relates seven great things that the study of the Bible will do for us:

1. The Bible discovers sin and convicts us.
2. The Bible helps cleanse us from the pollutions of sin.
3. The Bible imparts strength.
4. The Bible instructs us in what we are to do.
5. The Bible provides us with a sword for victory over sin.
6. The Bible makes our lives fruitful.
7. The Bible gives us power to pray.

You do not need a whole library of books to study the Bible. The Bible is its own best commentator and interpreter.

With all of the instructive helps that you have in this new Bible, you have a whole lifetime of Bible study.

The Bible is written if two parts. The first if the Old Testament and the second is the New Testament. It is believed to cover the 6,000 years from the Garden of Eden. It is also believed the Moses wrote the first five books of the Bible. The Scribes were to record what was happening and did happen. We believe all scripture in the Bible is inspired by the Holy Spirit and is accurate and true. History does validate the Bible accounts to give even more authority to the Word of God.

The Old Testament "The Promise of the Messiah"

The forms of government in the Bible are described as:

1. <u>Patriarchal</u>. The family being the unit of life, the father as head of the family we the authoritative ruler
2. <u>Theocracy</u>. God was the direct ruler of His people
3. <u>Government by judges</u>. The people forgot God. God chastised tem by selling them into slavery to their enemies. Upon repentance God raised up military chieftains as deliverers.
4. <u>Monarchy</u>. This was begun by the coronation of Saul, reached its height in David and Solomon, and ended with the Babylonian captivity.

The Laws of the Old Testament

Commandments relating to God

In the book of Exodus 20:1-17 (KJV) are listed the Ten Commandments that God gave to Moses; for the Hebrews he led out of Egypt and bondage from slavery. They were written by the Hand of God on Mount Sinai when Moses went up the mountain to seek God and found Him in the burning bush.

1. I am the Lord thy God, which have brought thee out of the land of Egypt, out of the house of bondage.

2. Thou shalt not make unto thee any grave image, or any likeness of any thing that is in heaven above, or that is in the earth beneath, or that is in the water under the earth:

3. Thou shalt not bow down thy self to them, nor serve them: for I the Lord thy God am a jealous God, visiting the iniquity of the fathers upon the children unto the third and fourth generation of them that hate me; And showing mercy unto thousands of them that love me, and keep my commandments.

4. Thou shalt not take the name of the lord thy God in vain; for the Lord will not hold him guiltless that taketh his name in vain.

5. Remember the Sabbath day, to keep it holy. Six days shalt thou labour, and do all they work, but the seventh day is the Sabbath of the Lord thy God. In it thou shalt not do any work, thou, nor they son, nor they daughter, thy manservant, nor thy maidservant, nor thy cattle, nor they stranger that is within thy gates. In six days the Lord made heaven and earth, the sea, and all that in them is, and rested the seventh day; wherefore the Lord blessed the Sabbath day, and hallowed it.

Commandments relating to man

6. Honour thy father and thy mother; that thy days man be long upon the land which the Lord thy God giveth thee.
7. Thou shalt not kill.
8. Thou shalt not commit adultery.
9. Thou shalt not steal.
10. Thou shalt not bear false witness against thy neighbor.

Thou shalt not covet thy neighbor's house; thou shalt not covet thy neighbor's wife, or his manservant, or his maidservant, or his ox, or his ass, or any thing that is thy neighbor's. (KJV)

All the laws are broken down into specifics in the book of Leviticus. Moses appointed the tribe of Levi to be the priests and carry out the duties of the Temple which was portable because of their wandering forty years in the desert. They finally reached the Promised Land, Moses was taken up to Heaven and Joshua took over as the leader of the Hebrew people.

Forgiveness by Works

God was very specific about sin and keeping the law. The consequences were very severe. It was important for any society to maintain order and the ability for human beings to live and work together in harmony. Moses was the first judge to determine decision that had to be made, whether between families, people or situations with livestock. Eventually it got too much for Moses so he appointed Judges to oversee the people and their problems. They also had to keep track of the people and the numbers that were accumulating. The book of Numbers is where the tracking of the people is recorded.

Forgiveness in the Old Testament was by works. You had to work your way into heaven. They had the prophets that did prophesy of the coming of the Messiah; the Savior of the world.

The concept of sacrifice was first seen in the Garden of Eden. After the sin of Adam and Eve, they realized their nakedness and hid from God. As God asked the question why they were hiding, even though He knew, they being ashamed responded to God. God provided a skin from an animal to cover them and this was the first animal sacrifice for sin.

After having to leave the Garden of Eden, God continued to demand a sacrifice for good and a sacrifice for sin. There had to be atonement for what was done. They also offered to God a sacrifice for plenty. They were to give back to God what He had given them an abundance of. Basically, it was their tithe of 10% established right from the beginning.

For the sacrifice of sin, it was the blood that was poured out and offered from an unblemished animal. The Hebrews were sheep herders so the choice of animal was a lamb. This is represented by Jesus being called the Lamb of God. In the laws of sacrifice which the priests did the sacrifice, there are specific laws to follow to be accepted by God. God has refused sacrifices that had a stench in His nostrils.

An expression we use today is that of a scapegoat. This comes from Biblical times when they used a goat to represent sin.

"Aaron is to offer the bull for his own sin offering to make atonement for himself and his household. Then he is to take the two goats and present them before the Lord at the entrance to the Tent of Meeting. He is to cast lots for the two goats – one lot for the Lord and the other for the scapegoat. Aaron shall bring the goat whose lot falls to the Lord and sacrifice it for a sin offering. But the goat chosen by lot as the scapegoat shall be presented alive before the Lord to be used for making atonement by sending it into the desert as a scapegoat. Leviticus 16:6-10 NIV

Between the Old and New Testament

The four hundred years between the prophecy of Malachi and the advent of Christ are frequently described as "silent", but they were in fact crowed with activity. Although no inspired prophet arose in Israel during those centuries, and the Old Testament was regarded as complete, events took place which gave to later Judaism its distinctive ideology and providentially prepared the way for the coming of Christ and the proclamation of His gospel.

A vase shatters, brushed by a careless elbow; a toy breaks, pushed beyond its limit by young fingers; and fabric rips, pulled by strong and angry hands. Spills and rips take time to clean up or repair and money to replace, but far more costly are shattered relationships. Unfaithfulness, untruths, hateful words, and forsaken vows tear delicate personal bonds and inflict wounds not easily healed. Most tragic, however, are broken relationships with God.

God loves perfectly and completely. And his love is a love of action – giving, guiding, and guarding. He is altogether faithful, true to his promises to his chosen people. But consistently they spurn their loving God, breaking the covenant, following other gods, and living for themselves. So the relationship is shattered.

But the breach is not irreparable; all hope is not lost. God can heal and mend and reweave the fabric. Forgiveness is available. And that is grace.

This is the message of Malachi, God's prophet in Jerusalem. His words reminded the Jews, God's chosen nation, of their willful disobedience, beginning with the priests and then including every person . They had shown contempt for God's name, offered false worship, led others into sin, broken God's laws, called evil "good", kept God's tithes and offerings for themselves, and became arrogant. The relationship was broken, and judgment and punishment would be theirs. In the midst of their wickedness, however, there were a faithful few – the remnant – who loved and honored

God. God would shower his blessings upon these men and women.

Malachi paints a stunning picture of Israel's unfaithfulness that clearly shows tem to be worthy of punishment, but woven throughout this message is hope – the possibility of forgiveness. This is beautifully express in 4:2 – *"But for you who revere my name, the sun of righteousness will rise with healing in its wings. And you will go out and leap like calves released from the stall"*.

Malachi concludes with a promise of the coming of "the prophet Elijah", who will offer God's forgiveness to all people through repentance and faith.

The book of Malachi forms a bridge between the Old Testament and the New Testament. If you would read the book of Malachi, you would see yourself as the recipient of this word of God to his people. Evaluate the depth of your commitment, the sincerity of your worship, and the direction of your life. Then allow God to restore your relationship with him through his love and forgiveness.

The Scarlet Thread

The Bible is a book of redemption. It is that or nothing at all. It is not merely a book of history, or of science, or of anthropology, or of cosmogony. It is a book of salvation and deliverance for lost mankind.

The idea in the word *redemption* is twofold: it refers to deliverance; and it refers to the price paid for that deliverance, a ransom. We are redeemed form the penalty of sin, from the power of Satan and evil, by the price Jesus paid on the cross for us; and we are redeemed to a new freedom from sin, a new relationship to God, and a new life of love by the appropriation of that atonement for our sins.

The whole of the Bible, whether the Old Testament or the New Testament, looks to the mighty, redemptive atonement of Christ. His blood sacrifice is the ransom paid for our deliverance. He took our sinful nature upon Himself in order that He might satisfy the demands of the law. His sacrifice is accepted as the payment for the debt the sinner owes to God, and His death is accepted as the full payment for man's deliverance.

Our Lord's redemptive work for us is threefold: first, it is closely associated with forgiveness, since we receive forgiveness through the redemptive price of Christ's death. Second, it involves justification, since the deliverance establishes us in a restored position of favor before God. Third, it promises final deliverance from the power of sin at the coming of the Lord. This redemption is "The Scarlet Thread."

The New Testament "The Arrival of the Messiah, Jesus"

1. <u>Birth and Preparation of Jesus, The King</u>

The people of Israel were waiting for the Messiah, their king. Matthew begins his book (the first book of the New Testament) by showing how Jesus Christ was a descendant of David. But Matthew goes on to show that God did not send Jesus to be an earthly king, but a heavenly king. His kingdom would be much greater than David's because it would never end. Even at Jesus' birth, many recognized him as a king. Herod, the ruler, as well as Satan, was afraid of Jesus' kingship and tried to stop him, but others worshiped him and brought royal gifts. We must be willing to recognize Jesus for who he really is and worship him as king of our lives.

2. **Message and Ministry of Jesus, the King**

Jesus gave the Sermon on the Mount, directions for living in his kingdom. He also told many parables about the difference between his kingdom and the kingdoms of earth. Forgiveness, peace, and putting others first are some of the characteristics that make one great in the future kingdom of God. And to be great in God's kingdom, we must live by God's standards right now. Jesus came to show us how to live as faithful subjects in his kingdom.

3. **Death and Resurrection of Jesus, The King.**

Jesus was formally presented to the nation of Israel, but rejected. How strange for the king to be accused, arrested, and crucified. But Jesus demonstrated his power even over death through his resurrection, and gained access for us into his kingdom. With all this evidence that Jesus is God's Son, we, too, should accept him as our Lord.

CHAPTER 3: **The Bible the Inspired Word of God**

As a Christian we believe that the bible is the inspired word of God. It was written by man, but the Holy Spirit gave the words to those who wrote the bible.

God would never want us to follow the bible if it were not His words we are to follow. He is God, and by the character of God, we know the bible has to be truth. Truth only has value if it is true.

The bible is our road map to heaven and our relationships with our brothers and sisters here on earth. Just knowing what the bible says is not enough. You have to believe that what it says is the word of God.

Believing in God is the answer. That is the only thing that matters. The bible tells us what we need to do. It is our faith in believing that what God says is true and if we do what the bible tells us too, we will go to heaven.

Love God

In the New Testament God is specific about what He calls the New Commandments. They are love the Lord your God with you whole heart and love your neighbor as you love yourself. On these two commandments give us all of what God wants for us so we do spend eternity with Him.

We cannot go any farther until we acknowledge God, that He is real, and that He must come first in our lives. This relationship has to be natural and a way of life just as your relationship with your mate. You have to learn to love Him, trust Him, depend on Him and live for His approval of your life. With that knowledge ever so present in my mind, my spirit has a chance to grow, develop, mature and life looks different. I see life through the eyes of God and not the eyes of the world. I believe God wants us to continue seeing life through the eyes of a child, simple, secure and comfortable.

Learn to Know Him

Putting God first is a journey that takes a lifetime. We think we are and then something happens that sets us back. As we go through our daily life, so many obstacles challenge us. We set God back and try to do whatever on our own. We have to learn to know God so we can make Him the center of our lives. In order to know Him, we have to learn about the character of God: *the total of qualities making up an individual and moral excellence...*

The bible is the one and only place to learn the truth of God's character. All through the bible, verse after verse, tells of how God dealt with His people through love, kindness, mercy, discipline, and forgiveness. God's actions were a sign of divine character. His faithfulness and being true to His word, shows how we can trust Him and desire to put Him first in our lives.

Another way to know who God is attend church. Attending a bible believing, bible teaching church; listening to the preacher and service praising; and regular attendance will all open the doorway to an opportunity of knowing God at a personal level. Even the smallest bible study group can aid you in finding a relationship with God through studying scripture, learning how to pray, and focusing on the truths of scripture.

Communication between you and God is paramount when it comes to knowing Him. It is no different than wanting to get to know anyone else better, especially if it is someone you want to spend your life together. And the awesome thing is, God desires nothing more than for you to communicate every heartfelt desire, every life long quest, and every painful journey with Him.

Christian fellowship is also a key factor in knowing God. Fellowship is time you learn of how others relate to God, as well as, how God had directly affected their life. Their struggles and triumphants are what you need to know so that when you are faced with adversity, you have known how others have struggled and how God has carried them through. You are experiencing His faithfulness. The relationship you develop with Christian friends and with their desire for you to succeed is what fellowship is all about. The caring and the kindness along with prayer are the tools for your growth and getting to know you can trust God with all your heart.

Learn to Love Him

Learning to love God is no different from learning to love your mate or your children. There is something that tells you inside, whether instinct or knowledge of the person, what you want of this person. Your children are an automatic love at first sight. There is a sense of knowing this person is right, and so it is with God. We are born with a sense of God and then through knowledge and experience, we learn of the reality of God. This sense of 'just knowing' is thought to pass from generation to generation or acquired from some other source, but God is real.

When we develop a relationship with God, we are developing the assurance of His existence. We can start by praising and worshipping Him in church. Giving praise is what we are saying to God to thank Him and giving worship is what God deserves from us. When we do that, the love we feel for God starts to grow. The more you praise and worship, the more His joy is fulfilling. He yearns for the praise and worship of His children. Only God deserves praise and worship. We do not put anything before God. This is His commandment.

When you learn to give yourself to God mentally, physically and emotionally your love relationship has grown. You become whole and ready to accept anything; however, if we truly evaluate life circumstances and how we act we often find we don't truly love God first. Whether you are single or married, something comes up that validates a sense that you are not 'complete'.

It is common for us to put ourselves or someone else before God. It is not intentional, but we do it because we always have. The moment things are happening, you have to put yourself in a place of accountability and think…"Is this what God would do?", or "Would God want me to do this, or wait on Him?"

Saying "NO" is often so hard but you need to put God first with any decision. God always answers prayer. Sometimes it is "YES", sometimes it is "NO" or sometimes it is "WAIT". Your love for God will grow when you learn to seek His face for the cares, concerns and even joys in your life. "Just keep praising the Lord".

Learn to Live for Him

Learning to live for God is rather simple but not easy to do. Every decision you make, you think about how God would feel about that decision and would it please Him.

You need to know the Bible to know what he expects of us. In the Old Testament, there are the Ten Commandments (Exodus 20), which God gave to His people to let them know what He expected of them. They are basic, loving God and loving your neighbor. You learn how God wants us to treat Him and how we are to treat our neighbor. It is very clear.

Living for God is a way of life. God would never leave us here without help He knows we are weak but with Him, we are strong. He left the Holy Spirit here for us to be our comforter, guide, and our help. The Holy Spirit is our instructor and he teaches each of us about the things of God; what God wants for us; and how God would react. I am certain you have experienced that 'gut wrenching experience' that just grabs your whole inner being and makes you feel uncomfortable. That sensation my friend is the Holy Spirit!

If we listen and act upon the warning, we will be all right. We are living for God, and listening to the Holy Spirit. If we ignore that feeling, proceed with what we know is wrong, than we are not living for God. Experience will make you realize that following God is the only way to be happy and develop a relationship with Him. Putting Him first will bring your relationship to where you will know, love and live for Him even better.

Love your Neighbor

My neighbor is anyone in this world. It includes your family, your co-workers, the people in the store, anywhere you go no matter where you go, that is your neighbor. No matter how beautiful or how unpleasant, this is your neighbor.

In the New Testament, God had two commandments:

1. Love God with all your heart.
2. Love your neighbor as yourself.

We should be able to keep two commandments, or we think we should; however, what if that neighbor caused you pain or hurt one of your own. What if that neighbor is a thief and steals from you, or vandalized your property? What if that neighbor had a disease that was unpleasant and they asked you to care for them? What if the two people you trusted like your mother and father, mentally, physically, and/or emotionally abused you as a child? What if your best friend betrayed a trust you had that was to be confidential? What if your boyfriend or girlfriend starting spreading rumors that we not true? What if someone was so hurtful, started spreading half-truths or rumors about you, and destroyed your reputation with false testimonies? What if you found out that someone you would trust with your life had violated that trust and caused you terrible pain?

What Is My Role

It might be easy to love my neighbor if they were a nice person, but what if they are the ones that hurt you. Our role in learning to love is learning to put into practice what He tells us to do. We act out of love of God, not out of our feelings. It is practicing obedience, not whether I want to or not. If you have to force yourself at first, it does get easier. God looks at the intentions of the heart, and the Holy Spirit will give you the courage. You would be so surprised at what you will feel if you do an act of kindness, not because the person deserves it, but because it is pleasing to God.

They are on loan to us in this world from God and we are responsible for their well-being. If they were going to run into a moving car, you would not hesitate to stop them. Sometimes what they want is like them falling in front of a moving car, and if you are afraid to say no, than you are setting them up to fail or worse yet death.

Learning to say "NO" is powerful. The ability to discern with a mature mind builds trusting relationships. Your reputation will be such that people will be able to trust you because you will give the right help if you feel it is appropriate. Just saying "YES" because you are afraid to say "NO" is not loving your neighbor and not being responsible.

CHAPTER 4: **Our Foundation**

Faith to Believe

All through our lives, we put our faith in so many things. From the efficiency of the home we live in, to the job we work at every day, to how we perform in our marriage and with friendships, to the vehicle we are driving, and so much more. We have faith in our family, our children, and our mate. We believe in them because they are ours, either from our bodies or from the parents given to us from God.

We may not like things about them or their behavior, which is not   becoming to society or your value system, but no matter what, we will stick by them. Even in times of abuse, we will continue to believe "they love me". Love is such a strong emotion that can drive a human being in either good direction, or bad. We have faith to believe in them because they are a part of us.

God is a part of us. The part that comes from our spirit is where man communicates with God. Our make up is a body, a soul and a spirit. The body came alive when we were born. Our soul comes alive as we develop into the person and personality we acquire from our parent's genes and our environment. Our spirit comes alive when we give our lives to the Lord and we are born again. The first birth is coming into this world as an infant. The second birth is being in this world, and what God wants of us. We are now His.

Now we need the faith to believe in God. So much of what God speaks to us about is real, especially when it comes to relationships with people. We can see, think and feel because people are here and we live with them everyday.

Believing in God is more difficult because so many of the things of God are not visible. God is a Spirit, which by definition is an immaterial being. That is why He sent Jesus to us to be the example for us that God wants us to know and embrace. He sent Jesus to be the sacrifice we needed to be free of our sins, so we can commune with God, through our spirit. We have to believe what God tells us and it is our faith put in motion, believing what God tells us is true. We cannot see with our eyes but believe with our spirit. It takes time to have faith to believe, no matter what, but each situation that comes up we make a choice to believe God will because He said He would. I choose not to look at what I see, but believe God knows best and the truth. God always answers our prayers. Sometimes yes, sometimes it is no and sometimes it is just to wait. You have to learn, through your walk, to have faith to believe because God is true to His Word.

Learning to Trust

Trust is actually relinquishing control of you and giving power to someone else. Trust is putting your confidence in another person, saying to that person, I have absolute certainty in the trustworthiness of this person. Learning to trust comes from our experiences, especially as a child with our parents.

Our parents are the first encounter and knowledge of security to a child. How those parents take care of that child will determine how secure that child is from the beginning. The care the parents provide for the child will either elevate their self-image or take him or her to a place where they are insecure.

Children learn trust first from their parents. For in a child's mind the thought process follows like this: If they supply my need then, I can trust my parents in my care and keeping. If they disrespect my need, then I begin to learn to mistrust. If my parents who are supposed to love me do not take care of me, then how can I trust those who do not love me? The cycle begins at a very young age and can continue all through life if we do not learn to trust someone.

We learn trust, by example, from someone who does trust a special person. You can see the operation of trust in that person's life. Sometimes through observation, we can learn what trust is and begin to put faith in your relationships with other people. You may be hurt or you may find out that there are trustworthy people. God wants us to trust Him and believe what He tells us is true. He lays out a plan to let us know how to achieve the life that will bring us to a place where we will spend eternity with Him. We have to trust God at His Word. The more we put our trust in God with each situation, the more we build the relationship with Him where trust becomes easier each time.

Prove God's Faithfulness

In any relationship, it takes time to really believe in that person or situation. Many relationships last only for a short time. Those relationships tell us that we cannot put our trust in them and they will not be faithful to the commitment of that association. A connection we have with someone that does have substance and endurance, teaches us the faithfulness of a relationship that will last for more than a season. To link two people tighter in a tight bond will prove to be enduring and trustworthy.

We can prove God's faithfulness by committing our lives to Him and do what he tells us to do in each situation. The reliability of God and His Word will bring us to that point in our lives where we want to spend time with Him. When things are difficult, we need to consistently turn to God so He can prove His faithfulness. Leaving God out is such a mistake because no one loves us more than God does. No one can do more for us than God. Living for God is seeking what He wants for our lives. He will show you, if you give Him your time and a chance. Make God your first choice, not your last.

Sacrifice of Praise

The word sacrifice by definition is, "A loss sustained in the accomplishment of or as the result of something". There are times that the pain we feel is so deep that we have lost a battle we have been trying to sustain for a long time. There are situations that may be momentary, but hurt so deeply. Someone says or does something that is truly unexpected and leaving us with the overwhelming feeling that cuts so deep. In these times, it is so hard to pray because we are so distracted trying to figure out a solution. We feel the answer is up to us.

When praying is so difficult, it is imperative that we do turn to God. We know the scriptures, its promises, and we know they are true. The problem lies in the fact that the hurt we are feeling emotionally drains our ability to remove ourselves and concentrate on God and the answer. No matter what situation happens, we are still and always are human. Our tears are an expression of that human quality that gives us the emotional release needed to help deal with the hurt.

At these times, the best reaction is one that works and is pleasing to God. He knows how inadequate you feel and He knows you know the Word of God. Now, He wants you to praise Him, continually, because He is waiting for you to commune with Him. This may feel like a sacrifice to you, but He knows, at this time, your attention and focus has to turn to Him. The helplessness you are feeling will give you a little control. The sacrifice of praise is not only for God but it is for us to get us through. If we just praise the Lord for who He is and not for anything else, you will begin to feel the load pressing down on you begin to lift. The situation has not changed by our perspective about it, but the time spent praising the Lord has renewed our strength

CHAPTER 5: **Spiritual Beliefs**

Willing to Die for God

Stephen was the first martyr recorded in the book of Acts. He did die for his faith. He believed that if you did believe on Jesus who died on the cross for our salvation, you will go to heaven. This is what the New Testament is all about.

Because Jesus did die on the cross and rose from the grave we have heaven to look forward to. This gift from God is so generous but we may be called to have to give our life for the cause of Christ. I believe in my heart I would do so, but if it really came to that, would I?

Because of the love I have for my Lord, I do believe I would die for Him. It may be painful at the moment, but eternity is worth it. The cause and effect are so worth the opportunity to prove to myself and to my Lord that I am faithful.

Willing to Witness for God

We witness every day of our life by how we act, speak and how we treat others. God sees our heart and the intent of what we do. There are no secrets from God. He sees and knows all, so you are kidding yourself if you think there is such a thing as privacy.

God does not call everyone to be and do the same thing. He just expects us to do what He has called our life to say for the kingdom. There is nothing too small for God. Loving your neighbor could be giving your place in line, giving up your seat for someone else's comfort or just a kind word. He is not asking us to climb the highest mountain just be in your own life what you can.

If you can do more, than do it. There are times in our lives that circumstance change so we can do more. Sometimes we cannot do as much. God expects us to be sensitive to our situation and be intelligent. The opportunity at this particular time may not be good, than you are not expected to.

The Holy Spirit

God would never leave us hanging and unsettled without a way out. His provision has made it possible for us to do and be who He wants us to be. The gift of the Holy Spirit is the part of God left here on earth after Jesus' ascension into heaven. It was Pentecost when the Holy Spirit arrived with the gift of Tongues.

The Holy Spirit gives us the tools that we need, and the wisdom to know what is of God and what is not. The Holy Spirit opens up our spiritual eyes to see as Jesus and be as Jesus is to accomplish in us the things that He has called us to do.

The definition of Holy is, "worthy of worship or veneration; sacred, divine; consecrated or set apart for sacred us; loving according to a highly moral spiritual system". The definition of spirit is, "invisible, nonmaterial part of humans; supernatural being (third person of the Trinity)". The Holy Spirit is divine, invisible and can communicate with us in a supernatural way. It is the part of the Trinity that is inside of us. We cannot see Him but we are aware of His presence or lack of presence. Sin will separate us from the Holy Spirit and out of relationship with God. Jesus would never have left us alone here on earth when He ascended back to His Father in heaven; so He promised us the Holy Spirit and He kept His promise when the Apostles went into Jerusalem after Jesus' ascending. This is where the Holy Spirit came to the Apostles in the upper room.

Filled with the Holy Spirit

God gave us His Holy Spirit because He knew we could not be all He wanted us to be without the Holy Spirit. The Holy Spirit is God within us. Hi attributes minister to us and for us. He lives in us like an idea or thought. You cannot see it but you know it is there. He may be invisible, but He is very real and without the Holy Spirit we could not be and do what the bible tells us. The Holy spirit s there to:

➤ Give us strength

➤ Helps us speak for Christ

➤ Is the Third Person of the Trinity (Mark 1:10-11)

➤ Makes our reform last

➤ Helps us understand the bible

➤ Helps us worship

➤ Urges us toward salvation

➤ Brings deep and lasting peace

➤ Guides us away from wrong places

➤ Gives us power to live the Christian Life

➤ Prays for us

➤ Helps us know God's thoughts

➤ Imparts glory to each believer

➤ Produces "Spiritual Fruit" in us

➤ Helps us discern false teaching

The Gift of the Holy Spirit

The gift of the Holy Spirit, as you can see, was meant to strengthen our flesh so we could become spiritually minded. Without the Holy Spirit we would be just man filled with flesh. Because of the Him, we are man filled with spirit, just as Jesus was. The Holy Spirit that lived in Jesus while here on earth is the same Holy Spirit that lives in us. Jesus knew we needed the Holy Spirit to overcome the flesh as He did. He could not have done and been who He was without the Holy Spirit living in Him. When Jesus was here on earth He put aside His Deity to become flesh. This is why we can look to Jesus as our example and He does not expect more from us than He knows is possible.

As a child of God, we are so blessed to have the Holy Spirit. This is not just a clique', it is the truth. Jesus knew that if we are to be successful, we need spiritual help. More than that, we have to know and understand who the Holy Spirit is and how that Holy Spirit affects our lives. The Holy Spirit is there to minister to us and be what we need.

CHAPTER 6: **Christianity**

Christianity is the belief in the bible and every word written and inspired by God. As a Christian we love and respect the bible because it is the guideline we follow to please God. Jesus is the example set before us. To be a Christian is to be like Jesus.

Be Like Christ

Once we have professed our faith as a Christian, we are expected to be like Jesus. If we fall or faultier, He is there to pick us up. Our belief in Jesus, His dying on the cross for us and then His resurrection, proves His Deity. If we sin, He is there to forgive us if we repent. We do have the knowledge we are going to heaven if we follow what Jesus tells us in His word, the bible.

As a Christian, God does expect us to become a worker for the cause of Christ. He has laid down ten tenants for us to follow to help bring others to the knowledge of Him. He saved us so we would turn to others and tell them the Good News. We are not to sit still and let life go by. We have a job to do.

Commission

Give us a watchword for the hour,

A thrilling word of power;

A battle cry, a flaming breath,

A call to conquest or to death;

A word to rouse the church from rest,

To heed the Master's high behest,

The call is given, ye hosts arise,

The watchword is EVANGELIZE!

To fallen men, a dying race,

Make known the gift of gospel grace.

The world that now in darkness lies,

O Church of Christ, EVANGELIZE!

"And Jesus came and spake unto them, saying, All power is given unto me in heaven and in earth. Go ye therefore, and teach all nations, baptizing them in the name of the Father, and the Son, and of the Holy Ghost: Teaching them to observe all things whatsoever I have commanded you: and, lo, I am with you always, even unto the end of the world. Amen" (Matthew 28:18-20).

"But ye shall receive power, after that the Holy Ghost is come upon you: and ye shall be witnesses unto me both in Jerusalem, and in all Judea, and in Samaria, and unto the uttermost part of the earth" (Acts 1:8).

"So thou, O son of man, I have set thee a watchman unto the house of Israel, therefore thou shalt hear the word at my mouth, and warn them from me. When I say unto the wicked, O wicked man, thou shalt surely die; if thou dost not speak to warn the wicked from his way, that wicked man shall die in his iniquity; but his blood will I require at thine hand: (Ezekiel 33:7, 8)

"Ye are the salt of the earth; but if the salt have lost his savor, wherewith shall it be salted? It is thenceforth good for nothing, but to be cast out, and to be trodden under foot of men. Ye are the light of the world. A city that is set on a hill cannot be hid. Neither do men light a candle, and put it under a bushel, but on a candlestick; nor it giveth light unto all that are in the house. Let your light so shine before men, that they may see your good works, and glorify your Father which is in heaven" (Matthew 5:13-16).

Compassion

The story is told that Martinelli received $25,000 for singing only twice. Paul and Silas sang one night in prison. Their song was not rendered with the skill or harmony of that of Maritnelli's, but its tenderness touched the heart of the keeper of the prison and echoed through the angel-crowed streets of heaven; and the listening King of kings rewarded those who sang with crowds of glory that will gleam in beauty throughout eternal ages.

An immortal soul is beyond all price. There is no trouble too great, no humiliation too deep; not suffering too severe, not love too strong, no labor too hard, no expense too large but that it is worth it, if it is spent in the effort to win a soul.

God loves the soul more than all creation. He fashioned it after His own image, and made it like unto Himself. Every soul has departed form God and gone astray, and God has bought the soul back again wit a price.

That price was in, and through, and by Jesus Christ. God loves the soul with an everlasting love.

Satan hates the soul. In Satan's enmity toward God he is using all his energy, using every snare his utmost cunning, employing every means *with the single purpose of ruining the soul of man.*

When a million eternities have each lived their endless ages and have rolled by into the unthinkable past and time to no more, the soul will still be living, *a conscious personality* endowed with perpetual life reunited with the body.

God has said, "He that winneth souls is wise" (Proverbs 11:30).

The Bible says: "And they that be wise shall shine as the brightness of the firmament; and they that turn many to righteousness as the stars for ever and ever" (Daniel 12:3).

Compassion was the heartbeat of our Savior's ministry. "But when he saw the multitudes, he was moved with compassion on them, because they fainted, and were scattered abroad, as sheep having no shepherd" (Matthew 9:36).

"But thou, O Lord, art a God full of compassion, and gracious, longsuffering, and plenteous in mercy and truth" (Psalm 86:15).

Heaven is geared for redemption. "I say unto you, that likewise joy shall be in heaven over one sinner that repenteth, more than over ninety and nine just persons, which need no repentance" (Luke 16:28).

No man who ever had a glimpse of hell would ever want a fellow human being to go there (see Luke 16:28).

"They that sow in tears shall reap in joy. He that goeth forth and weepeth, bearing precious seed, shall doubtless come again with rejoicing, bringing his sheaves with him" (Psalms 126:5, 6).

Concern

One of the first questions raised in recorded history was, "Am I my brother's keeper?" (Genesis4: 9). *Do I have moral obligations toward others?*

"And I sought for a man among them, that should make up the hedge, and stand in the gap before me for the land, that I should not destroy it: but I found none" (Ezekiel 22:30).

"My sheep wandered through all the mountains, and upon every high hill: yea, my flock was scattered upon all the face of the earth, and none did search or seek after them" (Ezekiel 34:6).

"And if thou draw out thy soul to the hungry, and satisfy the afflicted soul; then shall thy light rise in obscurity and thy darkness be as the noon day" (Isaiah 58:10).

"I say the truth in Christ, I lie not, my conscience also bearing me witness in the Holy Ghost, that I have great heaviness and continual sorrow in my heart. For I could wish that myself were accursed from Christ for my brethren, my kinsmen according to the flesh" (Romans 9:1-3).

Intercession is the way that leads to the winning of souls. No church can prosper without it. No Christian can grow without it. The law of life demands reproduction – that kind should beget kind.

Jesus interceded for each of us. "Therefore will I divide him a portion with the great, and he shall divide the spoil with the strong; because he hath poured out his soul unto death: and he was numbered with the transgressors; and he bare the sin of many, and made intercession for the transgressors" (Isaiah 53:12).

Christ left this command to us: "Pray ye therefore the Lord of the harvest, that he will send forth labourers into his harvest" (Matthew 9:38).

Be the Bible: Stop Reading and Start Being

In order to be the bible, a reflection of God's Word showing in your life, you have to understand the Heart of God and the message He wants for His people. This does not come just by wanting; it has to come with studying, listening and praying. You need to be in the presence of Bible Believing Pastors and Ministers who teach and preach the Word of God. As a student of the Word, you become the teacher fulfilling the Great Commission God has given us to go into all parts of the world and tell them of Him. It begins with certain specifications and desires to learn about God and Who He is.

Know the Character of God

God impressed on me that we come to that place in our lives when we have to start being what God wants us to be. We go from church to church, bible study to bible study, look up scriptures, which are what we need to hear the voice of God. What does God want me to do in this situation or that one, and go to the Bible seeking answers? This is what God wants us to do, but after a long search when God has supplied your answers, He wants you to start "Being the Bible", and live the word He speaks to us.

We may go from preacher to preacher listening for answers. That is what we are supposed to do. We are learning. Then there is graduation day where we put the studies behind us, leave the teachers for those who are still learning, and become what your teaching opened up your eyes to.

To put that much trust in someone, you need to know their character and you need to know how true they are to their character. Do they do what they say should be done? Are they consistent in how they live and how they treat other people? If we find that such a person does have these characteristics, then we can say they have good character. They are someone we could put our trust in, and believe that what they say would be true. It takes time to get to know someone and see if their life lives up to the words they speak. They have a lot of integrity and you respect them and believe that who they say they are is exactly the person you believe them to be.

It is no different from learning about God and getting to know His character. The bible tells us what God wants of us, and it tells us about God. His plan for our lives is so much more than we can even image. The true blessing is that He sent Jesus here to earth so He can be the perfect example of what God wants us to be and how to do that.

Jesus taught us by His life how to be a child of God. Jesus was willing to be everything we need to have a relationship with the Father. When Jesus was here on earth, He was God but became man for us. We would never be able to have any relationship with God because of our human nature. Jesus showed us when He went back to heaven that we need the Holy Spirit and He left Him here for us. Now we are human filled with the Holy Spirit and can commune with God.

Through the life of Jesus, we can observe the character of God. Jesus revealed to us through his actions and speaking in parables that we could do all things if we trust, believe, and have faith in God for our life journey. Jesus never lied, deceived, hurt or did harm to anyone. His life was filled with trials, tribulation, and salvation through prayer and seeking God's will. The greatest gift from Jesus was his death on the cross. No greater love has a man if he lays down his life for his brother. Jesus laid down his life for his enemies.

Jesus had the love that is so powerful that we could never do what He did. God is not asking us to, just love Him and love our neighbor as we love ourselves. Jesus was perfect and while here on earth, he lived with the same spirit in him as we have in us. That is why God never asks of us more than what we can do. He has given us the Holy Spirit to be our guide, our comforter, our teacher and so much more.

When you realize the character of God, and then you learn of the character of God, you have to go one-step further. You have to believe in the character of God. When you believe in the character of God, then you will start being the child he wants you to be.

God Wants Us to Be the Fruit of the Spirit

Galatians 5:22-23, *"But the fruit of the Spirit is love, joy, peace, patience, kindness, goodness, faithfulness, gentleness and self-control. Against such things there* is no *law."*(NIV). "The fruit of the Spirit is the spontaneous work of the Holy Spirit in us. The Spirit produces the character traits that are in the nature of Christ. They are the by-products of Christ's control – we cannot obtain them without His help. If we want the fruit of the Spirit to grow in us, we must join our lives to His. We must know Him, love Him, remember Him, and imitate Him. As a result, we will fulfill the intended purpose of the law - to love God and our neighbors. Which of these qualities do you want the Spirit to produce in you?"(NIV commentary Gal.5: 22-23).

Jesus is the perfect example, and he did posses all these qualities. The Son of God, Jesus Christ, has the same Holy Spirit that dwells in us in Him. What I do know is that there comes a time in our walk with Jesus that He expects us to do just that. It is possible if you release all those things that have held you in bondage, and start being what God wants us to be. He wants us to be love, be joyful, be peaceful, be patient, be kind, be good, be faithful, be gentle and be disciplined (self-control). We have to start doing whether or not we feel like it. Obedience is better than sacrifice. We are to make the first move. Whether the other person responds the way you think they should does not matter. God sees your heart and He knows your level of sincerity.

Walk in the Light

Galatians 5: 24-26 (NIV). "Those who belong to Christ Jesus have crucified the sinful nature with its passions and desires. Since we live by the Spirit, let us keep in step with the Spirit. Let us not become conceited, provoking and envying each other."

When I say walking in the light, another scripture I want to refer to is, 1John1: 5-7(NIV), *"This is the message we have heard from Him and declare to you: God is light: in Him there is no darkness at all. If we claim to have fellowship with Him yet walk in the darkness, we lie and do not live by the truth. But if we walk in the light, His Son purifies us from all sin."* Seeing the light of truth has responsibility we have to respond to, if we expect a deeper walk with the Lord. If we found out something about our children, we would not hesitate to react.

Light represents what is good and darkness represents bad or a place we are not comfortable. We want our life to shine in the light of God's grace. We want our life to be an example of what Jesus was talking about while here on earth. The Old Testament was about law and sacrifice (animal sacrifice). In order to get to heaven you had to be right with God through your good works. Jesus came to save us from all that and in the New Testament it is believing in Jesus, the sacrifice He made dying on the cross and then rose from the grave to prove He was God. Once we believe, then we have to live for Him. Put aside the old man and become new. Get rid of the old nature and put on the nature of Christ.

The time has come when you have to start being the Bible. You are to continue reading God's word, but instead of going here and there, put what you know in practice and be the living word of God. We are to love, be kind, etc. God had revealed this to me a long time ago and it has become a reality. I just remain faithful, do what I feel He wants me to do and go where I believe He wants me to go. My life has to shine as the light of Jesus, not expecting to be perfect as He was, but trying to be the best for Jesus that I can. I have come to feel that I am standing alone with a yellow light around me and I know this is Jesus. He is standing between the outside world and me. He is my all sufficiency, everything I will ever need. He guides me with His light; as I walk in that light through the world, He wants me to show those around me Him (Jesus), by my life. (Open Bible "A Guide to Christian Workers" P.1339, KJV)

CHAPTER 7: **Sand Castles / Bible Analogy**

Some things, like sandcastles, don't survive the changing tides. But love, family, and friendship, just as fragile, have a way of standing against anything. It will take nothing short of a miracle to heal the rift between father and daughter, husband and wife, the past and the present, but a miracle is exactly what is in the works at Star of the Sea Academy. The only question is: Do you believe?

(Sandcastles – Cast library; Google search)

Construction

The mystery of the Sandcastle we can equate with God. Our spiritual Heritage is weaved with God which in itself is a mystery and a miracle.

When we construct our Spiritual life, we need that strong foundation. If we add water to the sand, you have consistency. We will believe that the Bible is the water that holds the sand together. Knowledge is so important so we can believe. Faith is the spiritual water that gives us belief without seeing. Together we have the foundation of Christianity.

The Physics of Sandcastles

July 11,2002: Give a plastic bucket and a shovel to a child, then turn her loose on a beach full of sand. She'll happily toil the day away building the sandcastle to end all sandcastles. It's pure fun. It is also serious physics.

Sandcastles are built from grains – billions of tiny sharp-edged particles that rub and tumble together. The strength of ta sandcastle depends on how the gains interact. What happens when they're wet? How do they respond to a jolt? It's not only beachgoers who are interested; farmers, physicists and engineers want to know, too.

When kids work on a sandcastle, they begin by gathering water from the ocean to wet the sand. Not too much – just enough to make sand stick together without oozing. (Emergency planners: think of predicting a devastating mudslide.) Nest they pack the damp sand into a bucket, and flip it over to create an extra-strong base for a tower (Engineers: think of designing compacted road foundations.)

Kids love to build the towers taller and taller – until a wall suddenly caves and the tower slides into the moat. (Farmers: think of grain in a silo sticking together, then suddenly collapsing and destroying the silo.) They might even decorate the castle by letting watery sand drip from their fingertips, solidifying in place to form odd-looking stalagmites. (Artists: don't forget, physics is beautiful.)

Scientists mostly understand why sand on a beach behaves as it does. Damp sand sticks together because water forms little grain-to-grain bridges. Surface tension – the same force that lets some insects walk on the surface for a pond – acts like rubber bands between the grains. Adding water to damp sand fills spaces between the grains. The bridges vanish and the sand begins to flow more easily.

Experiments have uncovered many mysteries which have uncovered situations that puzzle scientists. They have sent sand experiments into space with interesting results. They have examined below surface sand in an earthquake, finding that the sand liquefies causing a collapse of the foundation. We look at sand as just small particles on the beach to play in, walk on and enjoy running into the water. (More research on www.science.nasa.gov)

Completion

We complete the sandcastle by adding more moist sand. As we construct it, our faith gives us courage to continue building. I have a picture and a goal in mind as my vision is taking form. The more I read the Bible, learn of God and His relationship with us and the purpose for His coming to earth to redeem us. The completion is giving our lives to Christ, living for others and sharing the Word.

The Tide Comes In

The tide comes in (Satan) to shake our foundation. It cannot be shaken if we take the precautions in the first place.

1. Build where the tide cannot reach.

2. Know the Word of God to cast out Satan.

3. Have faith to believe your Sandcastle is stronger than the enemy.

4. Live for God, be in the spirit, have strong relationships to fight the good fight.

Whether it is a sandcastle or some other form you can relate to, it does not matter. What is important is that as long as we live in this world, there will be problems. I have written a poem I would like to share with you.

Sandcastles

We pack tight many grains together
Of the sand on the beach wet with water,
We press; we squeeze to get the proper form
To make a picture of what is in our mind.

I start with an idea of what I want to say
Creating a form which I put on display,
I can pile the wet sand here and there
Step back and see what my mind wants to say.

The idea I have is a castle from the past
With many different rooms and a mote to protect,
As the castle is taking shape from those involved
I picture King Arthur and other great Kings.

My picture comes alive as the castle is almost done
Enjoying the moment I have within,
I have created this magnificent re-creation
A castle from the past which I am intrigued.

Then in an instant a wave rolls in
The tide has come up in its daily routine,
I say goodbye to the castle I built
But the endless sand will be there again.

CHAPTER 8: **The Great Spiritual Lie from Satan**

The Garden of Eden

One day I was thinking of the age of the earth while I was watching a Discovery program. Archeologists have determined the age of the earth as millions of years old. It is so fascinating to learn of prehistoric times when the dinosaurs roamed the earth. I do believe they were created and not a part of evolution. I do believe they evolved to accommodate themselves with their environment.

We also know that early man has been discovered to go back many years. I think he was created and not evolved from something else. I do believe man did evolve as he learned to adapt to the necessities of survival.

They were after the dinosaur era. Man was not meant to co-exist with the dinosaurs. Man could not have competed. What was around when early man came into existence had to be something he was able to co-exist with and be able to hunt for food. Survival of the fittest would be there life.

When I was in Bible College, we explored the book of Genesis and in Genesis 1:1-2 it tells us, *"In the beginning God created the heavens and the earth. Now the earth was formless and empty, darkness was over the surface of the deep, and the Spirit of God was hovering over the waters.*

We explored the thought that some have called this the "Gap Theory" meaning we do not know what happened in here. One commentary tells us, "The statement "the earth was formless and empty" provides the setting for the creation narrative that follows. During the second and third days of creation, God gave *form* to the universe; during the next three days, God *filled* the earth with living beings. The "darkness…over the surface of the deep" was dispelled on the first day, when God created light.

The image of the Spirit of God hovering over the waters is similar to a mother bird caring for and protecting its young. God's Spirit was actively involved in the creation of the world. God's care and protection are still active.

In Genesis 1:3-2:7 it gives us a time frame of creation and it tells us that God created the world in six days and on the seventh He rested. We believe Moses wrote the first five book of the Bible so Moses referenced each act as one day. How long did it take God to create the world? There are two basic views about the days of creation: (1) each day was a literal 24-hour period; (2) each day represents an indefinite period of time (even millions of years).

The Bible does not say how long these time periods were. The real question, however, is not how long God took, but how he did it. God created the earth in an orderly fashion (He did not make plants before light), and he created men and women as unique beings capable of communication with Him. No other part of creation can claim that remarkable privilege. It is not important how long it took God to create the world, whether a few days of a few billion years, but that he crated it just the way he wanted it."

The Spirit of God is shown in the beginning hovering over the earth. The Father, Son and Holy Spirit were all in the beginning of everything. Each person of the Trinity shows up when His person is needed for mankind. Jesus, the Son of God, shows up at the conception of Mary to come into this world as a man, still God, but put on the nature of man. The Holy Spirit shows up at Pentecost so man can have a relationship with Him as Jesus leaves the earth. The Three in One have existed always.

As I was exploring this in my mind God gave me a vision of the Garden of Eden. I knew the world is a lot older than the six thousand years recorded in the Bible when we see in Genesis the creation of man. My vision showed me the world as it was at that time and then in the center I could see a different world unfolding. It was as if it were a world inside a world. On the outside was the world that has existed for millions of years and then on the inside I see a beautiful garden exposed. It is almost as I remember in the movie "Shangri-La". On the outside were cold, wind and snow. It was almost impossible to make your way through. There are a group of people stranded in this blistery area when they come upon a cave to seek shelter. They were amazed to find a world in such a contrast to what they have come out of. It was a world of perfection where nothing dies. There is no sickness, disease or any of the human responses to life. As the story unfolds, one of the women falls in love with one of the strangers and decides to go back with him. Against the judgment of her peers, she decided to make the journey. As it turned out, because she left the protection of "Shangri-La", she deteriorated and died. She could not survive the unprotected place she was living.

This is a fictitious place but I am using it in an analogy to compare the Garden of Eden. As this picture unfolds of the garden, I see Adam and Eve walking in the garden in complete peace and perfection. The animals are existing as scriptures tells us in the thousand years on earth in the Millennium when the "lion will lay with the lamb". The Spirit of God is communing with them as a perfect relationship should be.

As I look at this vision with the world on the outside and the Garden of Eden in the middle. God gave me the knowledge that this is the beginning of Spiritual man. The Garden of Eden tells of the Garden and then the fall where mankind sins, changes the existence of the protection of the Garden and is cast out into the ordinary world. As we read the account as Moses tells in the Bible, this is the birth and lineage of the spirit of man and what journey we have had to take to be redeemed. We have the Old Testament where man had to live by the law and then the New Testament where redemption comes through the person of Jesus Christ and giving us grace. We still need the law but salvation comes through Jesus becoming the sacrifice for us all. We do not need to continually sacrifice animals for the redemption of sin but we have Jesus.

When God revealed this to me, I was so excited because I had a hard time figuring out Creation and the Garden of Eden. When God revealed to me that this was the beginning of the history of Spiritual man, I got it. This revelation is so exciting to me.

Temptation

By the definition of the word temptation the dictionary gives us these words to define:

1. Temptation – "Something that attracts, especially with the promise of pleasure or reward: allurement, bait, come-on, enticement, inducement, inveiglement, invitation, lure, seduction."
2. Tempter – "One that seduces: allurer, charmer, enticer, inveigles, lurer, seducer."
3. Tempting – "Pleasing to the eye or mind: attractive, bewitching, enchanting, engaging, enticing, fascination, fetching, glamorous, lovely, prepossessing, pretty, sweet, taking, winning, winsome."

The human condition is made up of needs to possess to be filled as a human being. There is our body, our mind and our spirit. The nature of man is to achieve the highest place of achievement in each of these areas. This is admirable but not at the expense of other people and by breaking the law. We are constantly surrounded by temptation because a part of this human condition is desire and fulfillment. These attributes can be used for good or for evil. There will always be a part of us that wants to fulfill the desires of the flesh. We need the balance to where we put God first, our family and then us. We are not to be first and elevated to a place we do not deserve.

Temptation is not a sin. In this world of good and evil, there will always be a struggle between your flesh and your spirit. Satan had his major victory in the Garden of Eden, when he tempted Eve, she gave in, and she ate the fruit. She then turned to Adam, he indulged, and history tells the rest. We are born sinners, and have to be redeemed.

What if Eve had not sinned? Temptation would not even be in our vocabulary. She did give in; and all humanity pays the price. If she had stayed with just the temptation and resisted, we would all be in the Garden right now.

Satan is after you because you are a child of God. If you were not, he would not have to worry about you because you would be going to hell anyway. His trophy is your very soul, turning you from God. This is his victory and desires to see everyone turn from God.

It takes strength and courage to resist sin. It is pleasurable; otherwise it would not be sin. We fight the enemy with the Word of God and refusing to let sin run your life. Your relationship with God is worth spending eternity with Him.

Temptation

Temptation is a ploy of Satan
God tells us in His Word,
Satan wants you to turn your eyes
Looking in the wrong direction.

Temptation is not a sin
Satan cannot read your mind,
But when we take our guard away,
He sees what your weakness is.

Sin becomes that very thing
That drives us in the flesh,
If we give into what is wrong
We please the passion from within.

It is pleasure for only a moment
Knowing it is not for our good,
Our flesh is satisfied, and now quiet
Just until the next time.

Temptation comes from many places
We have to learn to say "no",
It is with us every single day
It does not get any easier.

We receive the messages sin sends
Once you fall into the trap,
It can come through all of our senses
Beware, you have given up heaven.

God made our flesh in a way
There will always be something,
We want to serve God and please Him
Something wants to lead you astray.

We have taken what God gives us
And turned it to within our self,
Satan is happy because he knows
A child of God has fallen away.

("Resist the devil and he will flee from you" James 4:7 NIV)

Desire

We have built in us appetites which need to be fulfilled
This is how the human body tells us what we need,
If we do not listen to the urging that is calling us
We may not receive what our body is telling us to supply.

To desire something is a good thing because it tells us to want
But if the motives are more toward destruction, we overload,
If it is food we become too fat; if it is to obtain things limit
Unless we are in control, we have the knowledge of excess.

How many things in your life have you accumulated
We indulge our self to feel better; we feel we deserve it,
How much of your wants exceed your needs unknowing
We have over done what is necessary; we have abundance.?

When it comes to making choices examine your desire
Do I really need this or is it just a pacifier to fill a hole inside,
We use objects obtainable in life to satisfy our need to have
The question remains is it necessary or can I let it go?

To desire something can be a goal we set to achieve; work for
If it takes away from God, then it is wrong for you to do,
We do not need more stuff to fill the empty feeling inside
Turn to the Holy Spirit; Your need is spiritual not physical.

CHAPTER 9: **We Have Lost Our First Love**

God / Jesus

In the book of Revelation, it is recorded by John while exiled on the island of Patmos. God reveals to John the condition of the churches at that time, and has John write letters to these churches.

In the letter to the church at Ephesus, John tells them they have lost there first love. "Yet I hold this against you: You have forsaken your first love" (Revelation 2:4).

In the commentary, "Paul had once commended the church at Ephesus for its love for God and others (Ephesians 1:15), but many of the church founders had died, and many of the second-generation believers had lost their zeal for God. They were a busy church – the member did much to benefit themselves and the community – but they were acting out of the wrong motives. Work for God must be motivated by love for God or it will not last."

"Just as when a man and woman fall in love, so also new believers rejoice in their new found forgiveness. But when we lose sight of the seriousness of sin, we begin to lose the thrill of our forgiveness (see 2 Peter 1:9). In the first steps of your Christian life your may have had enthusiasm without knowledge. Do you now have enthusiasm without knowledge? Both are necessary if we are to keep love for God intense and untarnished (see Hebrews 10:32-35). Do you love God with the same fervor as when you were a new Christian?"

Our first love is Jesus. When we realize that Jesus is the Son of God, died on the cross for our sins, rose from the grave giving His life for all mankind. This is the redemptive power in the blood of Jesus. Because He died in the flesh we live in the spirit. Heaven is our home.

We can never take for granted this wonderful miracle given to us. All we have to do is believe this and live for Christ. The living for God is difficult after the initial warmth of accepting Jesus in our hearts. We have to stay focused and determined to live the way the bible maps out what God expects us to live.

America

We have lost our love for America. We criticize our leaders, are very vocal about our disappointments and even show hatred to our neighbor. What happened to the greatness in our heart for this country?

This country was founded on Godly principles and we put God first. Our fore fathers wanted the bible taught in school as a requirement. They prayed about what to do and what to write. I believe the bible is inspired by God and so is the Constitution. Both stress that "All men are created equal in the sight of God and should be treated as such."

We have moved so far left in this country that the bible is being challenged and limited to where we can read or display it. We have to go back to the roots of the bible where God wanted this country to reflect the principles of the bible.

The bible in America is still the most popular book sold and will be of all time. My concern is that our leaders are going to try to make the bible obsolete. Try to convince the American people that it is not relevant for today. There are religions that create the illusion that your conscience is your guide and that is what you follow. You need something to have truth to compare to and that has to be the bible. God meant it to be this way.

Man is trying to take the bible and re-word it to appeal to an audience that is humanistic. The flesh and the spirit are in war with each other. The spirit needs to overcome the flesh because the Holy Spirit will guide and direct us in the path that God wants us to follow. We have to know the truth by a source that is valid and credible.

America, You are Mine

America the beautiful are words that run true
To a land that I love and hold dear to my heart,
It makes me feel sad when there are those who disagree
This is their right because it is the land of the free.

America you are not perfect by any means
But considering you are made of human beings,
We do the best we can with what we have
A melting pot and a potpourri of different kinds.

Your greatness is expressed with those who give their life
Whether a politician, a president, a senator and a soldier,
We will define what is ours to possess and protect
From those who want to take from what we have fought.

As long as God is on our side as our prayers are sent to Him
We can be assured that we will be alright within,
But if we turn this country over to Satan and his imps
We will struggle for all that is good and precious to us.

Be assured that this country can only take so much
We have to go back to our roots that were expressed,
Our forefathers gave their life and soul for us
To be free and not to owe anyone anything.

PART 11: OUR HUMAN RIGHTS

CHAPTER 1: **Our Roots as an American: Our Forefathers**

The first recognition has to be the acknowledgement of the forty-three presidents of the United States starting in 1789 with George Washington and until today with President George W. Bush still in office today until 2009.

All the Presidents:

George Washington 1789-97

John Adams 1797-01

Thomas Jefferson 1801-09

James Madison 1809-17

James Monroe 1817-25

John Adams   1825-29

Andrew Jackson 1829-37

Martin Ban Buren 1837-41

William Henry Harrison 1841

John Tyler 1841-45

James Polk 1845-49

Zachary Taylor 1849-50

Millard Fillmore 1850-53

Franklin Pierce 1853-57

James Buchanan 1857-61

Abraham Lincoln 1861-65

Andrew Jackson 1865-69

Ulysses S. Grant 1869-77

Rutherford B. Hayes 1877-81

James Garfield 1881

Chester Arthur 1881-85

Benjamin Harrison 1885-93

Grover Cleveland 1893-1897

William McKinley 1897-01

Theodore Roosevelt 1901-09

William H. Taft 1909-13

Woodrow Wilson 1913-21

Warren Harding 1921-23

Calvin Coolidge 1923-29

Herbert Hoover 1929-33

Franklin D. Roosevelt 1933-45

Harry Truman 1945-53

Dwight Eisenhower 1953-61

John F. Kennedy 1961-63

Lyndon Johnson 1963-69

Richard Nixon 1969-74

Gerald Ford 1974-77

Jimmy Carter 1977-81

Ronald Reagan 1981-89

George H. W. Bush 1989-93

William J. Clinton 1993-2001

George Bush 2001-2009

Barack Obama 2009 - present

George Washington

Age 56: The First President of the United States

On April 30, 1789, George Washington, standing on the balcony of federal hall on Wall Street in New York, took his oath of office as the first President of the United States. "As the first of everything, in our situation will serve to establish a Precedent," he wrote James Madison, "it is devoutly wished on my part, that these precedents may be fixed on true principles". Born in 1732 into a Virginia planter family, he learned the morals, manners, and body of knowledge requisite from an 18th century Virginia gentleman.

He pursued two intertwined interests: military arts and western expansion. At 16 he helped survey Shenandoah lands for Thomas, Lord Fairfax. Commissioned a lieutenant colonel in 1754, he fought the first skirmishes of what grew into the French and Indian war. The next year, as an aide to Gen. Edward Braddock, he escaped injury although four bullets ripped his coat and two horses were shot from under him.

From 1759 to the outbreak of the American Revolution, Washington managed his lands around Mount Vernon and served in the Virginia House of Burgesses. Married to a widow, Martha Dandridge Curtis, he devoted himself to a busy and happy life. But like his fellow planters, Washington felt himself exploited by British merchants and hampered by British regulations. As the quarrel with the mother country grew acute, he moderately but firmly voiced his resistance to the restrictions.

When the Second Continental Congress assembled in Philadelphia in May 1775, Washington, one of the Virginia delegates, was elected Commander in Chief of the Continental Army. On July 3, 1775, at Cambridge, Massachusetts, he took command of his ill-trained troops and embarked upon a war that was to last six grueling years.

He realized early that the best strategy was to harass the British. He reported to Congress, "we should on all Occasions avoid a general Action, or put anything to the Risqué, unless compelled by a necessity, in which we ought never to be drawn." Ensuing battles saw him fall back slowly, then strike unexpectedly. Finally in 1781 with the aid of French allies-he forced the surrender of Cornwallis at Yorktown.

Washington longed to retire to his fields at Mount Vernon. But he soon realized that the Nation under its Articles of Confederation was not functioning well, so he became a prime mover in the steps leading to the Constitutional Convention at Philadelphia in 1787. When the new Constitution was ratified, the Electoral College unanimously elected Washington President.

He did not infringe upon the policy making powers that he felt the Constitution gave Congress. But the determination of foreign policy became preponderantly a Presidential concern. When the French Revolution led to a major war between France and England, Washington refused to accept entirely the recommendations of either his Secretary of the Treasury Alexander Hamilton, who was pro-British. Rather, he insisted upon a neutral course until the United States could grow stronger.

To his disappointment, two parties were developing by the end of his firs term. Wearied of politics, feeling old, he retired at the end of his second. In his Farewell Address, he urged his countrymen to forswear excessive party spirit and geographical distinctions. In foreign affairs, he warned against long-term alliances.

Washington enjoyed less than three years of retirement at Mount Vernon, for he died of a throat infection December 14, 1799. For months the Nation mourned him.

Washington and the Declaration of Independence
July 1776

By the summer of 1776, American and British forces have been engaged in armed conflict for fifteen months. On July 4, 1776, the Declaration of Independence changed the purpose and nature of that conflict. The two documents that follow concern Washington's reaction to receiving the Declaration of Independence from Congress. What is Washington's response to the news? What impact does he think the Declaration will be on his army?

George Washington, General Orders, July 9, 1776

<u>The Honor</u>: The Continental Congress, impelled by the dictates of duty, policy and necessity, having been pleased to dissolve the Connection which subsisted between this Country, and Great Britain, and to declare the United Colonies of North America, free and independent States: The several brigades are to be drawn up this evening on their respective Parades, at Six O'clock, when the declaration of Congress, showing the grounds and reasons of this measure, is to be read with a audible voice.

The General hopes this important Event will serve as a fresh incentive to every officer, and soldier, to act with Fidelity and Courage, as knowing that now the peace and safety of his Country depends (under God) solely on the success of our arms: And that he is now in the service of a State, possessed of sufficient power to reward his merit, and advance him to the highest Honors of a free Country.

Washington to Continental Congress, New York, July 10, 1776

<u>Sir:</u> I am now to acknowledge the receipt of your two favors of the 4th and 6th instants, which came duly to hand, with their important enclosures. I perceive that Congress have been employed in deliberating on measures of the most interesting nature. It is certain that it is not with us to determine in many instances what consequences will flow from our Counsels, but yet it behooves us to adopt such, as under the smiles of a Gracious and all kind Providence will be most likely to promote our happiness; I trust the late decisive part they have taken, is calculated for that end, and will secure us that freedom and those privileges, which have been, and are refused us, contrary to the voice of Nature and the British Constitution. Agreeable to the request of Congress I caused the Declaration to be proclaimed before all the Army under my immediate Command, and have the pleasure to inform them, that the measure seemed to have their most hearty assent; the Expressions and behaviors both of Officers and Men testifying their warmest approbation of it. I have transmitted a Copy to General Ward at Boston, requesting him to have it proclaimed to the Continental Troops in that Department.

Alexander Hamilton_(1755 or 1757-1804)

Alexander Hamilton was a noted statesman and political leader during the early years of the United States. He served in President George Washington's Cabinet as the nation's first secretary of the treasury. He also was a leader of the Federalist Party, one of the first political parties in the nation.

Hamilton was one of the boldest and most creative thinkers of his time. He supported the establishment of a strong federal government and believed that the U.S. Constitution should be interpreted loosely to give the government greater powers. Hamilton also favored the development of manufacturing to achieve and economic balance between agriculture and industry.

Many of Hamilton's policies were strongly opposed by Thomas Jefferson and other political leaders of the time. But today, scholars agree that Hamilton's ideas have had lasting importance.

His early political career was admitted to the bar in New York in 1782 and soon began to practice law there. Also in 1782, he became a delegate from New York to the Congress of the Confederation. The Congress had been established by the Articles of Confederation in 1781, but it had little power. In 1786, Hamilton wrote a proposal calling for a convention of the states for the purpose of strengthening the federal government.

The Constitutional Convention met in Philadelphia in 1787. Few of Hamilton's ideas were included in the U.S. Constitution, but he worked hard for its ratification by the states. Hamilton persuaded two other statesmen, John Jay and James Madison, to join him in writing letters to newspapers urging approval of the Constitution.

Hamilton became secretary of the treasury in 1789. He proposed that Congress establish a national bank to handle the government's financial operations. This measure was opposed by Secretary of State Thomas Jefferson, who did not believe that Congress had the power to establish such an institution. Hamilton then developed the *doctrine of implied powers*. This doctrine states that the government has implied powers. The Supreme Court later upheld this doctrine.

Hamilton wanted the government to encourage manufacturing, and he recommended measures for that purpose. Jefferson and Madison opposed such a program because they thought that it would hurt farming interests. Congress did not follow Hamilton's suggestions until many years later.

In the early 1790's, the conflicts between Hamilton and a group led by Jefferson and Madison resulted in the development of the nation's first two political parties. Hamilton led the Federalists Party, which favored a strong federal government. The Democratic-Republican Party, headed by Jefferson and Madison, wanted a weak national government.

In 1795, Hamilton resigned as treasury secretary because of personal financial problems and increased opposition in Congress. But he remained active in public life and in 1796, helped President Washington write his Farewell Address.

John Adams, a Federalist, became president in 1797. Adams and Hamilton had many personal disputes, and they also disagreed about foreign policy and other issues. Shortly before the election of 1800, Hamilton wrote a pamphlet attacking the president. The pamphlet widened a split among the Federalists. As a result, the Democratic-Republican candidates, Thomas Jefferson and Aaron Burr, won the election. Jefferson 9and Burr received an equal number of electoral votes. Under the voting procedure in use at the time, both men were eligible for the presidency. The House of Representatives had to decide the winner. Hamilton, who distrusted Burr more than he distrusted Jefferson, supported Jefferson for president. Jefferson won, and Burr became vice president.

Burr ran for governor of New York in 1804. Hamilton criticized Burr's character and worked to defeat him. Burr lost and then challenged Hamilton to a duel with pistols. The two men dueled in Weehawken, New Jersey, on July 11, 1804. Hamilton was shot, and he died the next day.

Abraham Lincoln (1809-1865)

Abraham Lincoln was one of the truly great men of all time. He led the United States during the Civil War (1861-1865), which was the greatest crisis in U.S. history. Lincoln helped end slavery in the nation and helped keep the American Union from splitting apart during the war. Lincoln thus believed that he proved to the world that democracy can be a lasting form of government. Lincoln's Gettysburg Address, second inaugural address, and many of his other speeches and writings are classic statements of democratic beliefs and goals. In conducting a bitter war, Lincoln never became bitter himself. He showed a nobility of character that has worldwide appeal, Lincoln, a Republican, was the first member of his party to become President. He was assassinated near the end o the Civil War and was succeeded by Vice President Andrew Johnson. Lincoln was the first U. S. President to be assassinated.

The American people knew little about Lincoln when he became President. Little in his past experience indicated that he could successfully deal with the deep differences between Northerners and Southerners over slavery. Lincoln received less that 40 per cent of the popular vote in winning the presidential election of 1860. But by 1865, he had become in the eyes of the world equal in importance to George Washington. Through the years, many people have regarded Lincoln as the greatest person in United States history.

During the Civil War, Lincoln's first task was to win the war. He had to view nearly all other matters in relation to the war. It was "the progress of our arms." He once said, "upon which all else depends." But Lincoln was a peace-loving man who had earlier described military glory as "that attractive rainbow, which rises in showers of blood-that serpent's eye that charms to destroy." The Civil War was by far the bloodiest was in U.S. history. In the Battle of Gettysburg, for example, the more than 45,000 total casualties (people killed, wounded, captured, or missing) exceeded the number of casualties in all previous American wars put together.

Lincoln became a remarkable war leader. Some historians believe he was the chief architect of the Union's victorious military strategy. This strategy called for Union armies to advance against the enemy on all fronts at the same time. Lincoln also insisted that the objective of the Union armies should be the destruction of opposing forces, not the conquest of territory. Lincoln changed generals several times because he could not find one who would fight the war the way he wanted it fought. When he finally found such a general, Ulysses S. Grant, Lincoln stood firmly behind him.

Lincoln's second great task was to keep up Northern morale through the horrible war in which many relatives in the North and South fought against one another. He understood that the Union's resources vastly exceeded those of the Confederacy, and that the Union would eventually triumph if it remained dedicated to victory. For this reason, Lincoln used his great writing and speechmaking abilities to spur on his people.

If the Union had been destroyed, the United States could have become two, or possibly more, nations. These nations separated could not have become as prosperous and important as the United States is today. By preserving the Union, Lincoln influenced the course of world history. By ending slavery, he helped assure the moral strength of the United States. His own life story, too, had been important. He rose from humble origin to the nation's highest office.

Millions of people regard Lincoln's career as proof that democracy offers all people the best hope of a full an free life.

Life in the United Sates during Lincoln's Administration revolved around the war. But almost miraculously, the nation also laid out a blueprint for modern America during the war years. Economic development played an important role in Lincoln's vision of America's future, in which all people would have the right to rise in life. National banking legislation provided for paper money as we know it today - and for federal controls to assure sound banking and credit. United States tariffs on European manufactured goods helped limit foreign competition and encouraged the growth of American industry. The administration encouraged labor unions. The government's homestead laws gave free land to settlers. Immigration was encouraged, as was the settlement of the West. Land was also granted for colleges that later became great state universities and for the construction of the nation's first transcontinental railroad. In addition, the nation's first income tax was levied to provide funds for the war.

Important dates in Lincoln's life

1809 Feb. 12) Born near present-day Hodgenville, Kentucky.

1834 Elected to the Illinois General Assembly.

1842 (Nov. 4) Married Mary Todd.

1846 Elected to the U.S. House of Representatives.

1858 Debated slavery with Stephen A. Douglas.

1860 (Nov.6) Elected president of the United States.

1864 (Nov. 8) Reelected president.

1865 (April 14) Shot by John Wilkes Booth.

1865 (April 15) Died in Washington, D.C.

The Men of the Declaration of Independence

John Adams_Age: 40 Lawyer

Adams was born in Braintree, Massachusetts, the son a farmer who came from a long line of farmers with roots deep in the history of Massachusetts. He entered Harvard, class of 1755, when he was fifteen. As the eldest son, he was expected to be the family tithe to the church. He graduated the year of Braddock's defeat in western Pennsylvania, an event that led him to predict that "if we can remove the turbulent Gallicks (Roman Catholics in France)…the only way to keep us from setting up for ourselves is to disunite us".

Adams left college uncertain of what he wanted to do with his life. To gain time to decide he took a teaching position in a back-country village of Worcester, some sixty miles west of Boston. He continued to teach until he settled on a career. After much thought he rejected the ministry. "As far as I can observe, people are not disposed to inquire for piety, integrity, good sense, or learning in a young preacher, but for stupidity". Against the advice of friends and family he finally chose to study law. He did not then think much of the legal profession – "a fumbling and raking amidst the rubbish of writs, indictment, pleas…that have neither harmony nor meaning" but it offered a young man from a middling background a chance to prosper. "Necessity drove me to this determination," he said, "but my inclination, I think, was to preach."

A lawyer in Boston who arranged for his admission to the bar offered several pieces of advice. "One is, to pursue the study of law, rather than the gain of it; purse the gain of it enough to keep out of the briers, but give your main attention to the study of it. The next is, not to marry early; for an early marriage will obstruct you improvement; and in the next place, it will involve you in expense. Another thing is, not to keep much company, for the application of a man who aims to be a lawyer must be incessant; his attention to his books must be constant, which is inconsistent with keeping much company".

Adams was determined to follow this advice but his diary reveals that he did turn to a life of sex, smoking and drinking. Putting these pleasures into his day, he had time to reflect on his behavior. He thought his lack of success was because of his choice in living the way he chose. He realized that virtue and wisdom should be aimed at. "He warned himself the reputation ought to be the perpetual subject of my thoughts, and aim of my behavior. How shall I gain a reputation! I feel vexed, fretted, chafed; the thought of no business mortifies me. But let me banish these fears; let me assume a fortitude, a greatness of mind".

He decided to move from the village of Braintree to Boston. He was overwhelmed by the distractions. He did stay for two years but with the death of his father, he went back to Braintree to live with his mother. He was elected as surveyor of the highways. He went at the job with vigor. He set up a system that lasted for over a half century. He tried to reform the town to three taverns realizing that they were affecting the lives of important people. His first major lesson in politics and patience was that he was creating enemies and opposition. He realized then it was difficult to do what he felt right but he did not want the ill will of the town. He decided to leave.

Adams turned to reform to building up his practice, cultivating popularity, and making money. He needed money now, for her had fallen in love with Abigail Smith. The courtship lasted four years; her parents did not think John Adams good enough for their daughter. It was an ordeal for both.

Finally, late in 1764, they married; he was then twenty-nine, she some ten years younger. The next year he reported in his diary the "1765 has been the most remarkable year of my life". Married life delighted him, he had picked up several clients in a tour of the court circuit, and been charmed by America's reaction to the Stamp act.

The Stamp Act itself embittered him. Lawyers' refusal to by the special stamps the act required for all legal documents caused the courts to be closed. Adams was just getting under sail when an embargo was set against the vessel he was to sail on. It was meant to ruin him as well as America and Great Britain.

The Stamp Act carried John Adams from local into provincial politics. He published a pamphlet attacking the act as contrary to the rights of man, "*rights* that cannot be repealed or restrained by human laws – *rights* derived from the great Legislator of the universe," In a set of instructions for Braintree's representative in the legislature he attacked the act as "burthensome", unconstitutional, and an "alarming extension of the power of the Courts of Admiralty". Within a year the Stamp Act was repealed, the courts were reopened in Massachusetts, and Adams found himself traveling the circuit, only now as one of the colony's leading lawyers. In order to deal more easily with his enlarged practice he moved back to Boston. When the customhouse sued John Hancock for treble (triple) the value of an illegal cargo of wine carried aboard his sloop *Liberty*, Hancock hired Adams to defend him. "A painful drudgery I had of his cause," Adams recalled. "There were few days through the whole winter when I was not summoned to attend the Court of Admiralty." When the government finally dropped charges, Adams was "weary and disgusted" with the case, the court "and even the tyrannical bell that dongled (deep sound) me out of my house every morning.

Adams took upon himself several cases where he defended unpopular cases but because of his legal talent, he argued their case and won. He felt better about this than anything else in his career but it took a tole on his life. He was then determined to leave public life and move from Boston back to Braintree. "Law and politics had exhausted my health, brought on a pain in my breast, and complaint in my lungs, which seriously threatened my life, and compelled me to throw off a great part of the load of business, both public and private, and return to my farm in the country". He left for the country with bitter thoughts. "I have stood by the people much longer than they would stand by themselves. But I have learned wisdom by experience; I shall certainly become more retired and cautious; I shall certainly mind by own farm and my own office".

John Hancock Age: 40 Merchant

No man enjoyed the pleasures wealth could give him more than John Hancock and, through it, he could give others. He rolled through life in a glorious array of colors, favoring lavender suits and bright yellow coaches, among other hues in the spectrum. He was graceful and prepossessing in manners, and very passionately addicted to what are called the elegant pleasures of life, to dancing, music, concerts, routs, assemblies, card parties, rich wines, social dinners and festivities. He relished what Jefferson called the "tinsel of life" but with such open satisfaction that few men resented the display.

Men who fell out over politics can at least agree on one thing – John Hancock had large failings mixed with modest virtue:

1. A BOSTON TORY: His understanding was of the dwarf size, but his ambition…was upon the gigantic He

was free from immoralities, and objects of charity often felt the effect his riches. His mind was a mere *tabula rasa,* and had he met with a good artist he would have enstamped upon it such character as would have made him a most useful member of society.

2. A BOSTON WHIG: Your old friend figures away in the usual style. Sometimes the pendulum swings one way, and sometimes the other – I mean with regard to Whiggism and Toryism- but never fails to swing uniformly against all that won't bow down and worship a very silly image.

3. A COLLEAGUE IN CONGRESS: He was fond of the ceremonies of public life, but anted industry and punctuality in business. His conversation was desultory, and his manners much influenced by frequent attacks of the gout, which gave a hypercritical peevishness to his temper. With all these infirmities he was a disinterested patriot, and made large sacrifices of an ample estate of the liberties and independence of his country.

As the son of a clergyman, Hancock had licked into his life of luxury. The father died when Hancock as nine, His mother soon after married and another clergyman of mediocre circumstances. She took Hancock's brother and sister with her, but a rich uncle, Thomas Hancock, carried John into his sumptuous house on Beacon Hill, where his childless wife Lydia made him "the object of her fondest affection on this side of heaven." Uncle Thomas sent him to Boston Latin, to Harvard College, then, as a clerk, drew him into his lucrative mercantile business. When twenty-three he went to London to meet the firm's agents, and while there he saw the funeral of George 11 and the coronation of George 111. He returned to Boston with his mind packed with memories of the way the rich lived abroad, but he repressed a yearning for the high life relished in London. Instead, he "became an example to all the young men of the town", said an incredulous friend. "Wholly devoted to business, he was regular and punctual at his store as the sun in his course".

Three years after his return Uncle Thomas died, and at the age of twenty-seven Hancock took control "of what was reputed to be the greatest fortune ever amassed in New England", a biographer has said.

It was fortunate that the business was substantial, for he lacked his uncle's acumen, and he was taking the helm in very difficult times". Parliament had recently passed a revenue act that forecast the end of the old "live and let live" policy toward the colonies. Customs collections were to be tightened up, smuggling attacked more vigorously. Then, in 1765, came news of the Stamp Act. Every bill of lading that passed through Hancock's firm, every legal document it filed in court, every advertisement for goods it took in the press would hereafter be taxed with stamps that had to be purchased through royal agents.

At first Hancock accepted the tax as a necessary evil. A few weeks later his opinion changed. He now believed that opposition to the Stamp Act is highly commendable. Soon he thought Americans were a gone people if they accepted the act; then he was convinced they would never suffer themselves to be made slaves of by a submission to that act.

The swing in sentiment owed much to Samuel Adams. It was remarked that Hancock was as closely attached to the hindermost part of Mr. Adams as the rattles are affixed to the tail of a rattlesnake. Before Hancock knew how it had happened he, who had said early in the agitation that I seldom meddle with politics, found himself in the provincial legislature. This town has done a wise thing today, Adams said after the election. They have made that young man's fortune their own. Adams manipulated his election to the council, then later as speaker *pro tem* of the legislature. Both times the governor vetoed the appointments, refusing to work with a declared enemy of the government.

It was an open secret Hancock was the colonies, if not the continent's, greatest smuggler. He had learned his craft from his Uncle Thomas. When one of his ships, the *Liberty*, arrived loaded with contraband wine, he crew locked up a curious customs officer, landed the cargo unmolested, and sent it on the way to customers. When the government sued for treble the value of the wine, he hired john Adams to fight the case. But when a few months later the British eased the pinch on his pocketbook nerve, he stepped back to reassess the situation. He now saw the Samuel Adams went further than appeared to him warrantable. He suggested the town meeting might investigate the great deficiency occasioned by Samuel Adams' tenure as tax collector. Governor Thomas Hutchinson rejoiced to hear Hancock had stopped going to Adam's political club and seems to have a new set of acquaintances. He approved Hancock's election as speaker of the house.

Yet within a year he had been enticed back to Adams' fold. The tax on tea imposed by parliament did not bother him so much as the fact that the subsidized East India Company would soon be unloading tea on the American market at cut-rate prices, cheaper than the smuggled Dutch tea people had been drinking. Hancock, it happened, had a warehouse full of the Dutch tea leaves. He now rejoined Samuel Adams' crusade for American freedom. As speaker, he approved publication of several Hutchinson's letters, stolen by Benjamin Franklin in London, which supposedly showed the governor working "to overthrow the government and to introduce arbitrary power into the province". He rejoined the committee of correspondence he had once abandoned. He helped organize the meeting that led to the dumping of the tea from London in Boston harbor. A few months later he delivered the annual oration Adams has decided to keep the Boston Massacre fresh in the people's memory. "Let every parent tell the shameful story to his listening children till tears of pity glisten in their eyes, and boiling passions shake their tender frames," he said in his ghost-written speech.

Two weeks after the Second Continental Congress convened, the Congress chose Hancock as its president. Benjamin Harrison, who could abide few Northerners, helped engineer the election. He had found Hancock a convivial companion who, shorn of his Boston accent, might pass for a gentleman. Hancock quickly proved to have been a superb choice. His benign presence helped alleviate Southern distaste for New England. He moderated the often bitter debates with skill. "Mr. Hancock had those talents which were calculated to make him appear to more advantage as chairman, than in the debates of a public body", a contemporary not especially fond of him remarked. "He discovered a fine address, a great impartiality, sufficient spirit to command attention, and preserve order. His voice and manner were much in his favor, and his experience, in public business, gave him ease and dignity".

But Hancock wished to be more than president of Congress. He wanted to be commander in chief of the continental army. When John Adams rose to propose a candidate for the post, Hancock listened "with visible pleasure; but when I came to describe Washington for the commander, I never remarked a more sudden and striking change of countenance. Mortification and resentment were expressed as forcibly as his face could exhibit them. Mr. Samuel Adams seconded the action, and that did not soften the President's physiognomy".

Hancock resigned himself to the decision – later he named a son after Washington – and settled down to running Congress with good humor and tact. Sometimes he let matters slide that called for prompt attention, but colleagues excused the fault. "The great and important business in which he is constantly employed and the almost immense number of letters which he is constantly receiving on the most interesting subjects said it impossible for him to attend to them all and lesser matters much be neglected", a delegate explained to a friend who insist on having wine", it was said – self-interest, too, may have been involved – and if so the ploy worked. "I do not know what to think of these men" from New England, Harrison told Washington. "They seem exceeding hearty in the cause but still want to keep everything among themselves. Our President is quite a different cast – noble, disinterested, and generous to a very great degree".

To escape the heat of Philadelphia, Congress in 1775 took off the month of August. The holiday ended with news of one "of the most unlikely things within the whole compass of possibility" – John Hancock had married Dorothy Quincy. He brought his "agreeable lady" back to Philadelphia, and she honors us with her presence and contributes much to our good humor as well as to the happiness of the President, so much so that the day the delegates gathered for their first session, Mr. Hancock having a touch of gout, there was no President in the chair.

After the holiday those who favored independence began to campaign relentlessly for their cause. Not once during the next ten months did they relax the pressure. Hancock stayed above the battle, though it was rumored that he favored those for reconciliation with Britain. He supposedly courted James Duane of New York and John Dickinson of Pennsylvania, then the leaders of the anti-dependence faction, and leaned so partially in their favor, that Mr. Samuel Adams had become very bitter against Mr. Hancock, and spoke of him with great asperity in private circles. Still, during the great debates in June and early July 1776 Hancock could, with his now good friend Harrison serving as chairman of the committee of the whole, have spoken from the floor against independence if he had wished. Apparently he did not; otherwise John Adams would have passed the work to posterity.

Shortly after the bell in the State House tower rang the hour of ten on June 7 Hancock rapped the delegates to order. Although they were on the whole hard-working, punctuality did not number among their virtues. As a rule they straggled in through the morning, many of them delayed by committee meetings often held before Congress convened. On days when important matters were to be debated, Hancock had to plead for "the delegates to be upon honor to meet punctually at ten o'clock". This morning he saw at once he had a quorum present and nodded to Andrew McNair, the doorkeeper, who swung shut the doors, took up his post outside, and was ready to bar all but tardy delegates from joining the secret discussion within.

In life the trivial often adulterates the momentous. This day that Samuel Adams thought the most important question "ever agitated in America would be decided" opened on a minor note. The delegates began by pondering the problem of a ship that had been commandeered by the commodore of the continental fleet. They resolved that the owner should be paid for his loss. Next, they discussed the quality of "powder manufactured at Mr. O. Eve's mill". These matters settled, Richard Henry Lee of Virginia, as the senior member of his delegation, rose to introduce his resolution.

Roger Sherman_Age: 55 Politician

It embarrassed a colleague from Connecticut to have Sherman in the delegation to the First Congress. "Mr. Sherman is cleaver in private," he conceded, "but I will only say he is as badly calculated to appear in such a company as a chestnut bur is for an eye stone. He occasioned some shrewd countenances among the company, and not a few oaths, by the odd questions he asked, and the very odd questions he asked, and the very odd and countrified cadence with which he spoke."

Odd was the word for Mr. Sherman. He was infuriatingly pious. "Mr. Sherman (would to heaven he were well at New Haven) is against our sending our carriages over the ferry this evening," a companion wrote, "because it is Sunday; so we shall have a scorching sun to drive forty miles in tomorrow." Once when Congress was backed up with business, it resolved to meet on Sunday. Mr. Sherman objected – out of "a regard of the commands of his Maker." After he heard that the continental army had been defeated on Long Island, although entrenched behind a chain of hills, he turned to a colleague and said: "Truly in vain is salvation hoped for from the hills and from the multitude of mountains."

He was odd and depressingly gave. To his face delegates addressed him as "Judge Sherman," but behind is back called him "Father Sherman." Once while absent from home he wrote his wife:

"This is your birthday. Mine was the 30th of last month. May we so number our days as to apply our hearts to wisdom, that is, true religion. Psalm 90:12. I remain affectionately yours, Roger Sherman."

He disliked bawdy tales – "prognostiferous observations," he called them – and lived by such lugubrious sayings as: "Intestine jars are worse than foreign wars... Plain downright honesty is the beauty and elegance of life... All men desire happiness but "tis only the virtuous that attain it... The gods are slow but sure paymasters".

Then there was his deviousness. "But of my old colleague Sherman, suffice it to say that if the order of the Jesuits is extinct their practices are not out of fashion," a victim remarked. The man "is as cunning as the Devil," said another, "and if you attack him, you ought to know him well; he is not easily managed, but if he suspects you are trying to take him in, you may as well catch an eel by the tail."

Odd! "Mr. Sherman exhibits the oddest shaped character I ever remember to have met with," said a delegate, attempting to sum up the man. "He is awkward, unmeaning, and unaccountably strange in his manner. But in his train of thinking, there is something regular, deep and comprehensive; yet the oddity of his address, the vulgarisms that accompany his public speaking, and that strange New England cant which runs through his public as well as private speaking make everything that is connected with him grotesque and laughable – and yet he deserves infinite praise – no man has a better heart or clearer head. If he cannot embellish he can furnish thoughts that are wise and useful. He is an able politician and extremely artful in accomplishing any particular object; - it is remarked that he seldom fails." That complimentary judgment seemed too temperate for Thomas Jefferson. "That is Mr. Sherman of Connecticut," he said one day, pointing out delegates to a visitor, "a man who never said a foolish thing in his life."

Connecticut could not be blamed for Sherman's countrified cadence." He was born and reared in Massachusetts, trained there a a shoemaker, and not until the age of twenty-two did he travel – by foot with his tools and clothes on his back, according to tradition – to New Milford, Connecticut, where his older brother lived. He pieced out a living as a shoemaker and filled his "leisure hours in the study of *mathematics,* then put the pastime to practical use as the county surveyor. He married at twenty-eight, when he felt prosperous enough to support a family. A year alter he and his brother opened a general store in New Milford, and Sherman began publishing an almanac that contained his own astronomical calculations and "everything that I thought would be useful." His energy was endless. Angered at the depreciated paper money of neighboring colonies that the store had to accept at face value, he published *A Caveat Against Injustice, or an Enquiry into the Evil Consequences of a Fluctuating Medium of Exchange.* While running the store and preparing the annual edition of the almanac, he amused himself reading law. The year he turned thirty-four and began practicing law he handled one hundred twenty-five cases, kept a hand in the store, accepted election to the provincial assembly, served as a justice of the peace and put out a new edition of the almanac.

This routine continued until 1760, when Sherman's wife died and left him with seven children to rear. After his wife's death he moved to New Haven and soon became the town's leading citizen – again a member of the provincial assembly, a justice of the peace, treasurer of Yale College, and, after a few years passed, judge of the superior court and member of the provincial council. He married again, this time to a striking young lady, twenty years is junior, who eventually added eight more children to his family.

Sherman opposed the Stamp Act but the "practice of great numbers of people assembling and assuming a kind of legislative authority passing and making resolves: against that act bothered him. He though such assemblies would "tend to weaken the authority of the government" and lead to such disorders and confusions as will not be easily suppressed or reformed." Opposition must follow the rules laid down in "our happy constitution." Bimperial policy flouted those rules by taxing the colonists without their consent, but that did not justify similar disreputable behavior in the citizens of Connecticut. Parliament, as Sherman saw matters, had no right at all to legislate for the colonies in any way, even in the regulation of trade, and he carried that view down to the First Congress, where it was judge too radical to be respectable. News of the battle at Lexington pushed him even further out ahead of the pack. Soon after her arrived at the Second Congress he said that the delegates must "not neglect any probable means for reconciliation with Great Britain" but that he had "no expectation that administration will be reconciled, unless the colonies submit to their arbitrary system or convince them that it is not in their power to carry it into execution."

This bold stand a year before independence did little damage to his reputation, which, now that Congress had become accustomed to his oddities, surpassed that of all members save possibly John Adams. He served on virtually every important committee created by the Second

Congress, including the board of war, the marine committee, and the board of treasury. Among their principal assignments, a friendly compiler has remarked, "were those to prepare instructions for the operations of the army in Canada; - to establish regulations and restrictions on the trade of the United Colonies; - to regulate the currency of the country; to purchase and furnish supplied for the army; to devise ways and means for providing for ten millions of dollars for the expense of the current year; to concert a plan of military operations for the campaign of "76; - to prepare and digest a form of confederation; - to repair to headquarters near New York and examine into the state of the army, and the best means of supply for their wants; etc., etc. "Naturally he was chosen to the committee created to draw up the Declaration of Independence. "He was so regular in business, and so democratic in his principles," and admiring delegate remarked, "that he was called by one of his friends' a republican machine.'"

A few generalizations can be made about the politicians in Congress. More northerners than Southerners made a career of politics and more men from New England that from the Middle Colonies. All, or nearly all, were mighty men within their colonies, but none ever achieved much of a reputation on the national scene. No man, except Benjamin Franklin, was better known or more admired within Pennsylvania and less know outside the colony than John Morton.

Philip Livingston Age: 61 Merchant

On the eve of independence there were four members of the Livingston clan in Congress: Philip, his younger brother William (fifty-three years old), young John Jay (thirty-one), married to William's daughter, and the still younger Robert R. (thirty). Philip and William came from the branch of the family that belonged to the Presbyterian Church; Robert and John Jay were Anglicans. But blood and background united where religion might have divided. All worked hard down to the end for reconciliation with England. Colleagues questioned which of the four most irked those in Congress who agitated for independence. It was probably Philip.

"In his temper Mr. Livingston was somewhat irritable," a charitable contemporary remarked. "There was a dignity, with a mixture of austerity, in his deportment, which rendered it difficult for strangers to approach him, and which made him a terror to those who swerved from the line, or faltered in the path of personal virtue and patriotic duty". A final observation – "he was silent and reserved, and seldom indulged with much freedom in conversation" – failed to fit the man known to Congress. There he was neither silent nor reserved, although he did not converse. He "is a great, rough, rapid mortal", said one member. "There is no holding conversation with him. He blusters away". He could be embarrassingly blunt. Once when someone leaked a secret of Congress he proposed that every member publicly swear he had not been the guilty party. In that way, he said, "the rascal might add the sin of perjury to that of treachery and thereby damn his soul forever". He detested "the leveling spirit" of New England. He dreaded independence because once cut adrift" we should go instantly to civil wars among ourselves to determine which colony should govern all the rest".

Livingston came from an aggressive, acquisitive clan long accustomed to power and wealth. He was born on the family manor near Albany, graduated in the class of 1737 from Yale, married a socially acceptable well-to-do girl from Albany, then set up in business as an importer in New York City. Family connections coupled with intelligence and energy quickly brought him a fortune. He lived in a handsome house on lower Manhattan except during the torrid summers when the family moved to a country house across the East River on Brooklyn Heights. With money enough to satisfy him, Livingston branched out. He had a hand in founding the New York Society Library, the St. Andrew's Society, the city's chamber of commerce, the New York Hospital, and King's College. To all these ventures he brought a blustery drive slightly softened by something akin to good-humored tolerance. He could be a rigid Presbyterian when fighting Anglican control of King's College, then the next moment contribute to the building of a Methodist meeting house or pause to censure the people of Massachusetts for persecuting Quakers. He could slip a scatological passage into a political pamphlet one day and on another endow a chair in divinity at Yale.

As he approached forty, Livingston eased into politics as a member of the city's board of alderman. Four years later he moved on to the provincial assembly where he joined the ancient battle between the colony's two great families, the Delaney's and the Livingston's, a battle for power in which neither side seemed concerned with what was best for the colony. Livingston reacted predictably to the Stamp Act: he opposed it and also the riots that resistance to it had occasioned. He was among those chosen to represent the colony at the Stamp Act Congress, where he met several gentlemen who would later turn up in the Second Congress, among them McKean and Rodney. The assembly chose him speaker in 1769. After failing to reconcile differences with the Delaney's – He feared that the split among the elite might permit the radical sons of

Liberty to take control of the colony – he was defeated for re-election. From outside the legislature he worked with one hand to smother the Sons of Liberty and with the other wrote and spoke steadily against British oppression. The assembly sent him and his brother William to the First Congress. He accepted all that body's measures, although the nonimportation agreement imposed serious financial losses upon him. In the Second Congress he served on several important committees, among them the marine committee, the committee on Indian affairs, the committee on commerce, and the treasury board. "He was very useful", a delegate said, "in committees where a knowledge in figure or commercial subjects was required".

The views Philip Livingston carried into the Second Congress were summarized by his cousin in a letter written three days after Lexington and Concord. "Every good man wishes that America may remain free", Robert R. Livingston, Sr., said; "in this I join heartily; at the same time I do not desire she should be wholly independent of the mother country. How to reconcile their jarring principles, I profess I am altogether at a loss". Philip and the three other congressional members of the clan held that view down to the day Congress voted for independence. Once the decision had been made all four, good politicians who could end to reality, abandoned their position. When the day came to sign the Declaration, Philip alone of the clan was in Congress. He signed for the family.

Thomas Jefferson_Age 33: Lawyer

Mr. Jefferson as seen by one of his overseers;

Mr. Jefferson was six feet tow and half inches high, well proportioned, and straight as a gun-barrel. He was like a fine horse – he had no surplus flesh. He had an iron constitution, and was very strong. He had a machine for measuring strength. There were very few men that I have seen try it, that were as strong in the arms as his son-in-law Col. Thomas Mann Randolph; but Mr. Jefferson was stronger than he. He always enjoyed the best of health. His skin was very clear and pure – just like he was in principle. He had blue eyes. His countenance was always mild and pleasant. You never saw it ruffled. No odds what happened, it always maintained the same expression. When I was sometimes very much fretted and disturbed, his countenance was perfectly unmoved. I remember one case in particular. We had about eleven thousand bushels of wheat in the mill, and coopers and everything else employed. There was a big freshet – the first after the dam was finished. It was raining powerfully. I got up early in the morning, and went up to the dam. Whiled I stood there, it began to break, and I stood and saw the freshet sweep it all away. I never felt worse. I did not know what we should do. I went up to see Mr. Jefferson. He had just come from breakfast.

"Well, sir," said he, "have you heard from the river?"

I said: "Yes, sir; I have just come from there with very bad news. The mill dam is all swept away."

"Well, sir," said he, just as calm and quiet as though nothing had happened, "we can't make a new dam this summer, but we will get Lewis' ferry-boat, with our own, and get the hands from all the quarters, and boat in rock enough in place of the dam, to answer for the present and next summer. I will send to Baltimore and get ship-bolts, and we will make a dam that the freshet can't wash away."

He then went on and explained to me in detail just how he would have the dam built. We repaired the dam s he suggested, and the next summer we made a new dam, that I reckon must be there yet.

Mr. Jefferson was always an early rise – arose at daybreak, or before. The sun never found him in bed. I used sometimes to think, when I went up there very early in the morning that I would find him in bed; but there he would be before me, walking on the terrace.

He never had a servant make a fire in his room in the morning, or at any other time, when he was at home. He always had a box filled with nice dry wood in his room, and when he wanted fire he would open it and put on the wood. He would always have a good many ashes in his fireplace, and when he went out he would cover up his fire very carefully, and when he came back he would uncover the coals and make a fire for himself.

He did not use tobacco in any form. He never used a profane word or anything like it. He never played cards. I never saw a card in the house at Monticello, and I had particular orders from him to suppress card-playing among the Negroes, who, you know, are generally very fond of it. I never saw any dancing in his house, and if there had been any there during the twenty years I was with him I should certainly have known it. He never eat much hog-meat. He often told me, as I was giving out meat for the servants, that what I gave one of them for a week would be more than he would use in six months.

When he was coming home I generally knew it, and got ready for him, and waited at the house to give him the keys. After saying "How are all?" and talking awhile, he would say, "What have you got that is good?" I knew mighty well what suited him. He was especially fond of Guinea fowls; and for meant he preferred good beef, mutton, and lambs. He was very fond of vegetables and fruit, and raised every variety f them. He was very ingenious. He invented a plough that was considered a great improvement on any that had ever been used. He got a great many premiums and medals for it. He planned his own carriage, buildings, garden, fences, and a good many other things. He was nearly always busy upon some plan or model.

Every day, most as regularly as the day came, unless the weather was very bad, he would have his horse brought out and take his ride. The boy who took care of his horse knew what time he started, and would bring him out for him, and hitches him in his place. He generally started about nine o'clock. He was an uncommonly fine rider – sat easily upon his horse, and always had him in the most perfect control.

He was always very neat in his dress, wore short breeches and bright shoe buckles. When he rode on horseback he had a pair of overalls that he always put on.

Mr. Jefferson never debarred himself from hearing any preacher that came along. There was a Mr. Hiter, a Baptist preacher that used to preach occasionally at the Charlottesville Court House. He had no regular church, but was a kind of missionary – rode all over the country and preached. He wasn't much of a preacher, was uneducated, but he was a good man. Everybody had confidence in him, and they went to hear him on that account. Mr. Jefferson nearly always went to hear him when he came around. I remember his being there one day I particular. His servant came with him and brought a seat – a kind of camp stool. Upon which he sat. After the sermon there was a proposition to pass round the hat and raise money to buy the preacher a horse. Mr. Jefferson did not wait for the hat. I saw him unbutton his overalls, and get his hand into his pocket, and take out a handful of silver, I don't know how much. He then walked across the Court House to Mr. Hiter, and gave it into his hand. He bowed very politely to Mr. Jefferson, and seemed to be very much pleased.

At the first meeting of the committee of five Jefferson suggested, as a courteous gentleman, that Adams, who had worked harder and longer for separation, should write the Declaration. Adams argued with Jefferson because Adams felt Jefferson was better at writing and the people liked him more. Jefferson agreed and Adams told him they would have a meeting as soon as it was drawn up.

This gracious exchange took some effort on Adams' part. He was at the time more distinguished than Jefferson and eight years his senior. However, relinquishing the chance to write the document he had for so many months urged on Congress came easier because he was not admired and liked Jefferson. He later recalled that the Virginian had soon impressed him upon arriving in Philadelphia in 1775 as "prompt, frank, explicit, and decisive upon committees and in conversation," so much so "that he soon seized upon my heart." The judgment is all the more remarkable because he two men outwardly held so little in common. Jefferson towered more than a half foot above the stubby Adams. He was a rich man who spent money easily; Adams owned a modest farm and the small income it gave him led to constant worry about money. Jefferson had traveled to Philadelphia with four horses and two slaves as servants; Adams traveled from Massachusetts astride his horse. Adams lived in a boarding house, but Jefferson, to escape the heat of the city, had taken a small apartment on the outskirts of town.

Jefferson had been reared in a world strange to John Adams. At the age of fourteen Jefferson had inherited from his father, who had recently died, twenty-seven hundred acres of land, sixty slaves, twenty-five horses, two hundred hogs, and seventy head of cattle – in short, a plantation which, transplanted to Massachusetts, would have made him one of the colony's richest landowners. When he was sixteen, he left the plantation to overseers to run and traveled from his home in the back country down to Williamsburg, the colony's capital, to attend William and Mary College. There he built on the foundation of Latin, Greek, and French acquired from a clergyman who had tutored him and won the reputation he would win again in Congress, of being a great "rubber off of dust". Then, as all through life, he rose with the sun, worked an hour or two before breakfast, and continued to work through the day. Often in the twilight he jogged a mile or so out into the countryside to clear the brain for an evening of further study. It is hard to accept his later confession that he fell into "bad company" in college and that he remained forever astonished he "did not turn off with some of them, and become as worthless to society as they were".

Jefferson left college after two years but remained in Williamsburg to read law with George Wythe, Virginia's most distinguished legal mind. Wythe introduced him to Governor Francis Fauquier. Jefferson said that during the evenings he spent in the Palace, as the governor's mansion was called, he "heard more good sense, more rational and philosophic conversation, than in all my life besides." There was music, too, for the governor was all my life besides." There was music, too, for the governor was fond of it, and when he learned that Jefferson played the violin, he "associated [him] with two or three other amateurs in his weekly concerts."

Under Wythe's guidance, Jefferson continued his dawn to past-dark reading schedule. He read in philosophy, science, and religion, as well as law, and found time for poetry and novels, for "everything is useful which contributes to fix us in the principles of virtue." He always read to a purpose. The Greek and Latin authors taught him that a man born to wealth had a duty to serve the people and that a man who pursued happiness found it only by living moderately, reasonably, and virtuously.

The year of the Stamp Act, when John Adams first immersed himself in politics, Jefferson also lifted his head out of his books. He was on hand when Patrick Henry rose in the House of Burgesses to denounce the Stamp Act, and for years afterward could recall the "torrents of sublime eloquence from Mr. Henry" and that the debate that afternoon had been "most bloody." The next year he traveled up to Philadelphia to be inoculated against smallpox, an act that suited his cautiously bold character; many of the day viewed inoculation with live smallpox germs a needless risk, except when an epidemic was upon them. He was admitted to the Virginia bar the following year. After practicing for two years his name and face were known throughout the county. He ran for the House of Burgesses, was elected, and took his seat in early May 1769. He prepared for the new career in the same thorough way he did everything – by buying a small library of books on government.

Shortly before his twenty-ninth birthday Jefferson married a wealthy widow, whose estate joined to his made him one of the largest landowners in Virginia. The house to which he carried his bride sat on a mountaintop. He called it Monticello, and Italian word meaning "little mountain," and upon it he would lavish all the thought and energy he gave to any project he undertook. "They was forty years at work on the house before Mr. Jefferson stopped building," one of his slaves said.

In 1774 Jefferson had served six years in the House but had not achieved enough stature to be sent to the First Continental Congress that convened that autumn. Back at Monticello he wrote a pamphlet which came out under the title *A Summary View of the Rights of British America.* It was an incredibly bold – brash even – attack against George 111. If the king expects things to settle down in America, said Jefferson, he would do well to mend his ways. He has many sins to account for. He has delayed consideration of our laws; endeavored to take from the people the right of representation; dissolved representative bodies doing their duty; delayed the issue of writs for choice of new representatives; perpetuated feudal landholding practices; and sent troops among us. Jefferson dared even to accuse he king of forcing slavery upon the colonies, an evil which insults "the rights of human nature." He ended the essay with some impudent advice from a young man to his monarch: "The whole art of government consists in the art of being honest. Only aim to do your duty, and mankind will give you credit where you fail."

The pamphlet made Jefferson famous overnight, and led the Virginia convention – the governor had refused to let the legislature meet and so the members convened informally and illegally in a convention – to send him to the Second Congress in May of 1775. The delegates in Philadelphia studied the young man who had dared insult the king with care. He wore "a loose, shackling air" about him, it was observed, "a rambling vacant look" and ambled along at an "easy and swinging" pace. He had long arms and legs, large wrists, a jutting chin, light red hair, and a brick-colored face. A slave of his called him "as neat a built man as ever was seen in Vaginny, I reckon, or any place – a straight-up man, long face, high nose," but others less generous likened him to "a tall large-boned farmer." He almost never spoke from the floor of Congress and away from Congress rarely talked about himself, always turning the conversation "to subjects most familiar to those with whom he conversed, whether laborer, mechanic, or other." He impressed his colleagues as a solid, able delegate. Few noticed that "it constituted a part of Mr. Jefferson's pride," as friend remarked, "to run before the times in which he lived."

Jefferson attended Congress irregularly. His wife's constant ill-health kept him in suspense "too terrible to be endured" and drew him often home to Monticello. The early months of 1776 found him in Virginia, leaving it to others to prod Congress to declare independence. Not until mid-May did he return to Philadelphia. Even then he came reluctantly; he wanted to be in Virginia, where the convention was about to draw up a constitution for the colony. "It is work of the most interesting nature and such as every individual would wish to have his voice in," he said. "In truth, it is the whole subject of the present controversy."

He resumed his seat in Congress on May 14 but gave little time to the campaign for independence. Instead, he worked on a constitution for Virginia. His draft opened with a long list of the king's wrongs; these justified Virginia creating a constitution for itself. Jefferson then went on to advance a number of innovations for the new government. He thought the right to vote should be extended to virtually all white adult males in the colony. "Whoever intends to live in a country must wish that country well," he said, "and has a natural right of assisting in the preservation of it." He wanted to end the established that is, the state-supported and protected church and allow "all persons to" have full and free liberty of religious opinion. In a day when a man who stole a silver spoon risked death by hanging he dared to call for an end to all capital punishment except for the crime of murder. He also wanted to end slavery and inserted a clause in his draft that said "no person hereafter coming into this country shall be held in slavery under any pretext whatever."

Jefferson did all he could to get recalled to Virginia in order to present his draft to the constitutional convention, but he knew that the long-postponed vacation due to Richard Henry Lee and George Wythe meant he must stay in Philadelphia. Thus, against his own desire, he found himself in Congress on June 11 when the delegates chose him to head the committee created to draw up the Declaration of Independence.

Six months earlier Thomas Paine in Common Sense has defined the task the Congress had handed Jefferson. He urged that a manifesto "be published and dispatched to foreign courts, setting forth the miseries we have endured and the peaceful methods which we have ineffectually used for redress." This manifesto should declare to the world "that not being able any longer to live happily or safely under the cruel disposition of the British court, we had been driven to the necessity f breaking off al connections with her." Since the monarchs of Europe were bound to be suspicious of colonies rebelling against one of their brethren, the document should assure "all such courts of our peaceable disposition toward them, and of our desire of entering into trade with them." Such a document, Paine concluded, "Would produce more good effects to this continent than if a ship were freighted with petitions to Britain."

Consciously or not, Jefferson followed Pain's suggestions when he began the Declaration of

Independence as if they were orders. He knew his manifesto must appeal to the American people as well as foreign courts, but like Paine he also knew that the main job of the paper was to convince the world that what America was doing was right, that she "had been driven to the necessity" of breaking away from Great Britain.

Consciously or not, Jefferson followed Paine's suggestions when he began the Declaration of Independence as if they were orders. He knew his manifesto must appeal to the American people as well as foreign courts, but like Paine he also knew that the main job of the paper was to convince the world that what America was doing was right, that she "had been driven to the necessity" of breaking away from Great Britain.

Jefferson wrote his paper in the quiet of the second-floor apartment he had moved to in order to escape "the excessive heats of the city" and to "have the benefit of a freely circulating air." He worked at a portable desk light enough to rest comfortably on his knees. He wrote quickly, probably taking no more than a morning to complete the first draft. He began with a statement of purpose, which would be substantially revised before the world saw it:

When in the course of human events it becomes necessary for a people to advance from that subordination I which they have hitherto remained, & to assume among the powers of the earth the equal & independent station to which the laws of nature & of nature's god entitled them, a decent respect to the opinions of mankind requires that thy should declare the causes which impel them to the change.

No one in Congress except John Adams had read more widely in political literature than Jefferson, but in his opening lines he made clear he would draw principally, for his argument, from a book all the delegates were familiar with – John Locke's *Two Treatises of Government.* In that book Locke developed a justification for the "right of rebellion". Men were born free, in a state of nature and unhampered by government. The laws of nature endowed them with certain "self-evident" natural rights, among which were the rights to life, liberty, and property. Now, the state of nature is difficult to maintain, for evil exists in the world and there are times when a man alone cannot cope with it. To protect their rights, men voluntarily band together and make a compact or agreement whereby one of their own is chosen to rule over them. This ruler, with the people's consent, creates a government whose sole purpose is to protect men's natural rights. If the ruler fails to protect these rights, fails to carry out his duties, the people have the right to rebel, for their ruler has broken the original compact they made with him. But before they rebel, they must tell the world "the causes which impel them to the change."

Jefferson's next sentence, which would also be much rewritten, develops these ideas of Locke:

We hold these truths to be sacred and undeniable; hat all men are created equal & independent, that from that equal creation they derive rights inherent & inalienable, among which are the preservation of life, & liberty & the pursuit of happiness.

But here Jefferson made a major change. From Locke's trio of natural rights – life, liberty, and property – he dropped the last and added a new one. He did this with reason. His manifesto must appeal to all Americans, and many who were fighting to win America's freedom owned little or no property. The words he substituted for property - the pursuit of happiness – were borrowed from a friend who had written of man's right of "pursuing and obtaining happiness". Jefferson changed the wording, because he knew that while man had a right to pursue happiness he did not necessarily have a right to obtain it.

The theoretical basis for revolt had been laid down. Jefferson now moved on to submit "facts to a candid world," or as Paine put it, to set "forth the miseries we have endured" that justified the American revolt. He did not have to rummage through his mind to collect these facts. The lost of charges against the king he had drawn up as a preface for his draft of a constitution for Virginia were slipped in here. But in copying over the list Jefferson dreamed up several new charges, one of them a lengthy paragraph that blamed the imposition of slavery upon America on the king. George 111, said Jefferson, has "determined to keep open a market where MEN should be bought and sold, he ha prostituted his negative for suppressing every legislative attempt to prohibit or to restrain this execrable commerce."

Some, upon first meeting Jefferson, found him a cool gentleman – "nay, even cold," said one – but nothing in the concluding paragraphs of his manifesto reveals this side of his character. He writes with almost unrestrained passion. "These facts have given the last stab to agonizing affection and manly spirit bids us to renounce forever these unfeeling brethren," goes one sentence. Some of his most vivid phrases now come forth: Our former brethren we must now hold "as we hold the rest of mankind, enemies in war, in peace friends." We must now climb alone "the road to happiness and to glory;" From these lines he moves to a formal renouncement of all ties to Great Britain, and then ends with one of the great sentences in the English language:

And for the support of this declaration we mutually pledge to each other our lives, our fortunes, & our sacred honour.

With the first draft completed, Jefferson began tinkering with his handiwork, cutting out a word here, adding one there he decided, for example, that it sounded better to say "We hold these truths to be self-evident," rather than that they were "sacred & undeniable." The polishing done, he showed the document to John Adams, who liked it so much that he took time to make his own copy.

Between the time Adams returned the draft to Jefferson and when it was laid before Congress some thirty-one changes were made in the paper by Jefferson and members of the committee. The first two sentences were polished to their final form, and three new charges against the king were added. All other changes were minor. Everyone seemed highly satisfied with what Jefferson had done.

And exactly what had he done? He had, most skillfully, courted sympathy abroad. The eloquent but restrained opening passages, followed by the long list of the king's abuses of his power, revealed that the American people were acting only after endless suffering. Jefferson had carefully avoided attacking the monarchical form of government – to do so would have angered all the crowned heads of Europe – and centered his blast on a single misguided king, George 111. No hint of praise for a republican government appeared in the document. Americans were made to appear not as rebels but as a long-suffering, much put upon people who with great reluctance were breaking away from their mother country because of an evil monarch who had attempted to corrupt their way of life.

Jefferson managed at the same time he appealed to Europe to promote unity at home. The catalogue of George 111's transgressions touched on every section of the country. Few colonists could read the list without feeling that somewhere along the line they had been directly injured by the king. This was a remarkable achievement, considering the splits that have divided Congress the past several months. There was little in the paper, except possibly the indictment against slavery, likely to irritate any delegate, regardless of what part of the continent he came from.

As if this were not enough, Jefferson did more. In announcing America's independence, he made the new nation appear as a land of promise. We will climb "the road to happiness & glory," he said. We are a virtuous people and whatever corruption exists among us was imposed on us by Great Britain. Separation, he implied, would bring much more than a change of masters. Exactly what it would bring was unclear, but no hint of doubt that great changes were in the making turns up in the paper. By the substitution of the phrase "pursuit of happiness" for the word "Property," Jefferson made America seem a place where human rights ranked above all others, especially the rights of property.

For all its virtues, Jefferson's paper had a major flaw. He had simplified the highly complex issues dividing the colonies from Britain into a drama of good versus evil. It was, perhaps, hardly possible in a short paper appealing to world opinion for Jefferson to have done otherwise, but the result of this approach would be unfortunate in the long run. All the arguments in the great debate in Congress early in June had centered on what was best for America, what would do the most to promote the colonies' own interests. By obscuring the role of self-interest in shaping the decision on independence, Jefferson's paper propagated an unrealistic picture of how and why political decisions are made. But before the paper was given to the world Congress must approve it. Perhaps the delegates would edit Jefferson's paper in a way that would alleviate its single flaw.

A Difficult Time for Mr. Jefferson

Congress began to edit Jefferson's Declaration of Independence in the early afternoon of July 2 and continued to revise, amend, and cut the paper through the next two days. No author likes to have someone he thinks knows little about writing slash away at his sentences; he likes it less if the surgery is performed in public. Jefferson recorded that Benjamin Franklin, "who perceived that I was not insensible to these mutilations", leaned over from his adjacent seat and tried to divert him with a story.

Benjamin Franklin_Age 70: Retired Printer

The news of Lexington was still the talk of the town when Benjamin Franklin returned from England on May 5, 1775. His arrival in Philadelphia was "announced by ringing of bells, to the great joy of the city", and the provincial assembly, then in session, instantly added his name to the Pennsylvania delegation chosen for the Second Congress. When Congress convened four days later, Franklin was in his seat. For over two decades delegates had heard about the "prodigious genius" of Doctor Franklin. His "iron points" dotted roof tops in every village. He had lived in England some sixteen years and com home a man of world renown, the single American whose name was familiar in every household the length of the land. Now here he sat, "a short, fat trunched old man in a plain dress, bald pate, and short white locks". And he sat saying nothing, in *"expressive silence"*.

So great was his reputation that men hardly dared to consider what the effect would have been if, within a few days after his return, Franklin had announced for or against independence. But such and "if" would have required him to act against his nature. He had never been a man to hurry a decision and now, nearly seventy, he was even less prone to haste. Nor was he eager to find himself on the losing side of a cause. "Didst thee ever know Dr. Franklin to be in a minority"? a Quaker once asked rhetorically. So Franklin held his peace until he saw what was best for his interests and America's.

The first month and a half he kept to his house and went abroad only on public business. Those for reconciliation hoped he would use his influence to make Congress act with moderation. Rumors circulated that he planned soon to sail back to London on a peace mission, then his long silence evoked gossip of another sort. It was whispered about the city that the delegates in Congress "begin to entertain a great suspicion that Dr. Franklin came rather as a spy that as a friend, and that he means to discover our weak side to make his peace with the ministers by discovering information with regard to affairs a home, but hitherto he has been silent on that head and in every respect behaved more like a spectator than a member". A British agent in Philadelphia knew Franklin was no spy, but he knew little else. "By every intelligence I can get", he reported home in May, "Dr. Franklin keeps much on the reserve, and has not hitherto opined in the manner that was expected; if he is not blinded by faction, he can be of more use to Great Britain and America than any man in this country". A month later the spy reported that Franklin remained "among those who are for moderation and bringing about reconciliatory measures, but," he added "as he is a deep, designing man, it is not easy coming at this real intention". Franklin's reticence "highly offended" the volatile Richard Henry Lee of Virginia.

The rumors had died away by mid-July. By then he had told his old political ally Joseph Galloway and his son William, governor of New Jersey – both of whom would become Loyalists – that he favored independence. "The suspicions against Dr. Franklin have died away", a citizen reported; "whatever his design at coming over here, I believe he has now chosen his side, and favors our cause." But he did little inside and nothing outside Congress to promote independence, made no public speeches, wrote any articles for the press. The people must decide the question without his help.

"Dr. Franklin has been very constant in his attendance on Congress from the beginning," John Adams told his wife on July 23, and then proceeded to chart the doctor's curious course with a precision and clarity even Franklin would have admired.

His conduct has been composed and grave and in the opinion of many gentlemen very reserved. He has not assumed anything, nor affected to take the lead; but has seemed to choose that the Congress should pursue their own principles and sentiments and adopt their own plans. Yet he has not been backward; has been very useful on many occasions, and discovered a disposition entirely American. He does not hesitate at our boldest measures, but rather seems to think us too irresolute and backward. He thinks us at present in an odd state, neither in peace nor war, neither dependent nor independent. But he thinks that we shall soon assume a character more decisive.

He thinks that we have the power of preserving ourselves, and that even if we should be driven to the disagreeable necessity of assuming a total independency, and set up a separate state, we could maintain it. The people of England have thought that the opposition in America was wholly owing to Dr. Franklin; and I suppose their scribblers will attribute the temper and proceedings of this Congress to him; but there cannot be a greater mistake. He has had b little share farther than to cooperate and assist.

Although Franklin, like Adams, had been reared in Massachusetts, he resembled no man ever met there by Adams, who never came close to understanding him. "More of a philosopher than a politician", he said of one of the most adept politicians in Congress, Samuel Adams not accepted. A politician to Adams, who thought politics to be a noble profession, took a firm stand on an issue, then fought for it. Franklin, however, when he saw others headed in the direction he was going, husbanded his energy, satisfied " to cooperate and assist" while his companions fought the battles. Adams raged at Franklin's "passion for reputation and fame", which even friends admitted to be one of the old man's weaknesses, but failed to see that he used that fame deftly for ends beyond the reach of lesser mortals. James Wilson had a story to prove it. There was a citizen who once proposed to divert the waters of a creek north of Philadelphia into the city for public use. The man was carried by his family into court "to prove him insane". Later Franklin donated 1000 pounds to get the project underway, "and obtained for his legacy the character of a wise and benevolent man".

On committees Franklin was always "punctual and indefatigable", but in Congress he spent "a great part of his time fast asleep in is chair", to John Adams' dismay. His indolence "will prevent any thorough reformation of anything, and his" – "cunning" was the word Adams anted and wrote but hardly dared use; he crossed it out – "and is silence and reserve render it very difficult to do anything with him:. Occasionally, thought, when politics was not involved, Franklin could be garrulous, as Adams knew from a night when the two shared a bed in a small tavern. Before blowing out the candle Adams closed the bedroom window.

"Oh!" said Franklin, "don't shut the window. We shall be suffocated".

Adams said he feared "the evening air".

"The air within this camber will soon be, and indeed is now worse than that without doors", Franklin said. "Come! Open the window and come to bed, and I will convince you. I believe you are not acquainted with my theory of colds".

Adams opened the window and leaped into bed, saying that he had so much curiosity to hear his reasons that he would run the risk of a cold. Thereupon, Franklin "began an harangue upon air and cold and respiration and perspiration, with which I was so much amused that I soon fell asleep and left him and his philosophy together".

What manner of man was this sometimes garrulous, more often silent, old gentleman?

A genius? "His understanding is good enough for common uses. But not good enough for uncommon ones", said Thomas Jefferson, who liked and admired him. "He has very moderate abilities. He knows nothing of philosophy, but his few experiments in electricity", said John Adams, who developed an intense dislike for him.

Dispassionate? "I always knew him to be a very factious man", said the philosopher David Hume, a friend. "I am afraid that B.F., whose face at times turns white as the driven snow, with the extremes of wrath, may assert facts not true", said a friend who later became an enemy.

Virtuous? The most "hypocritical old rascal that ever existed – a man who, if ever one goes to ell, he will", said Lord Hillsborough, an enemy who had known him well in d "I have a very high opinion of B.F.'s, virtue and uncorrupted honest", said another, "but party zeal throws down all the poles of truth and candor and lays all the soul waste to temptation without knowing or suspecting it".

Beloved? "I never really was much of an admirer of the doctor", remarked a citizen of Pennsylvania after listening to companions tear apart Franklin's character, "but I could hardly find it in my heart to paint the devil so bad". A once close friend, later an enemy, called him "a very artful, insinuating fellow, and very ready at expedients". John Dickinson, who headed the Pennsylvania delegation when Franklin arrived in Congress, hated him so much he refused to have a lightning rod on his city mansion, an obstinacy later paid for when lightning struck the house.

Congress for several months treated its world-famous sage circumspectly. Gradually, it dawned upon the delegates that any session where wit, intelligence, and diplomacy might be of use must involve Franklin, and he, in turn, no matter how arduous the assignment, accepted it. In October 1775 he traveled up to Cambridge with Lynch and Harrison to confer with Washington about the siege of Boston. In March 1776, before the snows had cleared from the ground and traveling remained tortuous, Franklin with Charles Carroll and Carroll's cousin Father John Carroll trekked up to Canada seeking to cajole the citizens there to join the American cause. He returned from that ordeal in May, not only weary but in blinding pain from one of his recurring bouts with the gout. He spent the month of June recuperation on a friend's farm not far from the city. Jefferson sent his draft of the Declaration out to the farm on June 21. Franklin made only a few minor changers in the paper. He was well enough – or pretended to be – to attend Congress on July 2 to vote for independence, then stay on to watch the editing of the Declaration.

I have made it a rule, "Franklin said to Jefferson, as the young man writhed in his seat, "whenever in my power, to avoid becoming a draughtsman of papers to be reviewed by a public body. I took my lesson from an incident which I will relate to you".

When I was a journeyman printer one of my companions, an apprentice hatter, having served out his time, was about to open shop for himself. His first concern was to have a handsome signboard, with a proper inscription. He composed it in these words:

JOHN THOMPSON HATTER: MAKES AND SELLS HATS FOR READY MONEY

With a figure of a hat subjoined. But he thought he would submit it to his friends for their amendments. The first he showed it to thought the word "hatter" tautologous, because followed by the words "makes hats" which show he was a hatter. It was stuck out. The next observed that the word "makes" might as well be omitted, because the customers would not care who made the hats. If good and to their mind, they would buy, by whoever made. He struck t out. A third said he thought the words "for ready money" were useless, as it was not the custom for the place to sell on credit. Everyone who purchased expected to pay. They were parted with, and the inscription now stood:

John Thompson sells hats

"*Sells* hats" says his next friend. "Why, nobody will expect you to give them away. What then is the use of that word"? It was stricken out, and "hats" followed it, the rather, as there was one painted on the board. So his inscription was reduced ultimately to

"JOHN THOMPSON" with the figure of a hat subjoined.

Despite John Dickinson's heated objections to the Declaration, it looked at first as thought the paper would survive better than John Thompson's sigh. The opening paragraphs slid through with only a few minor changes. So, too, did the first fifteen of the charges against the king. The slight editing carried out here sought only to increase th3e accuracy of the charge. For instance, "He has suffered the administration of justice totally to cease in some of these states..."became" he has obstructed the administration of justice..." for it could be argued that the king had not closed the courts nor had the administration of justice "totally" ceased. In another charge Jefferson censured the standing armies and ships of war sent to America during peace time. Congress accepted the objection against standing armies, but ships of war protected America's shores and trade; that part of the charge was dropped. Only in the sixteenth charge did Congress finally feel the need to shore up Jefferson's prose. That charge dealt with the use of foreign troops. To underscore the cruelty and perfidy of this act they added – their additions are in italics – that it was "*scarcely paralleled in the most barbarous ages and totally* unworthy of the head of a civilized nation".

Congress had now covered over half the Declaration. The minor alterations made thus far should have bothered Jefferson little. The easy sailing ended when the delegates reached the last of his charges, the dealing with slavery. The entire paragraph was thrown out. It went out, Jefferson said bitterly, "in complaisance to South Carolina and Georgia, who had never attempted to restrain the importation of slaves, and who on the contrary still wished to continue it. Our Northern brethren also, I believe, felt a little tender under those censures; for tho' their people have very few slaves themselves, yet they had been pretty considerable carriers of them to others". He might have added that most of the Northern delegates also owned or had owned slaves – Benjamin Franklin among them – and were equally embarrassed by Jefferson's paragraph.

The misery had only begun for Jefferson. Nearly every line of the concluding paragraphs was assailed by someone in the room. Earlier Jefferson had attacked George 111 in his capacity as king.

When, however, at the start of the concluding section he wrote that:

> Future ages will scarce believe that the hardiness of one man, adventured within the short compass of twelve years only, to build a foundation, so broad & undisguised, for tyranny over a people fostered & fixed in principles of freedom he censured George as an individual. John Adams thought the attack "too personal, for I never believed George to be a tyrant in disposition and in nature", and Congress agreed with him. The passage was struck out.

The run of criticisms continued. Out went the obviously untrue statement that all who had migrated to America had been "unassisted by the wealth or the strength of Great Britain". Congress also deleted the judgment that "submission to their parliament was no part of our constitution, nor ever in idea, if history may be credited", for there were too many instances in the past of America's accepting Parliamentary jurisdiction without complaint. Then came the most agonizing blow: Congress reflected all of the last half of Jefferson's first concluding paragraph, which dealt mainly with those "unfeeling brethren", the English people. The decision kept away some of Jefferson's happiest phrases – "the road to happiness and glory is open to us too; we will climb it apart from them" 0 but there were sound reasons for the cut. America was breaking its ties with Great Britain not because of the iniquiti3es of the British people, but because of the king's crimes against America.

The final paragraph was reworked to include the original working of Lee's resolution of June 7. Several of the delegates felt Jefferson had been remiss in his references to God. Two more were added to the last paragraph. One appealed "to the supreme judge of the world for the rectitude of our intentions". The other went into Jefferson's final sentence:

And for the support of this declaration *with a firm reliance on the protection of divine providence,* we mutually pledge to each other our lives, our fortunes, & our sacred honor.

Congress completed its revision of the Declaration in the early evening of July 4. What had the delegates achieved during the two and a half days spent on Jefferson's paper" They had, in spite of some forty additions and extensive cuts that reduced the length by one-quarter, left the document pretty much intact, especially that part of it that would appeal to future generations. Jefferson said years later that the Declaration's "authority rest…on the harmonizing sentiments of the day:, and as far as pointing up those sentiments went, Congress improved his paper at every point. It eliminated any remark that tended to divide America – out went the diatribe against slavery, which especially angered the South, and along with it a reference to Scotch mercenaries, which jarred the sensibilities of an ethnic group – and added what it could to strengthen the union, as, for example, the reference to God which ought to satisfy the devout of the nation that the Revolution was being carried out under divine guidance.

The process of making Jefferson's Declaration into an American Declaration did more than improve the paper. It revealed that, despite strong divisive forces within the new nation, there appeared to exist a solid ideological basis for unity. Thirteen states, whose representatives only two years earlier had first met in Philadelphia and been appalled at the diversity of customs, laws, and traditions among the colonies, and who only three weeks earlier had been at loggerheads over the practical question of independence, had with little difficulty been able to agree on a set of fundamental political beliefs.

The thirteen clocks had been timed to strike as one, and also to strike the same tone. This, as the delegates knew, was remarkable and perhaps the most notable aspect of the Declaration of Independence as it left Congress. There may have been much in Jefferson's paper that dissatisfied or perturbed the delegates. Quite likely they voiced their complaints to the end, but when it seemed apparent that this was the best that could be produced to satisfy thirteen distinctly various colonies, defeat was accepted with the same grace, in the same spirit of realistic compromise, with which it had been accepted when independence itself, horrifying as it was to many of the delegates, became inevitable. Jefferson and Congress, then, could e equally pleased with their joint handiwork. Now, the delegates might begin to ask themselves, how would America, and the world, too, for that matter, react to what John Dickinson had called "this skiff made of paper?" We are now, sir," one member of Congress wrote on the morning of July 4, "embarked on a most tempestuous sea; life very uncertain, deceiving danger scattered thick around us, plots against the military, and it is whispered against the senate. Let us prepare for the worst, we can die but once".

Bibliography:

"Honorable Treason"

The Declaration of Independence and the Men who Signed It

David Freeman Hawke

The Viking Press, N.Y.; Copyright 1976 by David Freeman Hawke; Published in 1976.

JEFFERSON AND THE MEMBERS of the Second Continental Congress had not understood what they were doing in quite the way on July 4, 1776. For them, it was enough for the Declaration to be "merely revolutionary". Their text would not risk becoming wadding left to rot on the battlefield until the war with Britain was over, a memorial to the dead past until time had silenced the contests of their day. They sought to extend support for their cause and enhance the chances of victory; more they did not ask. In many ways, Douglas's history was more faithful to the past and to the views of Thomas Jefferson, who to the end of his life saw the Declaration of Independence as a revolutionary manifesto, and who understood that slavery violated the values of the Revolution but say federal coercion of Western slaveholders in exactly the same way. Lincoln's view of the past, like Jefferson's in the 1770s, was a product of political controversy, not research, and his version of what the founders meant was full of wishful suppositions.

But Lincoln was the greater statesman. By the mid-nineteenth century, when the standard of revolution had passed to radical Abolitionists and Southern secessionists who wanted to dismember the Union, the Declaration of Independence was in need of another reading. In Lincoln's hands, the Declaration of Independence became first and foremost a living document for an established society, a set of goals to be realized over time, and so an explanation less of the colonists' decision to separate from Britain that of their victory in the War for Independence. Men would not fight and endure as our fathers did", Lincoln wrote in a fragment probably composed early I 1861, "without the promise of something better, than a mere change of masters". He understood the Northern cause in the Civil war in much the same way; the North fought not only to save the Union, but to save a form of government, as Lincoln told Congress on July 4, 1861, "whose leading object is to elevate the condition of men; to lift artificial weights from all shoulders – to clear the paths of laudable pursuit for all – to afford all, an unfettered start and a fair chance in the race of life." The rebellion it opposed was at base an effort "to overthrow the principle that all men were created equal".

The deaths of Adams and Jefferson on the Fourth of July in 1826 had reinforced the belief that the United States held a special place in God's plans for the world. Surely Divine Providence was again at work when the turning point of the Civil war, the Northern victory at Gettysburg – as well as that at Vicksburg I the west – coincided with the celebration of Independence Day in 1863, six months after Lincoln issued the Emancipation Proclamation, freeing the slaves in rebel states. In Lincoln's hands that Union triumph because a vindication of the "proposition that all men are created equal" to which the new nation's "fathers" had committed it in 1776, "four score and seven years ago", and a challenge, as he said in dedication the cemetery at Gettysburg the following November, to complete the "unfinished work" of the Union dead and bring to "this nation, under God, a new birth of freedom.

In time, Lincoln's Gettysburg Address became itself an American sacred text. It started briefly and eloquently deep convictions that he had developed over the previous decade, convictions that on point after point echoed earlier Americans – the eulogists Peleg Sprague and John Sergeant in 1826, John Cooke in the Virginia constitutional convention a few years lat3r, Henry Clay in 1842, Benjamin Wade in Senate debates on the Kansas-Nebraska bill, and others who had also struggled to understand the practical implications of their revolutionary heritage, some of whose remarks Lincoln knew as well as many whose arguments were unknown to him but who had followed the same logic to the same conclusions. No less than Thomas Jefferson, then, Abraham Lincoln gave expression to a powerful strain in the American mind, not what all Americans thought but what many did. The values he emphasized – equality, human rights, government by consent – had in fact been part and parcel of the Revolution, and as much the subject of controversy than as later. Lincoln and those who shared his convictions did not therefore give the nation a new past or revolutionize the Revolution. But as descendants of the revolutionaries and of their English ancestors, they felt the need for a document that stated those values in a way that could guide the nation, a document that the founding fathers had failed to supply. And so they made one, pouring old wine into an old vessel manufactured for another purpose, creating a testament whose continuing usefulness depended not on the faithfulness with which it described the intentions of the signers but its capacity to convince and inspire living Americans.

The Declaration of Independence Lincoln left posterity, the "charter of our liberties", was not and could not have been his solitary creation. It was hat the American people chose to make o it. At once a legacy and a new conception, a document that spoke both for the revolutionaries and for their descendants, who confronted issues the country's fathers had never known or failed to resolve, binding one g3neration after another in a continuing act of national self-definition.

Bibliography:

"American Scripture"

Making the Declaration of Independence

Pauline Maier

Copyright 1997 by Pauline Maier; Published Alfred A. Knopf, Inc., N.Y.

CHAPTER 2: **The American Government**

Democracy

Democracy is a form of government, a way of life, a goal or ideal, and a political philosophy. The term also refers to a country that has a democratic form of government. The word *democracy* means *rule by the people.* United States President Abraham Lincoln described such self-government as "government of the people, by the people, for the people."

The citizens of a democracy take part in government either directly or indirectly. In a *direct democracy,* also called a *pure democracy,* the people meet in one place to make the laws for their community. Such democracy was practiced in the ancient Greek city-state of Athens and exists today in the New England town meeting.

Most5 modern democracy is *indirect democracy,* which is also known as *representative democracy.* In large communities-cities, states, provinces, or countries-it is impossible for all the people to meet as a group. Instead, they elect a certain number of their fellow citizens to represent them in making decisions about laws and other matters. An assembly of representatives may be called a council, a legislature, a parliament, or a congress. Government by the people through their freely elected representative is sometimes called a *republican government* or a *democratic republic.*

Many voting decisions in democracies are based on *majority rule* – that is, more than half the votes cast. A decision by *plurality* may be used when three or more candidates stand for election. A candidate with a plurality receives more votes than any other candidate, but does not necessarily have a majority of the votes. In several democracies, elections to legislative bodies are conduced according to *proportional representation*. Such representation awards a political party a percentage of seats in the legislature in proportion to its share of the total vote cast.

Throughout history, the most important aspects of the democratic way of life have been the principles of individual equality and freedom. Accordingly, citizens in a democracy should be entitled to equal protection of their persons, possessions, and rights; have equal opportunity to pursue their lives and careers; and have equal right of political participation. In addition, the people should enjoy freedom from undue interference and domination by government. They should be free, within the framework of the law, to believe, behave, and express them as they wish. Democratic societies seek to guarantee their citizens certain freedoms, including freedom of religion, freedom of the press, and freedom of speech. Ideally, citizens also should be guaranteed freedom of association and of assembly, freedom from arbitrary arrest and imprisonment, and freedom to work and live where and how they choose.

Some people in democratic states have been eager to increase the role of government in society in order to make material conditions more equal for everyone. But other people have been concerned that the extension of government's role in such areas as welfare, education, employment, and housing may decrease the freedom of the people and subject them to too much government regulation. The division between these groups has helped furnish one of the main themes of controversy and discussion in modern democratic societies.

Applying democratic principles in everyday life can be challenging. In the United States, for example, freedom of speech, press, religion, and assembly are protected by the First Amendment to the Constitution. In guarding these freedoms, the U.S. Judiciary has tried to balance the interests of individuals against possible injury and damage to other people and community. Thus, the right of free speech does not allow people to falsely damage the reputations of others.

Politics
Political –

1. Concerned with the science or art of politics.
2. Connected to a political party.
3. Exercising or seeking power in the governmental or public affairs of state or municipality.
4. Engaged in or connected with a civil Administration.
5. Having a definite policy or system of government.
6. Pertaining to Citizens.

Politicians –

1. A person who is active I in party politics.
2. A seeker or holder of public office.
3. More concerned about winning favor or retaining power than maintaining principles.
4. A person skilled in political government.
5. An expert in politics or political government.
6. A person who seeks power and advancement within an organization in ways that are generally disapproved.

The Constitution and The Bill of Rights
Definition of the Constitution and the Bill of Rights

Article 1:   The Legislative Branch

    Section 2   The House of Representatives

    Section 3   The Senate

    Section 4   Organization of Congress

The Bill of Rights

Amendment 12: Election of the President and Vice President

Amendment 13: Abolition of slavery

Amendment 14: Civil rights

Amendment 15: Black suffrage

Amendment 16: Income taxes

Amendment 17: Direct election of senators

Amendment18: Prohibition of liquor

Amendment 19: Woman suffrage

Amendment 20: Terms of the President and Congress

Amendment 21: Repeal of prohibition

Amendment 22: Limitation of Presidents to two terms

Amendment 23: Suffrage in the District of Columbia

Amendment 24: Poll taxes

Amendment 25: Presidential disability and succession

Amendment 26: Suffrage for 18-year-olds

Amendment 27: Congressional salaries

The Charters of Freedom

Or

The Nation's Vital Documents

1) The Constitution
2) The Bill of Rights
3) Declaration of Independence

Copied on Parchment in 1776; the Constitutional Convention 1787.

The British invaded Aug. 1814.

The Constitution has become a tangible remnant of the revolution which its children can still cling. What we are struggling to preserve from time is, however, not a physical body but a physical document that was written to perform a Constitutional function. That, too, involves some irony. The heroic efforts invested in conserving the document by which the United States declared its Independence from Britain testify to the powerful and enduring influence of English constitutional tradition on American political culture.

The committee that drafted the Declaration of Independence was:

1. Ben Franklin,
2. John Adams,
3. Roger Sherman,
4. Robert R. Livingston,
5. Thomas Jefferson.
6. George Washington was with his Continental Army in New York.

THE CONSTITUTION

What does our Constitution mean to you, and why should you bother studying it? When it comes to your rights and liberties, it would be dangerous to be indifferent. True, the U.S. Constitution has stood the test of time for more than two hundred years, preserving our rights, preventing despotism, and adjusting to the needs of an ever-growing nation. Yet despite its appearance of strength and stability, time and again constitutional rights and liberties have been imperiled and might have crumbled if taken for granted.

The U.S. Constitution has never been perfect. Like all laws, constitutions involve compromises. The original Constitution was a remarkable document, wise in construction and broad and balanced in powers but it contained serious flaws. The First Congress addressed a flaw of omission by hastily adding the Bill of Rights to the Constitution. A decade later Congress quickly repaired problems that had surfaced with the electoral college. The Constitution's most damaging compromise was its tolerance of slavery, an issue that eventually led to a constitutional breakdown and terrible Civil War. Out of that war came the amendments to the Constitution abolishing slavery ad guaranteeing the equal protection of the law to all citizens, regardless of race.

There were other unresolved issues that required additional amendments. Women struggled for a century to achieve political equality with men by gaining the right to vote. Young men between the ages of eighteen and twenty-one were subject to the military draft without having the right to elect the leaders who might send them into combat. States charged poll taxes that prevented poor people from casting ballots. Some issues were more structural, but still had significant consequences for every citizen because they involved national leadership; the long delay between a Presidential election and the inauguration; the ability of Presidents to run for an unlimited number of terms; the succession to the Presidency and Vice Presidency if the incumbent became ill, died, or resigned.

Beyond amendments, our lives have been influenced by thousands of laws enacted in Congress, by executive orders signed by Presidents, and by judicial decisions of the Supreme Court. These affect your education, your wages and hours, your taxes, and your pensions. The continuing debates over how to interpret the Constitution influence your freedom to worship, to read what you want, to speak your mind, and to protest injustices. They involve your life, liberty, and property, everything that you consider valuable. For these reasons, it is in your interest to know your constitutional rights. You will have the opportunity to choose your leaders – perhaps become one yourself. That carries with it a civic responsibility to understand how government works, to know its powers and its limits, and the meaning of a constitution written in the name of "we he people".

(Bibliography: Introduction "Our Constitution" Donald A. Ritchie & JusticeLearning.org; A Project of the Annenberg Foundation Trust at Sunny lands)

THE UNITED STATES CONSTITUTION

PREAMBLE
WHAT IT SAYS

We the People of the United States, in Order to form a more perfect Union, establish Justice, insure domestic Tranquility, provide for the common defense, promote the general welfare, and secure the Blessings of Liberty to ourselves and our Posterity, do ordain and establish this Constitution for the United States of America.

WHAT IT MEANS

The preamble expresses the purpose of the U.S. Constitution. The federal government gains its power from the people rather than from the states. The government exists to maintain peace at home, provide national defense, promote the well-being of the people, and protect their liberties. Importantly, the Supreme Court has held, in *Jacobson* vs. *Massachusetts* (1905), that the preamble itself is not a source of federal power or individual rights. Rather, all rights and powers are set out in the articles and amendments that follow.

ARTICLE 1: SECTION 1

WHAT IT SAYS

All legislative Powers herein granted shall be vested in a Congress of the United States, which shall consist of a Senate and House of Representatives.

WHAT IT MEANS

The framers of the Constitution separated the powers of government into three branches, granting legislative power (the power to pass laws) to Congress, executive power (the power to administer the laws) to the President, and Judicial power (the power to interpret laws and decide legal disputes) to the courts. The unique and limited powers of the Congress are specified in Article 1.

This separation of powers ensures that no one person or group could create, administer, and interpret the laws at the same time, and that each branch would serve as a check on the power of the other two branches. In some instances, the spheres of the three branches overlap, such as when Senate approval is required to confirm the President's nominees to the Supreme Court, or when the President can veto acts of Congress or pardon convicted criminals.

Section 1 also specifies that the Congress of the United States shall be bicameral, that is, it will be divided into two houses, the Senate and the House of Representatives. The previous government under the Articles of Confederation had only a single lawmaking body, as did some of the states. The creation of two legislative bodies reflected a compromise between the power of the states and the power of the people. The number of seats in the House of Representatives is based on population.

ARTICLE 1: SECTION 2

Clauses 1-2

WHAT IT SAYS

1) The House of Representatives shall be composed of members chosen every second Year by the People of the several States, and the Electors in each State shall have the Qualifications requisite for Electors of the most numerous Branch of the State Legislature.
2) No Person shall be a Representative who shall not have attained to the Age of twenty five Years, and been seven Years a Citizen of the United States, and who shall not, when elected, be an Inhabitant of the State in which he shall be chosen.

WHAT IT MEANS

The House of Representatives is composed of members chosen every two years by the voters of each state. There are only three qualifications: representatives must be at least twenty-five years old, must have been citizens of the United States for at least seven years, and must live in the state from which they are chosen. The states may not add any further controls on members of Congress, such as term limits or recall – special elections in which voters can remove public official's midterm- because these provisions are not specified by the Constitution. The Constitution allows the states to determine who is eligible to vote (the Constitution calls the voters "electors"). Whatever requirements are necessary to cast a vote for member so the larger house of the state legislatures will be sufficient to vote for the U.S House of Representatives.

In recent years, the Supreme Court has used the notion "by the people of several states" in Article 1 along with the Fourteenth Amendment's "equal protection" clause to require that each congressional district contain roughly the same number of people. This ensures that each person has an equal vote in a congressional election.

ARTICLE 1: SECTION 2
Clauses 3-5
WHAT IT SAYS

3) (Representative and direct Taxes shall be apportioned among the several States which may be included within this Union, according to their respective Numbers, which shall be determined by adding to the whole Number of free Persons, including those bound to Service for a Term of Years, and excluding Indians not taxed, three fifths of all other Persons.) The actual Enumeration shall be made within three Years after the first meeting of the Congress of the United States, and within every subsequent Term of ten Years, in such manner as they shall by Law direct. The Number of

Representatives shall not exceed one for every thirty Thousand, but each State shall have at Least one Representative; and until such enumeration shall be made, the State of New Hampshire shall be entitled to chose three, Massachusetts eight, Rhode-Island and Providence Plantations one, Connecticut five, New-York six, New Jersey four, Pennsylvania eight, Delaware one, Maryland six, Virginia ten, North Carolina five, South Carolina five, and Georgia three.

4) When vacancies happen in the Representation from any State, the Executive Authority thereof shall issue Writs of Elections to fill such vacancies.

5) The House of Representatives shall chose their Speaker and other Officers; and shall have the sole Power of Impeachment

WHAT IT MEANS

The Constitution set the number of members of the first House of Representatives from each of the original thirteen states and declared that the amount of direct taxes would depend on the number of citizens in each state. At the time, when slavery was still legal, it specified that slaves did not count as full citizens. The "three-fifths compromise" at the Constitutional Convention counted slaves as three-fifths of a citizen for purposes of state representation and taxation. This provision was changed following the Civil War with the passage of the Thirteenth, Fourteenth, and Fifteenth Amendments that abolished slavery, guaranteed equal protection, and extended voting rights to African Americans. Since then, all citizens, regardless of race, are fully counted in each census.

Clause 3 also establishes that the census (enumeration or headcount) will be conducted every ten years. Every adult in the country must answer a survey, which Congress then uses to determine how many representatives are to come from each state and how to distribute federal funds among the states. Every state must have at least one representative, but Congress sets the maximum number of members.

The Constitution specified the original number of representatives each state should have, but did not draw the district lines, a function it left to the states. As a result, the political party in power in each state legislature is able to define districts in such a way that benefits its own candidates. Extreme cases, which result in oddly shaped districts, are called gerrymandering, after a plan devised when Elbridge Gerry was governor of Massachusetts in 1812. An editorial cartoonist, looking at such a district, compared it to the mythical lizard-like creature the salamander, added the governor's name and coined the term gerrymander.

If a member of the House dies or resigns in midterm, the governor of the representative's state can call for a special election, with a "writ of election," to fill the vacancy. Unlike the Senate, where a governor can appoint someone to serve until the next election, no one has ever been appointed to the House of Representatives.

The Constitution authorizes the House to elect its own Speaker. The Speaker of the House presides over its meetings or authorizes another member to preside in his place. By act of Congress, the Speaker is next in line to become President, if both the President and Vice President are unable to serve. The House may also choose other officers, such as its chaplain, clerk of the House, and sergeant of arms.

The house also holds the power of impeachment. Akin to an indictment, impeachment of a federal officer- whether a judge, a cabinet secretary, or the President- requires only a simple majority in the House. A two-thirds vote of the Senate is then required to convict and remove from office the impeached official. Members of the House act as prosecutors during the trial in the Senate chamber. If a President is impeached, the chief justice of the United States presides over the Senate trial, rather than the Vice President, who stands to benefit from the President's removal.

SECTION 3

Clauses 1-3

WHAT IT SAYS

1) The Senate of the United States shall e composed of two Senators form each state, (chosen by the Legislature) thereof, for six Years; and each Senator shall have one Vote.
2) Immediately after they shall be assembled in Consequence of the first Election, they shall be divided as equally as may be into three Classes. The Seats of the Senators of the first Class shall be vacated at the Expiration of the second Year, of the second Class at the Expiration of the fourth Year; and of the third Class at the Expiration of the sixth Year; so that one-third may be chosen every second year; (and if Vacancies happen by Resignation, or otherwise, during the Recess of the Legislature of any State, the Executive thereof may make temporary Appointments until the next meeting of the Legislature, which shall then fill such Vacancies).
3) No Person shall be a Senator who shall not have attained to the Age of thirty Years, and been nine Years a Citizen of the United States, and who shall not, when elected, be an Inhabitant of that State for which he shall be chosen.

WHAT IT MEANS

The Senate, which now has one hundred members, has two senators from each state. Originally elected by state legislatures, senators have been directly elected by the people since ratification of the Seventeenth Amendment in 1913. Senators must be more than thirty years old, must have been an American citizen for at least nine years, and must live in the state they represent. Senators can serve for an unlimited number of six-year terms.

The Senate is divided into three "classes," and elections are held on a staggered basis so that one class, or one-third of the senators, stands for election every two years. When a state entered the Union, its first senators flipped a coin to determine which class they would enter, with the result that one received a longer term than the other, If senators leave office before the end of their terms, the state legislature may authorize the governor of their state to appoint someone to fill the vacant seat until the next election.

ARTICLE 1: SECTION 3

Clauses 4-7

WHAT IT SAYS

4) The Vice President of the United States shall be President of the Senate, but shall have no Vote, unless they be equally divided.
5) The Senate shall choose their other Officers, ad also a President pro tempore, in the absence of the Vice President, or when he shall exercise the Office of President of the United States.
6) The Senate shall have the sole Power to try all Impeachments. When sitting for that Purpose, they shall be on Oath or Affirmation. When the President of the

United States is tried, the Chief Justice shall preside: And no Person shall be convicted without the Concurrence of two-thirds of the Members present.

7) Judgment in Cases of Impeachment shall not extend further than to removal from Office, and disqualification to hold and enjoy any Office of honor, Trust or Profit under the United States: but the Party convicted shall nevertheless be liable and subject to Indictment, Trial, Judgment and Punishment, according to Law.

WHAT THIS MEANS

The Vice President of the United States is also the president of the Senate. The Vice President may preside over the Senate but can vote only to break a tie. To preside in the absence of the Vice president, the Senate elects a president pro tempore (literally, for the time being). Like the Speaker of the House, the president pro tempore is in the line of Presidential succession. By modern custom the president pro tempore is the senior member of the Senate's majority party. The Senate may also create and fill its other offices, such as the chaplain, secretary of the Senate, and sergeant at arms.

If the House of Representatives votes to impeach a federal official, the Senate holds a trial to convict or acquit that officer. The Vice President presides, except when a President has been impeached. The chief Justice of the United States presides over Presidential trials. A vote of two-thirds of the senators present (sixty-seven if all one hundred are present) is necessary to remove someone from office. This means that while a simple majority in the House may impeach an official, a larger consensus in the Senate is needed for conviction. In cases of impeached Presidents Andrew Johnson and Bill Clinton, fewer that two-thirds of the senators voted to convict them, and they were acquitted. Those convicted by the

Senate are removed from office, but Congress can inflict no further punishment on them, other than barring them from holding future office. Officials who have been removed may still be prosecuted criminally or sued, just like any other citizen.

ARTICLE 1: SECTION 4
Clauses 1-2
WHAT IT SAYS

1) The Times, Places and manner of holding Elections for Senators and Representatives, shall be prescribed in each State by the Legislature thereof; but the Congress may at any time by Law make or alter such Regulations, except as the Places of choosing Senators.
2) The Congress shall assemble at least once in every year, and such Meeting shall (be on the first Monday in December,) unless they shall by Law appoint a different Day.

WHAT IT MEANS

The Constitution gives the state legislatures the task of determining how congressional elections are held. For example, the state legislatures determine when elections are scheduled, how voters can register, and where they can cast their ballots. But, Congress has the right to change these state rules to set a uniform date for federal elections and to provide national protection for the right to vote. The first federal election law prohibited false registrations, bribery of election officials, and reporting false election returns. Congress passed this law after the Civil War as a means of enforcing the prohibitions against racial discrimination in voting contained in the Fifteenth amendment. With the passage of the Civil Rights Acts of 1957 and 1964 and the Voting Rights Act of

1965, Congress enacted greater protections for the right to vote in federal, state, and local elections.

As a general rule, Congress sets its own schedule for how frequently it meets. The Constitution provides only that it must meet once a year. Originally, congress convened on the first Monday in December, a year and a month after the congressional elections. In 1933 the Twentieth Amendment moved this date forward to January 3, unless the members specify a different schedule.

ARTICLE 1: SECTION 5

Clauses 1-4

WHAT IT SAYS

1. Each house shall be the Judge of the Elections, Returns and Qualifications of its own Members, and a Majority of each shall constitute a Quorum to do Business; but a smaller Number may adjourn from day to day, and may be authorized to compel the Attendance of absent Members, in such Manner, and under such Penalties as each House may provide.
2. Each House may determine the Rules of its Proceedings, punish its Members for disorderly Behavior, and with the Concurrence of two thirds expel a Member.
3. Each House shall keep a Journal of its Proceedings, and from time to time publish the same, excepting such Parts as may in their Judgment require Secrecy; and the Yeas and Nays of the Members of either House on any question shall, at the Desire of one fifth of those Present, be entered on the Journal.
4. Neither House, during the Session of Congress, shall, without the Consent of the other, adjourn for more than

three days, nor to any other Place than that in which the two Houses shall be sitting.

WHAT IT MEANS

Both the House of Representatives and the Senate are in charge of determining whether an election of one of its own members is legitimate. The losing candidate in an election may bring charges before the appropriate House or Senate committee, which will sift through the evidence and render a judgment. Similarly, the House and Senate can establish their own rules, punish members for disorderly behavior, and, if two-thirds of its members agree, expel a member.

Both the house and Senate need a quorum to do business - meaning that a majority of members must be present. A full majority need not always be present in the chamber but must be close enough to respond to quorum calls. Business in the chamber stops if a member calls attention to the absence of a quorum. Bells then ring through the Capitol and office buildings summoning enough members to establish a quorum. Each house may authorize its sergeant at arms to arrest absent members and compel their attendance to establish a quorum to do business.

Both bodies must keep and publish a journal of their proceedings, including how members voted. Congress can decide that some discussions and votes are to be kept secret, but if one-fifth of the members demand that a vote be recorded, it must be. To keep the two chambers operating on similar schedules, the Constitution requires that neither the House nor the Senate can close down or move proceedings from their usual location for a period longer than three days without the consent of the other chamber. To avoid having to ask each other's permission, either the House or the Senate will often hold pro forma (for form) sessions, where only a few members are present and no business in conducted, at times when the other body is meeting. So, for instance, if the House is meeting to handle some unfinished business, but the Senate has nothing on its agendas, and most senators are out of town that week, one senator will agree to stay behind and call the Senate to order each day, and then immediately adjourn. The presiding senator sometimes tries to see how fast he or she can strike the gavel calling the Senate to order and then immediately adjourning it, as a sort of game. This meets the constitutional requirements that both houses be in session at the same time.

ARTICLE 1: SECTION 6

Clauses 1-2

WHAT IT SAYS

1. The Senators and Representatives shall receive a Compensation for their Services, to be ascertained by Law, and paid out of the Treasury of the United States. They shall in all Cases, except Treason, Felony and Breach of the Peace, be privileged from Arrest during their Attendance a the Session of their respective Houses, and in going to and returning from the same; and for any Speech or Debate in either House, they shall not be questioned in any other Place.
2. No Senator or Representative shall, during the Time for which he was elected, be appointed to any civil Office under the Authority of the United States, which shall have been created, or the Emoluments whereof shall have been increased during such time; an no Person holding any Office under the United states, shall be a Member of either Hours during his Continuance in Office.

WHAT IT MEANS

Member of Congress are entitled to be paid for their service from the U.S. Treasury. Because members must vote to raise their own salaries, the Twenty-seventh Amendment, ratified in 1992, provides that salary increases can take effect only after the next election, giving voters a chance to register their approval or disapproval at the polls.

The Constitution protects legislators from arrests I civil lawsuits while they are I session, but they may be arrested in criminal matters. Member of Congress are granted immunity for criminal prosecution and civil lawsuits for the things they say and the work they do as legislators. This protection prevents prosecutors and others from using the courts to intimidate legislators because they do not like their views.

To ensure the separation of powers between the legislative, executive, and judicial branches of government, senators and representatives are prohibited from holding any other federal office during their service in Congress

ARTICLE 1: SECTION 7

Clauses 1-3

WHAT IT SAYS

1. All Bills for raising Revenue shall originate in the House of Representatives; but the Senate may propose or concur with Amendments as on other Bills.
2. Every Bill which shall have passed the House of Representatives and the Senate, shall, before it becomes a Law, be presented to the President of the United States; if he approve he shall sign it, but if not he shall return it, with his Objections to the House in which it shall have originated, who shall enter the Objections as large on their Journal, and proceed to reconsider it. If

after such Reconsideration two thirds of the House shall agree to pass the Bill, it shall be sent, tighter with the Objections, to the other House, by which it shall likewise be reconsidered, and if approved by two thirds of the House, it shall become a Law. But in all such Cases the Votes of both Houses shall be determined by yeas and Nays, and the Names of the Persons voting for and against the Bill shall be entered on the Journal of each House respectively. If any Bill shall not be returned by the President within ten Days (Sundays excepted) after it shall have been presented to him, the Same shall be a Law, in like Manner as if he had signed it, unless the Congress by their Adjournment prevent its Return in which Case it shall not be a Law.

3. Every Order, Resolution, or Vote to which the Concurrence of the Senate and House of Representatives may be necessary (except on a question of Adjournment) shall be presented to the President of the United States; and before the Same shall take Effect, shall be approved by him, or being disapproved by him, shall be repassed by two thirds of the senate and House of Representatives, according to the Rules and Limitations prescribed in the Case of a Bill.

WHAT IT MEANS

When it comes to raising and spending money, the House of Representatives must begin the process. The Senate can offer changes ad must ultimately approve the bills before they can go to the president. If the President signs the bill, it becomes a law. If the President does nothing for ten days, not including Sundays, the bill also automatically becomes law, except during the last few days of a congressional session. In that period of time, the President can use a "pocket veto." By doing nothing, the President automatically vetoes the bill. If the President sends a vetoed bill back to Congress with objections, it takes a two-thirds vote in both the House and Senate to override the veto in order for the bill to become law. Congress can also change the bill to make it more acceptable to the President. For political reasons, Presidents may be cautious about vetoing legislation, but just a threat of a veto may press members of Congress to work out a compromise. Similarly, if Congress has the necessary votes to override a veto, it is likely that the President will make every effort to compromise on the issue.

ARTICLE 1: SECTION 8

Clauses 1-4

WHAT IT SAYS

1. The Congress shall have Power To lay and collect Taxes, Duties, Imposts and Excises, to pay the Debts and provide for the common Defense and general Welfare of the United States; but all Duties, Imposts and Excises shall be uniform throughout the United States;
2. To borrow Money on the credit of the United States;
3. To regulate Commerce with foreign Nations, and among the several States and with the Indian Tribes;
4. To establish an uniform Rule of Naturalization, and uniform Laws on the subject of Bankruptcies throughout the United States.

WHAT IT MEANS

The eighteen clauses of Article 1, section 8 specify the powers of Congress in great detail. These powers are limited to those listed and those that are "necessary and proper" to carry them out. All other law-making powers are left to the states. The First Congress, concerned that the limited nature of the federal government was not clear enough in the original Constitution, adopted the Tenth Amendment, which reserved to the states all the powers not specifically granted to the federal government.

Over time, federal legislation has dealt with many matters that the states had previously managed. In passing these laws, Congress has often relied on the power granted it by the commerce clause (clause 3), which allows Congress to regulate business activities "among the states," because so much business today, either in manufacturing or distribution, crosses state lines. But the commerce clause powers are not unlimited. In recent years, the Supreme Court has expressed greater concern for states' rights. It has issued a series of rulings that limit the power of Congress to pass legislation under the commerce clause or other powers contained in Article 1, section 8. For example, these rulings have found unconstitutional federal laws aimed at protecting battered women or protecting schools from gun violence on the ground that these types of police matters are usually managed by the states.

The most important of the specific powers that the Constitution enumerates is the power to set taxes, tariffs (which the Constitution refers to as imposts), and other means of raising federal revenue, and to authorize the expenditure of all federal funds. In addition to the tax powers in Article 1, the Sixteenth Amendment (1913) authorized Congress to establish a national income tax. The power to appropriate federal funds is known as the "power of the purse." It gives Congress its greatest authority over the executive branch, which must appeal to Congress for all its funding.

The federal government borrows money by issuing bonds. This crates a national debt, which the United States is obligated to repay. Congress also determines how individuals and corporations can declare bankruptcy. It also has the responsibility for determining naturalization – how immigrants become citizens. Such laws must apply uniformly to all states and cannot be modified by the states. Although bankruptcy and immigration are unrelated, they are linked in this clause by the Constitution's intention to set uniform laws on such national issues.

ARTICLE 1: SECTION 8

Clauses 5-8

WHAT IT SAYS

5. To coin Money, regulate the Value thereof, and of foreign Coin, and fix the standard of Weights and Measures;
6. To provide for the Punishment of counterfeiting the Securities and current Coin of the United States;
7. To establish Post Offices and post Roads;
8. To promote the Progress of Science and useful Arts, by securing for limited Times to Authors and Inventors the exclusive Right to their respective Writings and Discoveries

WHAT IT MEANS

Congress determines what type of money the federal government will issue, both coins and bills, and sets punishments for anyone who tries to counterfeit that currency. In order to deliver the mail across the country, the Constitution authorized Congress to create the necessary infrastructure – post offices and roads. For the general improvement of society, Congress has the right to establish copyright laws and provide patent protection for authors and inventors, so their creative work cannot be pirated.

ARTICLE 1: SECTION 8

Clauses 9-11

WHAT IT SAYS

9. To constitute Tribunals inferior to the supreme Court;
10. To define and punish Piracies and Felonies committed on the high Seas, and Offences against the Law of Nations;
11. To declare War, grant Letters of Marque and Reprisal and make Rules concerning Captures on Land and Water;

WHAT IT MEANS

In Article 111 the Constitution established the Supreme Court, but it was left to Congress to create the lower federal court system, such as federal district courts and courts of appeal. Congress may also enact laws to protect American shipping on the seas beyond the national boundaries.

Although the President is the commander in chief, Congress has the constitutional responsibility to declare war. However, Congress has not formally declared war since World War 11. Since then it has generally passed resolutions authorizing Presidents to use military forces where necessary. Congress has also relied more on the power of the purse to shape military policy, most notably when it cut off funds for further military action in Southeast Asia in 1975.

Letters of Marque and reprisal were eighteenth-century documents that authorized "privateers," or private merchant to seize other nations' ships and cargoes in reprisal for having been pirated themselves. This section of the Constitution has become obsolete over time.

ARTICLE 1: SECTION 8

Clauses 12-16

WHAT IT SAYS

12. To raise and support Armies, but no Appropriation of Money to that Use shall be for a longer Term the two Years;
13. To provide and maintain a Navy;
14. To make Rules for the Government and Regulation of the land and naval Forces;
15. To provide for calling forth the Militia to execute the Laws of the Union, suppress Insurrections and repel Invasions;
16. To provide for organizing, arming, and disciplining the Militia, and for governing such Part of them as may be employed in the Service of the United States, reserving to the States respectively, the Appointment of the Officers, and the Authority of training the Militia according to the discipline prescribed by Congress;

WHAT IT MEANS

Congress grants the military authority and appropriations to maintain forts, arsenals, and naval yards. The executive branch can spend only what Congress appropriates, and Congress may not pass any appropriation of finds for longer than two years. Traditionally, Congress makes only annual appropriations, requiring all military and civilian agencies to request funds every year. The "power of the purse" gives Congress the opportunity to review and to influence military policy.

The states operate militias, such as the National Guard, under the laws passed by Congress. The federal government may call up these forces in times of national emergency. For instance, in 1795, Congress authorized President George Washington to use the militia to suppress the antitax Whiskey Rebellion in western Pennsylvania. In 1957, President Dwight D. Eisenhower used the Arkansas National Guard to protect students integrating a Little Rock high school. In 2003, President George W. Bush sent National Guard troops into combat in Iraq.

ARTICLE 1; SECTION 8

Clauses 17-18

WHAT IT SAYS

17. To exercise exclusive Legislation in all Cases whatsoever, over such District (not exceeding ten Miles square) as may, by Cession of particular States, and the exception of Congress, become the Seat of the Government of the United States, and to exercise like Authority over all Places purchased by the Consent of the Legislature of the State in which the Same shall be, for the Erection of Forts, magazines, Arsenals, dock-Yards, and other needful Buildings; - And

18. To make all Laws which shall be necessary and proper for carrying in Execution the foregoing Powers, and all other Powers vested by this Constitution in the Government of the United States, or in any Department or Officer thereof.

WHAT IT MEANS

Since 1800, the federal government has operated within the District of Columbia, an area consisting of land ceded by the states of Maryland and Virginia. For many years, Congress directly governed the District, but in 1967 it established a locally elected government. Even with such "home rule," Congress retained oversight over the District's laws and budget.

Because the framers of the Constitution could not anticipate the range of issues that Congress would face in the future, they gave Congress great latitude in making all laws "necessary and proper" to carry out its general powers. This is known as the "elastic clause," and it enables Congress to address new problems as they arise so long as these laws are consistent with the powers stated above.

ARTICLE 1: SECTION 9

Clauses 1-4

WHAT IT SAYS

1. (The Migration or Importation of Such Persons as any of the States now existing shall think proper to admit, shall not be prohibited by the Congress prior to the Year one thousand eight hundred and eight, but a tax or duty may be imposed on such Importation, not exceeding ten dollars for each Person.)
2. The Privilege of he Writ of Habeas Corpus shall not be suspended, unless when in Cases of Rebellion or Invasion the public Safety may require it.
3. No Bill of Attainder or ex post facto Law shall be passed.
4. (No capitation, or other direct, Tax shall be laid, unless in Proportion to the Census or Enumeration herein before directed to be taken.)

WHAT IT MEANS

Article 1, section 9, details areas in which Congress cannot legislate. In the first clause, the Constitution banned Congress from ending the slave trade before the year 1808.

In the second and third clauses, the Constitution specifically guarantees right to those accused of crimes. It provides that a writ of habeas corpus (a Latin phrase meaning "produce the body"), which allows prisoners the right to challenge their detention, cannot be suspended except under extreme circumstances, such as rebellion or invasion, when there is a public danger. Habeas corpus has been suspended only on are occasions in American history. For example, President Abraham Lincoln suspended the writ during the Civil War. In 1871, the federal government also suspended habeas corpus in South Carolina to combat the Ku Klux Klan.

The Constitution similarly prohibits bills of attainder, which are laws directed against specific individuals or groups, declaring them guilty of a serious crime – such as treason – by legislation rather than by a jury trial. This ban was intended to ensure that the legislative branch did not bypass the courts and deny people the protections designed for criminal defendants and guaranteed elsewhere in the Constitution. In addition, there can be no "ex post facto" (Latin for "after the fact") laws – or laws passed to make an action illegal after it has already happened. This protection guarantees that individuals are warned ahead of time that their actions are illegal.

The fourth clause, which prevented the imposition of direct taxes, caused the Supreme Court to strike down a national income tax in 1895. To expand federal revenues, Congress proposed and the states ratified the Sixteenth Amendment (1913), permitting the federal government to levy an income tax.

ARTICLE 1: SECTION 9

Clauses 5-8

WHAT IT SAYS

5. No Tax or Duty shall be laid on Articles exported from any State.
6. No Preference shall be given by any Regulation f Commerce or Revenue to the Ports of one State over those of another; nor shall Vessels bound to, or from, one State, e obliged to enter, clear, or pay Duties in another.
7. No Money shall be drawn from the Treasury, but in Consequence of Appropriations made by Law; and a regular Statement and Account of the Receipts and Expenditures of all public Money shall be published from time to time.
8. No Title of Nobility shall be granted by the United States: And no Person holding any Office of Profit or Trust under them, shall, without the Consent of the Congress, accept of any present, Emolument, Office, or Title, of any kind whatever, from any King, Prince, or foreign State.

WHAT IT MEANS

In order to ensure equality between the states, the Constitution prohibits states from imposing taxes upon goods coming into their states from another state and prevents Congress from favoring the ports of one state over the ports of others. This provision makes the entire United States a free trade zone, where no fees would be charged to import or export goods from state to state. Further, Congress could enact tariffs on goods imported from abroad, but it could not tax goods exported from any of the states.

The government cannot spend any public money unless Congress has appropriated it. Furthermore, Congress is required to produce a regular accounting of all the money the government spends.

Having fought a revolution to end aristocratic rule, and rejecting government by monarchy, the framers of the Constitution forbid Congress from establishing any American titles of nobility. It prohibited federal officials from accepting a title of nobility, office, or gifts from any foreign nation without congressional authorization.

ARTICLE 1: SECTION 10

Clauses 1-3

WHAT IT SAYS

1. No State shall enter into any Treaty, Alliance, or Confederation, grant Letters of Marque and Reprisal; coin Money; emit Bills of Credit; make any Thing but gold and silver Coin a Tender in Payment of Debts; pass any Bill of Attainder, ex post facto Law, or Law impairing the Obligation of Contracts, or grant any Title of Nobility.

2. No state shall, without the Consent of the Congress, lay any Imports or Duties on Imports or Export, except what may be absolutely necessary for executing its inspection Laws; and the net Produce of all Duties and imposts., laid by any State on Imports or Exports, shall be for the Use of the Treasury of the United states; and all such Laws shall be subject to the Revision and Control of the Congress.

3. No State shall, without the Consent of Congress, lay any duty of Tonnage, keep Troops, or ships of War in time of Peace, enter into any agreement or Compact with another state, or with a foreign Power, or engage

in war, unless actually invaded, or in such imminent Danger as will not admit of delay.

WHAT IT MEANS

Article 1, section 10 limits the power of the states. No state may enter into a treaty with a foreign nation as that power belongs to the President, with the advice and consent of two-thirds of the Senate. States cannot make their own money nor can they grant any titles of nobility. Like Congress, the states are prohibited from passing laws the assign guilt to someone without court proceedings (bills of attainder), that make some act illegal retroactively (ex post facto laws), or that interfere with legal contracts.

Under the federal system, the states retain sovereignty but the Constitution prohibits them from exercising powers granted to Congress, such as collecting taxes on exports and imports, building an army or keeping warships in time of peach, or otherwise engaging in war unless invaded or in imminent danger. States are also prohibited from charging "duties of tonnage," which refers to fees on the cargo-carrying capabilities of any ship.

ARTICLE 11: SECTION 1

Clauses 1-3

WHAT IT SAYS

1. The executive Power shall be vested in a President of the United States of America. He shall hold his Office during the Term of four years, and, together with the Vice-President, chosen for the same Term, be elected, as follows:
2. Each state shall appoint, in such Manner as the Legislature thereof may direct, a Number of Electors, equal to the whole Number of Senators and

Representatives to which the State may be entitled in the Congress: but no Senator or Representative, or Person holding an Office of Trust or Profit under the United States, shall be appointed an Elector.

(The Electors shall meet in their respective States, and vote by Ballot for two Persons, of whom one at least shall not be an Inhabitant of the same State with themselves. And they shall not be an Inhabitant of the same State with themselves. And they shall make a List of all the Persons voted for, and of the Number of votes for each; which List they shall sign and certify, and transmit sealed to the Seat of the Government of the United States, directed to the President of the Senate. The President of the senate shall, in the Certificates, and the Votes shall then be counted. The Person having the greatest Number of Votes shall be the President, if such Number be a Majority of the whole Number of Electors appointed; and if there be more than one who have such Majority, and have an equal number of Votes, then the House of Representatives shall immediately chuse by Ballot one of them for president; and if no Person have a majority, then from the five highest on the List the said House shall in like Manner chuse the President. But in chusing the President, the Votes shall be taken by States, the Representation from each State having one Vote; A quorum for this Purpose shall consist of a Member or Members from two-thirds of the States, and a Majority of all the States shall be necessary to a Choice. In every Case, after the Choice of the President, the Person having the greatest Number of Votes of the Electors shall be the Vice-President. But if there should remain two or more who have equal

Votes, the Senate shall chuse from them by Ballot the Vice-President.)

3. The Congress may determine the Time of chusing the Electors, and the Day on which they shall give their Votes; which Day shall be the same throughout the United States.

WHAT IT MEANS

The Constitution establishes that the President of the United States has the power to run the executive branch of the government. This section, later modified by the Twelfth amendment, establishes the Electoral College (the process by which the president and Vice President are elected).

This section says that the president and Vice President are elected at the same time and serve the same four-year term. Originally, there was no limit to the number of times a President could run for reelection. George Washington set the tradition of serving for no more than two terms. After Franklin Roosevelt was elected for four terms, the ratification of the Twenty-second Amendment limited presidents to no more than two four-year terms. A Vice President who assumes the presidency and serves more than two years of the remaining term is limited to one additional term.

Rather than being elected directly by the people, the President is elected by members of the Electoral College. It is not really a college but a group of people who are elected in each of the states. To keep elections national, rather than to favor any single state, the electors have to choose one candidate for president or Vice President who is not from their own states. The Electors then vote for the Presidential candidate who won the majority of the popular vote in their states. (In a few states, laws specify that electors will cast their ballots according to the percentage of votes that each candidate received). The number of electors from a state is equal to the number of senators and representatives from that state. Neither members of Congress nor other federal officials can serve as electors. The Electoral College give more weight to smaller states, rather than allowing the more populous states to control who becomes President, since all states have two Senators, regardless of the size of their population. Should no one receive a majority in the Electoral College, then the House of Representatives chooses the President and the Senate chooses the Vice President.

Presidential elections are held on the Tuesday that follows the first Monday in November. After the people cast their votes, the electors meet in their respective states to ballot on the Monday following the second Wednesday in December. The electoral ballots are than counted at a joint session of Congress, held on January 6.

ARTICLE 11: SECTION 1

Clauses 4-7

WHAT IT SAYS

4. No Person except a natural born Citizen, or a Citizen of the United States, at the time of the Adoption of this Constitution, shall be eligible to the Office of President; neither shall any person be eligible to that Office who shall not have attained to the Age of thirty-five Years, and been fourteen Years a Resident within the United States.

5. In Case of the Removal of the President from Office, or of his Death, resignation, or Inability to discharge the Powers and Duties of the said Office, the same shall devolve on the Vice President, and the Congress may by Law provide for the Case of Removal, Death, Resignation or Inability, both of the President and Vice

President, declaring what Officer shall then act as President, and such Officer shall act accordingly, until the Disability be removed, or a President shall be elected.

6. The President shall, at stated Times, receive for his Services, a compensation, which shall neither be increased nor diminished during the Period for which he shall have been elected, and he shall not receive within that Period any other Emolument from the United States, or any of them.

7. Before he enter on the Execution of his Office, he shall take the following Oath or Affirmation: - "I do solemnly swear (or affirm) that I will faithfully execute the Office of President of the United States, and will to the best of my Ability, preserve, protect and defend the Constitution of the United States."

WHAT IT MEANS

There are three minimum requirements to be President: one must be a natural-born citizen of the United States, have lived in the United States for at least fourteen years, and must be at last thirty-five years old. A natural – born citizen is a person either born in this country or born to American parents living abroad.

If the President dies or resigns, the Vice president becomes President. Congress has designated other officials to be in the line of succession, including the Speaker of the House, the president pro tempore of the Senate, and members of the cabinet. The Twenty-fifth Amendment, added in 1967, allowed for the appointment of a new Vice President in case that office becomes vacant.

Congress sets the president's salary. To prevent Congress from punishing or rewarding the President financially, the Constitution prohibits any change in salary during a President's current term, but it could be increased in a second term. The President is prohibited from receiving any other type of compensation while in office. However, Congress also provides funds to pay for Presidential expenses in operating the White House, hosting social functions, and traveling. Ethics laws also determine what gifts a President can accept and what belongs to the government.

On taking office, Presidents take an oath to do their best to uphold the United States Constitution as the law of the land. The wording of this oath is written into the Constitution. All other federal officers take an oath enacted by Congress.

ARTICLE 11: SECTION 2

Clauses 1-3

WHAT IT SAYS

1. The President shall be Commander in Chief of the Army and Navy of the United States, d of the Militia of the several States, when called into the actual Service of the United States; he may require the Opinion, in writing, or the principal Officer in each of the executive Departments, upon any Subject relating to the Duties of heir respect Offices, and he shall have Power to Grant Reprieves and Pardons for Offences against the United states, except in Cases of Impeachment.

2. He shall have Power, by and with the Advice and Consent of the Senate, to make Treaties, provided two-thirds of the Senators present concur; and he shall nominate, and by the with the Advice and Consent of the Senate, shall appoint Ambassadors, other public Ministers and Consuls, Judges of the supreme Court, and all other Officers of the United States, whose appointments are not herein otherwise provided for, and

which shall be established by law; but the Congress may by Law vest the Appointment of such inferior Officers, as they think proper, in the President alone, in the Courts of Law, or in the Heads of Departments.

3. The President shall have Power to fill up all Vacancies that may happen during the Recess of the senate, by granting commissions which shall expire at the End of their next Session.

WHAT IT MEANS

The President serves no only as head of the executive branch of government but also as the commander in chief of the armed forces (including the National Guard of each state when they are called upon to serve with the federal armed forces). All U.S. military forces are therefore subordinate to the civilian government. The President appoints a secretary of defense and other civilian officials to supervise the armed forces. Being commander in chief has given Presidents immense power in wartime, and over time has allowed them to assert greater control over foreign and military policy.

As chief executive, the President is responsible for the different executive offices. These include the high-level cabinet departments, such as the Department of the Treasury, and also many smaller, specialized agencies, such as the National Aeronautics and Space Administration (NASA).

With the permission of two-thirds of the Senate, the President can make treaties with other nations, and with the approval of majority of senators, the President appoints U.S. ambassadors to other countries, federal judges including Supreme Court justices, cabinet officers, agency heads, and other officers of the government. Congress may choose to allow the President to appoint lower-level positions without Senate approval. When the Senate is not in session, the president can appoint people without Senate approval. Know as "recess appointment," these appointees' terms end when the next Senate session ends – unless the Senate votes to confirm their nominations.

ARTICLE 11: SECTION 3-4

WHAT IT SAYS

He shall from time to time give to the Congress Information on the State of the Union, and recommend to their Consideration such Measures as he shall judge necessary and expedient; he may, on extraordinary Occasion, convene both Houses, or either of them, and in Case of Disagreement between them, with Respect to the Time of Adjournment, he may adjourn them to such Time as he shall think proper; he shall receive Ambassadors and other public Ministers; he shall take Care that the Laws be faithfully executed, and shall Commission all the Officers of the United States.

President, Vice President and all civil Officers of the United States, shall be removed from Office on Impeachment for, and Conviction of, Treason, Bribery, or other high Crimes and Misdemeanors.

WHAT IT MEANS

Most years the President reports to Congress about how things are going in the country. Although the Constitution only requires a State of the Union speech "from time to time," Presidents use the opportunity annually to present their agenda for legislative action. This section also grants the President the power to call the House of Representatives and the Senate back into special session after they have adjourned, to deal with a crisis or some other business that cannot wait. Although the President is also granted the power to adjourn Congress, that has never been done. The President meets with representatives of other nations on behalf of the United States and otherwise runs the country by enforcing the laws and directing its officers and staff.

The President, Vice President, and other federal officers can be removed from office through impeachment and conviction of treason, bribery, or other high crimes. The process begins in the House, where a simple majority is needed to impeach. The accused official then stands trial in the Senate, where a two-thirds vote must be achieved for conviction. President Richard Nixon resigned from office as the House prepared to vote to impeach him. Presidents Andrew Johnson and Bill Clinton were impeached in the House but acquitted in the Senate. If convicted, the official is removed from office.

ARTICLE 111: SECTION 1

WHAT IT SAYS

The judicial Power of the United States shall be vested in one Supreme Court, and in such inferior Courts as the Congress may from time to time ordain and establish. The Judges, both of the supreme and inferior Courts, shall hold their Offices during good Behavior, and shall, at stated Times, receive for their Services a compensation which shall not be diminished during their Continuance of Office.

WHAT IT MEANS

Article 111 establishes the federal court system. The first section creates the U.S. Supreme Court as the federal system's highest court. The Supreme Court has the final say on matters of federal law that come before it. The Constitution specifies that judges will serve "during good Behavior," meaning for life – so long as they do not violate their oath of office by taking an impeachable action – and that their salaries cannot be cut as a means of controlling or punishing them. This assures an independent judiciary. The Supreme Court today has nine members, who are appointed by the President with the consent of a majority of the Senate. Congress has the power to create and organize the lower federal courts, which operate in every state. A case is filed and tried in the federal district courts or in some specialty courts, such as admiralty or bankruptcy courts. The trial courts look at the facts of the case and decide guilt or innocence, or which side is right in a dispute. If the losing side appeals the outcome, the appellate courts determine whether the trial was fair and followed the rules, and whether the law was correctly applied. A case may be appealed as far as the Supreme Court, although the Supreme Court hears only a small number of cases.

ARTICLE 11: SECTION 2

Clauses 1-3

WHAT IT SAYS

1. The judicial Power shall extend to all Cases, in Law and Equity, arising under this Constitution, the Laws of the United States, and Treaties made, or which shall be made, under their Authority; - to all Cases affecting Ambassadors, other public ministers and Consuls; - to all Cases of admiralty and maritime Jurisdiction; - to Controversies to which the United States shall be a Party; - to Controversies between two or more States – between a State and Citizens of another State; - between Citizens of different States; - between Citizens of the same State claiming Lands under Grants of different States, and between a State, or the Citizens thereof, and foreign States, Citizens or subjects.
2. In all Cases affecting ambassadors, other public Ministers and Consuls, and those in which a State shall

be Party, the Supreme Court shall have original Jurisdiction. In all the other Cases before mentioned, the Supreme Court shall have appellate Jurisdiction, both as to Law and Fact, with such Exceptions, and under such Regulations as the Congress shall make.

3. The trial of all Crimes, except in Cases of Impeachment, shall be by Jury; and such Trial shall be held in the State where the said Crimes shall have been committed; but when not committed within any state, the Trial shall be at such Place or Places as the Congress may by Law have directed.

WHAT IT MEANS

The federal courts decide argument over how to interpret the Constitution, all laws passed by Congress, and the nation's rights and responsibilities in agreements with other nations. Federal courts can hear disputes that may arise between states, between citizens of different states and between states and the federal government.

In the case of *Marbury v. Madison* (1803), the Supreme Court interpreted Articles 111 and 1V as giving the federal courts the final say over the meaning of the Constitution and all federal laws, as well as the power to order state and federal officials to comply with its rulings. The federal courts can make decisions only on cases that are brought to them through the appeals process. Federal courts cannot create cases on their own – even if they believe that a law is unconstitutional. A person adversely affected by the law must bring suit against the government in order for the courts to rule on the matter.

Almost all federal cases start in the federal district court, where motions are decided and trials are held. Then, if the outcome of the trial is questioned by one of the parties, the cases are heard on appeal by the federal court of appeals and possibly by the Supreme Court. The Supreme Court accepts only a small number of cases for review, typically about eighty cases each year.

The federal courts also have final say over guilt or innocence in federal criminal cases, such as kidnapping, wiretapping, or narcotics smuggling. U.S. attorneys in the various states bring charges against those accused of breaking federal law. The Justice Department also brings suits and prosecutes alleged offenders. Defendants in criminal cases, except impeachment, have a right to have their cases heard by a jury in the state where the crime occurred.

ARTICLE 111: SECTION 3

Clauses 1-2

WHAT IT SAYS

1. Treason against the United States shall consist only in levying War against them, or in adhering to their Enemies, giving them Aid and Comfort. No Person shall be convicted of Treason unless on the Testimony of two Witnesses to the same overt Act, or on Confession in open Court.
2. The Congress shall have Power to declare the Punishment of Treason, but no Attainder of Treason shall work Corruption of Blood, or Forfeiture except during the Life of the Person attained.

WHAT IT MEANS

Treason is the only crime specifically defined in the Constitution. Individuals may be found guilty of treason if they go to war against the United States or give "aid or comfort" to its enemies. They do not have to physically pick up a o and fight in combat against U.S. troops. Actively helping the enemy by passing along classified information or supplying weapons can lead to the charge of treason. Vocal opposition to a U.S. war effort through protest and demonstration, however, is protected by the free speech clause the First Amendment.

A conviction of treason must be based either on an admission of guilt or on the testimony of two witnesses. Congress may set a punishment, but it must be directed only at the guilty persons and not against their friends or family, if they were not involved in the crime. The Constitution's strange reference to corrupt blood or forfeiture was intended to negate the English common law that prevented blood relatives of person convicted of treason from inheriting the person's property. This became an issue when the government was dealing with the property of Confederates after the Civil War.

ARTICLE 1V: SECTION 2

Clauses 1-3

WHAT IT SAYS

1. The Citizens of each State shall be entitled to all Privileges and Immunities of Citizens in the several States.
2. A Person charged in any State with Treason, Felony, or other Crime, who shall flee from Justice, and be found in another State, shall on demand of the executive Authority of the State from which he fled, be delivered up, to be removed to the State having Jurisdiction of the Crime.
3. (No Person held to Service or Labour in one state, under the Laws thereof, escaping into another, shall, in Consequence of any Law or Regulation therein, be discharged from such Service or Labour, but shall be

delivered up on Claim of the Party to whom such Service or Labour may be due.)

WHAT IT MEANS

States cannot discriminate against citizens of other states. A state must give people from other states the same fundamental rights it gives its own citizens. For example, Arizona cannot pass a law prohibiting residents of New Mexico from traveling, owning property, or working in Arizona, nor can the state impose substantially different taxes on residents and nonresidents. But certain distinctions between residents and nonresidents are permitted, such as giving state residents a right to by a hunting license at a lower cost.

When any person accused of committing a crime in one state flees to another, the second state is obligated to return the fugitive to the state where the crime was committed. The process used to return fugitives (called extradition) were created by Congress and originally enforced by the governors of each state. Today the state and federal courts enforce the return of accused prisoners. Fugitives do not need to have been charged with the crime in the first state in order to be captured in the second and sent back. Once returned, the state can charge the accused with any crime for which there is evidence. By contrast, when a foreign country returns a fugitive to a state for trial, the state is only allowed to try the fugitive on the charges named in the extradition papers (the formal, written request for the fugitive's return).

The "fugitives from labor" provision gave slave owners a nearly absolute right to recapture runaway slaves who fled to other states, even if slavery was outlawed in those states. This meant the state laws in free states intended to protect runaway slaves were unconstitutional because they interfered with the slave owners' right to their slave's return. After the Civil War, the adoption of the Thirteenth Amendment, which abolished slavery and prohibited "involuntary servitude," nullified this provision.

ARTICLE 1V: SECTION 3
Clauses 1-2
WHAT IT SAYS

1. New States may be admitted by the Congress into this Union; but no new State shall be formed or erected within the Jurisdiction of any other State; nor any State be formed by the Junction of two or more states, or parts of States, without the Consent of the Legislatures of the States concerned as well as of he Congress.
2. The Congress shall have Power to dispose of and make all needful Rules and Regulations respecting the Territory or other Property belonging to the United States; and nothing in this Constitution shall be so construed as to Prejudice any Claims of the United States, or of any particular State.

WHAT IT MEANS

Congress can admit new states into the Union, but a single state cannot create a new state within its boundaries. For instance, the state of New York cannot make New York City a separate state. Nor can two states, nor parts of states such as eastern Oregon and western Idaho, merge to form a new state without the consent of the various state legislatures and Congress. The Constitution does not specify that new states enter into the Union on an equal footing with the other states, but Congress has always granted new states equality with the existing states.

Not all the lands of the United States are states. Some lands are territories, and Congress has the power to sell off or regulate the territories. This includes allowing U.S. territories to become independent nations, which is what happened in the case of the former U.S. territory the Philippines, or regulating the affairs of such current U.S. territories as Guam and Puerto Rico. This provision also gives Congress the power to set rules for lands owned by the United States, such as national park land and notional forests. The last sentence of this clause makes sure that nothing in the Constitution will harm the rights of either the federal government or the states in disputes over territory or property.

ARTICLE 1V: SECTION 4

WHAT IT SAYS

The United States shall guarantee to every State in this Union a Republican Form of Government, and shall protect each of them against Invasion; and on Application of the Legislature, or of the Executive (when the Legislature cannot be convened) against domestic Violence.

WHAT IT MEANS

This provision, known as the guarantee clause, ensures that each state is run as a representative democracy, as opposed to allowing a monarchy or dictatorship to control the government. Courts have been reluctant to specify what a republican government means, leaving that decision to Congress.

Congress has the power, and the obligation, to protect the states from invasion by a foreign country or form significant violent uprising with each state. The Constitution authorizes the legislature of each state (or the governor, if the legislature cannot be assembled in time) to request federal help in the event of riots and other violence.

ARTICLE V
WHAT IT SAYS

The Congress, whenever two-thirds of both Houses shall deem it necessary, shall propose Amendments to this Constitution, or, on the Application of the Legislatures of two-thirds of the several States, shall call a Convention for proposing Amendments, which, in either Case, shall be valid to all Intents and Purposes, as Part of this Constitution, when ratified by the Legislatures of three-fourths of the several States, or by Conventions in three-fourths thereof, as the one or the other Mode of Ratification may be proposed by the Congress; Provided that no amendment which may be made prior to the Year One thousand eight hundred and eight shall in any Manner affect the first and fourth Clauses in the Ninth Section of the first Article; and that no State, without its Consent, shall be deprived of its equal Suffrage in the Senate.

WHAT IT MEANS

Realizing that over time the nation would want to make changes to the Constitution, its framers established a process to allow that to happen. Unlike laws and regulations that can be passed by simple majorities in Congress, the Constitution is more difficult to change.

Amendments are offered to the states once two-thirds of the Senate (67 of the 100 senators) and of the House (290 of 435 representatives) vote to approve the change, or when two-thirds of the states (34 of the 50 states), call for a national convention (at gathering of representative of each state) to propose a change.

Once the amendment is proposed, three-fourths of the state legislatures, or state conventions (38 of the 50 states, must vote to ratify the amendment before it becomes part of the Constitution. One portion of the Constitution is not subject to amendment. There can be no amendment that would deny a state its equal votes in the Senate, without that state's consent.

ARTICLE V1

Clauses 1-3

WHAT IT SAYS

1. All Debts contracted and Engagements entered into, before the Adoption of this Constitution, shall be as valid against the United States under this Constitution, as under the Confederation.
2. This Constitution, and the Laws of the United States which shall be made in Pursuance thereof; and all Treaties made, or which shall be made, under the Authority of the United Stated shall be the supreme Law of the Land; and the Judges in every State shall be found thereby, any Thing in the Constitution or Laws of any State to the Contrary notwithstanding.
3. The Senators and Representatives before mentioned, and the Members of the several State Legislatures, and all executive and judicial Officers, both of the United States and of the several States, shall be bound by Oath or Affirmation, to support this constitution; but no religious Test shall ever be required as a Qualification to any Office or public Trust under the United States.

WHAT IT MEANS

The new Constitution recognized that the debts of the previous government under the Articles of Confederation were still valid.

If a state law is in conflict with federal law, federal law must prevail. Referred to as the "supremacy clause," this article declares that the Constitution and the laws and treaties of the federal government are the highest in the land. While state courts rule on stated laws, the federal courts can stop and order charges if the state laws go against federal law.

All federal and state officials must take an oath of allegiance to the Constitution. Although state officials have a duty to obey there own state constitutions and laws, their first loyalty must be to the U.S. Constitution. To ensure freedom of religion, public officials cannot be required to practice or pledge allegiance to any particular religion in order to hold office.

ARTICLE V11

WHAT IT SAYS

The Ratification of the Conventions of nine States shall be sufficient for the Establishment of this Constitution between the States so ratifying the same.

<u>SIGNERS</u>

Done in Convention by the Unanimous Consent of the States present the Seventeenth Day of September in the Year of our Lord one thousand seven hundred and Eighty seven and of the Independence of the United States of America the Twelfth. In witness whereof We have here unto subscribed our Names,

George Washington, President and deputy from Virginia

New Hampshire	*Pennsylvania*	*Virginia*
John Langdon	Benjamin Franklin	John Blair
Nicholas Gilman	Thomas Mifflin	James Madison Jr.

Robert Morris
Massachusetts
Nathaniel Gorman
Connecticut
William Samuel
Johnson
Roger Sherman
Alexander Hamilton
New Jersey
William Brearley
William Paterson
William Paterson
Jonathan Dayton
Attest: Abraham Baldwin

George Clymer
Thomas Fitzsimons
Jared Ingersoll
Governor Morris
Delaware
Richard Bassett
Jacob Broom
Maryland
James McHenry
Daniel Livingston
Daniel of St. Thomas

North Carolina
William Blount
Richard Dobbs
Hugh Williamson
South Carolina
Charles Cotesworth
Charles Pinckney
Pierce Butler
Georgia
William Few

William Jackson, Secretary

WHAT IT MEANS

Unlike the Articles of Confederation, which needed the unanimous consent of the thirteen states to make changes in the structure of the government, the Constitution required ratification by only nine of the states for the new government to go into effect. All of the original thirteen states, except Rhode Island, held conventions to ratify the Constitution. North Carolina's convention adjourned without voting on the document. On December 7, 1787, Delaware became the first state to ratify the Constitution, followed by Pennsylvania, New Jersey, Georgia, Connecticut, Massachusetts, Maryland, and South Carolina. The ninth ratification, by New Hampshire, occurred on June 21, 1788. Virginia and New York ratified the Constitution shortly afterward. North Carolina and Rhode Island waited to ratify the Constitution until after Congress passed the Bill of Rights and sent it to the states for ratification.

Of the fifty-five delegates who attended the Constitutional Convention, thirty-nine signed the document. Some of the delegates who did not sign supported the new Constitution but were absent at the time of its signing. A few, however, raised objections to the Constitution and refuse to sign it. William Jackson was not a delegate but served as the secretary for the convention and authenticated the signatures of the delegates.

THE BILL OF RIGHTS

FIRST AMENDMENT (1791)
WHAT IT SAYS

Congress shall make no law respecting an establishment of religion, or prohibiting the free exercise thereof; or abridging the freedom of speech, or of the press; or the right of the people peaceably to assemble, and to petition the Government for a redress of grievances.

WHAT IT MEANS

The First Amendment may well be the best known of our constitutional protections, and possibly the least understood. The First Amendment's free speech, assembly, and press guarantees allow citizens to express and be exposed to a wide range of opinions. It was intended to ensure a free marketplace of ideas – even if the ideas are unpopular. Freedom of speech encompasses not only the spoken word, but also all kinds of expression (including nonverbal communications, such as sit-ins). Under its provision, the media – newspaper, television, radio, books, art, advertisements, and Internet – are fit to distribute news, information, ideas, and opinions. The amendment protects not only the speaker but also the person who receives the information. The ability to read, hear, see, and obtain different points of view is a First Amendment right, too.

The right to free speech is not absolute, however. The government may limit or ban libel (the communication of false statements about people that injures their reputations). The government can further restrict obscenity, "fight words" – insults intended to provoke a fight – and words that present a "clear and present danger" of causing violence, to use the phrase of Justice Oliver Wendell Holmes Jr. The government can also regulate speech through specific rules limiting the time, place, or manner in which it is made.

The First Amendment also protects the freedom of assembly, which can mean everything from gathering with a group of people to picket or protest to giving people the right to associate with one another in groups for economic, political, or religious purposes without unnecessary government regulation. Related to this is the right to petition the government, which includes everything from signing an actual petition to filing a lawsuit.

The First Amendment protects individuals' freedom of religion in two ways. It allows people to hold whatever religious beliefs they want and to "exercise" these beliefs, as by attending religious services or wearing religiously mandated items of clothing. The free exercise of religion also includes the right not to believe in any religion and not to participate in any religious "exercise". The amendment further prohibits the government from endorsing religion in general or one set of religious beliefs in particular. The free exercise clause and establishment clause sometimes clash, and courts have to help keep the balance between accommodating people's religious freedom and maintaining a neutral approach to religious believers and nonbelievers alike.

SECOND AMENDMENT (1791)

WHAT IT SAYS

A well regulated Militia, being necessary to the security of a free State, the right of the people to keep and bear Arms, shall not be infringed.

WHAT IT MEANS

The principal debate surrounding the Second Amendment concerns whether the right to bear arms applies to individuals or only to a militia. The proliferation of firearms, their use in crimes, and a high rate of deliberate and accidental shootings in the United States has caused many Americans to advocate tighter gun controls. They argue that the Second Amendment applies essentially to militias. Hunters, those who own weapons for self-protection, and other gun enthusiasts insist the Second Amendment prohibits any restrictions on their right to bear arms. Rather than limit the sale of guns, they argue, the government should enact stiffer penalties for those caught using a gun while committing a crime. The courts have held that the right does apply to individuals, but have also recognized certain limits on that right. Recent questions about the Second Amendment have centered around such issues as restrictions on concealed weapons. Ban on assault weapons, and mandatory background checks and waiting periods before weapons can be purchased. Both gun rights advocacy groups, such as Handgun control, Inc., have vigorously lobbied the government to decide these issues.

THIRD & FOURTH AMENDMENTS (1791)

WHAT IT SAYS

(Third Amendment) No Soldier shall, in time of peace be quartered in any house, without the consent of the Owner, nor in time of war, but in a manner to be prescribed by law.

(Fourth Amendment) The right of the people to be secure in their persons, houses, papers, and effects, against unreasonable searches and seizures, shall not be violated, and no Warrants shall issue, but upon probable cause, supported by Oath or affirmation, and particularly describing the place to be searched, and the persons or things to be seized.

WHAT IT MEANS

The Third and Fourth Amendments are intended to protect citizens' rights to the ownership and use of their property without government intrusion. The men who drafted the Constitution, like many other citizens of their era, were resentful of the pre-Revolutionary laws that allowed British soldiers to use private homes for their barracks. The Third Amendment therefore bars the government from forcing individuals to provide lodging, or quarters, for soldiers in their homes, except under very extreme circumstances when national security may override individuals' right to privacy.

The Third Amendment has never been the subject of a Supreme Court decision and has rarely been addressed in federal court cases. The Third Amendment has instead been cited by courts as evidence that the Constitution created a general right of privacy for individuals, to protect them from government intrusion o their personal affairs.

The Fourth Amendment protects people against unreasonable searches and seizures by government officials. A "search" can mean everything from being "frisked" by a police officer to taking a blood test to having one's home and car examined. A "seizure" refers to the government taking control of something in individuals' possession, including the individuals themselves. Items that are "seized" are often used against a person as evidence at trial.

As a general rule, before police can search anyone's property they must go to the courts for a warrant, which is granted on probable cause of finding evidence of a crime. The Fourth Amendment also suggests that some searches may be reasonable without a warrant. For instance, a car stopped for speeding can be subject to search if the police observe evidence of illegal narcotics. But the courts will not accept evidence seized without a warrant when the police stop cars randomly for safety purposes to check drivers' licenses.

The Fourth Amendment also protects people against arbitrary arrest. The courts will not accept as evidence a confession taken from a person who is being held in custody illegally, nor consider evidence that is collected as a result of unlawful arrest. However, there are certain "special needs" for which the courts have allowed searches without warrants, because they meet the constitutional requirement of reasonableness. For instance, prison authorities may search prisoners and their cells for weapons, school authorities may search students and their lockers for drugs, and airport authorities may search passengers and their luggage for explosives.

The invention of electronic eavesdropping equipment in the twentieth century complicated the definition of "search". At first the Supreme Court accepted evidence gathered by wiretapping, declaring it outside the Fourth Amendment's protections, as it involved no physical trespassing of a person's property, and that simply overhearing evidence was not a "seizure". But, Congress, in writing the Federal Communications Act of 1934, specifically prohibited the government from wiretapping without a warrant. And, in later years, the Supreme Court concluded that the Fourth Amendment protections went beyond "physical intrusion" and excluded evidence collected electronically.

The Fourth Amendment has been frequently cited as evidence that the Constitution recognizes the right to privacy, that is, people have a right to be "secure" from the government with regard to their bodies, homes, papers, and other effects.

FIFTH AMENDMENT (1791)

WHAT IT SAYS

No person shall be held to answer for a capital, or otherwise infamous crime, unless on a presentment or indictment of a Grand Jury, except in cases arising in the land or naval forces, or in the Militia, when in actual service in time of War or public danger; nor shall any person be subject for the same offenses to be twice put in jeopardy of life or limb; nor shall be compelled in any criminal case to be a witness against himself, not be deprived of life, liberty, or property, without due process of law; nor shall private property be taken for public use, without just compensation.

WHAT IT MEANS

Rooted in English common law, the Fifth Amendment seeks to provide fair methods for trying people accused of committing a crime. To avoid giving government unchecked powers, grand jurors are selected from the general population, and their work, conducted in secret, is not hampered by rigid rules about the type of evidence that can be heard. Grand jury charges can be issued against anyone except members of the military, who are subject to courts-marital in the military justice system. In the U.S. federal courts and some state courts, grand juries are panels of twelve to twenty-three citizens who serve for a month or more. If the jurors find there is sufficient evidence against individuals accused of crimes, the grand jury will indict them, that is, charge them with a crime. Once indicted, defendants stand trial before a petit (from the French word for "small") jury of six to twelve citizens who hear the evidence and testimony to determine whether the accused are guilty or innocent.

The Fifth Amendment protects people from being put in "double jeopardy," meaning they cannot be punished more than once for the same criminal act and that once found innocent of a crime they cannot be prosecuted again for the same crime. The double jeopardy clause reflects the idea the government should not have unlimited power to prosecute and punish criminal suspects, instead getting only one chance to make its case.

The Fifth Amendment's right against self-incrimination protects people from being forced to reveal to the police, a judge, or any other government agents any information that might subject them to criminal prosecution. Even if a person is guilty of a crime, the Fifth Amendment demands that the prosecutors find other evidence to prove their case. If police violated the Fifth Amendment by forcing a suspect to confess, a court may prohibit the confession from being used as evidence at trial. Popularly known as the "right to remain silent", this provision prevents evidence taken by coercive interrogation from being used in court and also means that defendants need not take the witness stand at all during their trials. Nor can the prosecution point to such silence as evidence of guilt. This right is limited to speaking, nodding, or writing. Other personal information that might be incriminating, such as blood or hair samples, DNA samples, or fingerprints, may be used as evidence, with or without the accuser's permission.

The right to due process of law protects those accused of crimes from being imprisoned without fair procedures. The due process clause applies to the federal government's conduct. The Fourteenth Amendment, ratified in 1868, contains a due process clause that applies to the actions of state governments as well. Court decisions interpreting the Fourteenth Amendment's due process rights generally apply to the Fifth Amendment and visa versa. Due process applies to all judicial proceedings, whether criminal or civil, that might deprive someone of "life, liberty, or property".

The "taking clause" of the Fifth Amendment strikes a balance between private property rights and the government's right to take property that benefits the public at large. The superior power the government can exert over private property is sometimes referred to a as "eminent domain". Government may use eminent domain, for instance, to acquire land to build a park or highway through a highly populated area, so long as it pays "just compensation" to the property owners for the loss.

SIXTH AMENDMENT (1791)

WHAT IT SAYS

In all criminal prosecutions, the accused shall enjoy the right to a speedy and public trial, by an impartial jury of the state and district wherein the crime shall have been committed, which district shall have been previously ascertained by law, and to be informed of the nature and cause of the accusation; to be confronted with witnesses against him; to have compulsory process for obtaining witnesses in his favor, and to have the Assistance of Counsel for his defense.

WHAT IT MEANS

The Sixth amendment further specifies the protections offered to people accused of committing crimes. It allows the accused to have their cases heard by an impartial jury make up of people from the surrounding community who have no connection to the case. In some instances when there has been a significant amount of news coverage of the crime, jury members may be picked from outside the place where the crime took place.

Without the Sixth Amendment's right to a speedy trial, criminal defendants could be held indefinitely, under a cloud of unproven accusations. A speedy trial is also critical to a fair trial, because if a trial takes too long to occur witnesses may die or leave the area, their memories may fade, and physical evidence may be lost. The public trial guarantee protects defendants from secret proceedings that might encourage abuse of the judicial system. Criminal defendants can voluntarily give up their right to a public proceeding – such a renunciation is called a waiver – and judges may limit public access to trials in certain circumstances, such as to protect witnesses' privacy or to keep order in the court.

A speedy, public trial heard by an impartial jury would be meaningless if a defendant did not know what crime he or she was being charged with and why. Criminal defendants further have the right to face their accusers, which requires that prosecutors put their witnesses on the stand to testify under oath. The defendant's counsel may then cross-examine the witnesses, which may reveal their testimony as unreliable.

The Sixth Amendment guarantees a criminal defendant the right to have an attorney. That right does not depend on the defendant's ability to pay an attorney. If a defendant cannot afford one, the government must provide one. The right to an effective defense does not guarantee a successful defense. A defendant can receive effective legal assistance and still be convicted.

SEVENTH & EIGHTH AMENDMENT (1791)

WHAT IT SAYS

(Seventh Amendment) In suits at common law, where the value in controversy shall exceed twenty dollars, the right of trial by jury shall be preserved, and no fact tried by a jury, shall be otherwise reexamined in any Court of the United States, than according to the rules of the common law.

(Eighth Amendment) Excessive bail shall not be required, nor excessive fines imposed, nor cruel and unusual punishments inflicted.

WHAT IT MEANS

The Seventh and Eighth Amendments add to the Constitution's protections for individuals in the judicial system. The Seventh Amendment guarantees a jury trial in common law – consisting of centuries of judicial precedents – civil cases such as personal injury cases arising from car accidents, disputes between corporations for breach of contract, or discrimination and employment cases. The parties in a federal civil trial have the right to have their case decided by a jury of their peers. In a civil case a plaintiff (who brings the suit) may obtain money damages or a court order preventing the defendant from engaging in certain conduct, but civil cases cannot send a defendant to jail. The Seventh Amendment has not been extended to the states, which may choose not to employ juries in civil cases.

In addition to defining what kinds of cases require a jury, the Seventh Amendment highlights the jury's role as "fact finder", and it imposes limits on the judge's ability to override the jury's conclusions. Under the common law, the jury hears the facts and decides the verdict, and the judge sets the penalty based on the jury's findings.

The Eighth Amendment deals with bail, the money that defendants pay in exchange for their release from jail before trial. This money is returned to the defendants when they appear at trial, but the government keeps the money if a defendant does not appear. Bail is an incentive for a defendant to remain in the area and participate in the trial. Bail also promotes the ideal of being "innocent until proven guilty", in that defendants are not punished with jail time prior to conviction and sentencing.

The Eight Amendment ensures that bail cannot be excessive, set so high that only the richest defendants can afford it. However, the Supreme Court has identified certain circumstance in which courts can refuse bail entirely, such as when a defendant shows a significant risk of fleeing or poses a danger to the community.

The better-known component of the Eighth Amendment is its prohibition against "cruel and unusual" punishment. The phrase was originally intended to outlaw gruesome methods of punishment, such as torture or burning at the stake, but the courts have broadened it over the years to protect against punishments that are deemed too harsh for the particular crime. Eighth amendment challenges to the death penalty have often focused on whether certain offenders, such as juveniles or the mentally retarded, should be subject to a sentence of death, and whether death sentences have been decided fairly or have been tainted by racial bias. The "cruel and unusual" provision has also been used to challenge grossly unsanitary or otherwise deficient prison conditions.

NINTH & TENTH AMENDMENT (1791)

WHAT IT SAYS

(Ninth Amendment) The enumeration in the Constitution, of certain rights, shall not be construed to deny or disparage others retained by the people.

(Tenth Amendment) The powers not delegated to the United States by the Constitution, nor prohibited by it to the States, and reserved to the States respectively, or to the people.

WHAT IT MEANS

The Ninth Amendment offers a constitutional safety net, intended to make it clear that Americans have other fundamental rights beyond those listed in the Bill of Rights. The amendment was added out of concern that it would be impossible to mention every fundamental right, and dangerous to list just some of them for fear of suggesting that the list was complete. Because the rights protected by the amendment are not specified, they are referred to as "unenumerated" rights, as opposed to those enumerated in the Constitution. It is up to the courts to interpret through their decisions exactly what rights the amendment does and does not protect.

The Tenth Amendment was included in the Bill of Rights to preserve the balance of power between the federal government and the states. The amendment limits the federal government's power to just what is written in the Constitution. Those powers not listed are left to each of the states. The Tenth Amendment does not specify what those "powers" are, however, leaving room for dispute between the federal and state government and need for interpretation by the courts. At different times in American history the courts have been more or less restrictive in deciding what the federal government can do and what responsibilities fall to the states.

ELEVENTH AMENDMENT (1795)

WHAT IT SAYS

The Judicial power of the United States shall not be construed to extend to any suit in law or equity, commenced or prosecuted against one of the United States by Citizens of another State, or by Citizens of Subjects of any Foreign State.

WHAT IT MEANS

After the U.S. Supreme Court ruled in 1793 that two South Carolina men could sue and collect debts from the state of Georgia, states'-rights advocates in Congress proposed what became the Eleventh amendment. This amendment specifically prohibits federal courts from hearing cases in which a state is sued by individuals from another state or country. Protecting states from certain types of legal liability is known as "sovereign immunity".

As initially interpreted, the Eleventh Amendment did not bar suits against the states when a matter of federal law was at issue, nor did it prevent suits against a state by its own citizens. Over time, the Supreme Court has expanded its interpretation of the amendment to reflect a broader view that states were immune from all suits in federal courts with their agreement, which seemed unlikely.

The Eleventh amendment refers to suits "in law or equity". In those cases where neither party in the suit has broken the law they can seek resolution through equity, by which the courts measure the fairness and justice of their claims.

TWELTH AMENDMENT (1804)

WHAT IT SAYS

The electors shall meet in their respective states, and vote by ballot for President and Vice-President, one of whom, at least, shall not be an inhabitant of the same state with themselves; they shall name in their ballots the person voted for, as President, and in district ballots the person voted for, as Vice-President, and they shall make district lists of all persons voted for as President, and of all persons voted for as Vice-President, and of the number of votes for each, which lists they shall sign and certify, and transmit sealed to the seat of the government of the United States, directed to the President of the Senate; - The President of the Senate shall, in the presence of the Senate and House of Representatives, open all the certificates and the votes shall then be counted; - The person having the greatest Number of votes for President, shall be the President, if such number be a majority of the whole number of Electors appointed; and if no person have such majority, then from the persons having the highest numbers not exceeding three on the list of those voted for a President, the House of Representatives shall choose immediately, by ballot, the President. But in choosing the President, the votes shall be taken by states, the representation from each state having one vote; a quorum for this purpose shall consist of a member or members from two-thirds of the states, and a majority of all the states shall be necessary to a choice. (And if the House of Representatives shall not choose a president whenever the right of choice shall devolve upon them, before the fourth day of March next following, then the Vice-President shall act as President, as in the case of the death or other constitutional disability of the President). The person having the greatest number of votes as Vice-President, shall be the Vice-president, if such number be a majority of the whole number of Electors appointed, and if no person have a majority, then from the two highest numbers on the list, the Senate shall choose the Vice-President; a quorum for the purpose shall consist of two-thirds of the whole number of Senators, and a majority of the whole number shall be necessary to a choice. But no person constitutionally ineligible to the office f President shall be eligible to that of Vice President of the United States.

WHAT IT MEANS

As the Electoral College was originally constituted, the candidates who received the most electoral votes became President and the runner-up became Vice president. With the rise of a two-party system, this meant that the president and Vice president might be chosen from different parties. This occurred in the election of 1796, when John Adams, a Federalist, received the most electoral votes, and his opponent, Thomas Jefferson, a Democratic-Republican, received the largest electoral vote and became Vice President. In 1800, Jefferson ran for President on the Democratic-Republican ticket with Aaron Burr. They won, but both received the same number of electoral votes. With the Electoral College unable to cast a majority of votes for either of them, the election was thrown into the House of Representatives, where the Federalist Party still had a majority. After numerous attempts to each a majority, the House finally elected Jefferson President and Burr Vice President.

The turmoil o the 1800 election urged the passing of the Twelfth amendment, which solved this problem by allowing for separate Electoral College votes for President and Vice President, and by allowing the parties to nominate a team for President and Vice President. The Twelfth Amendment strongly suggests that the President and Vice President not be from the same state, as electors from that state cannot vote for both offices.

If the Electoral College fails to elect a President, the House of Representatives will select the new President from the top three candidates. The vote within the House is by state, not by representatives. Lastly, the Twelfth Amendment extends all the eligibility requirements for the President (a natural-born citizen, at least thirty-five years of age, who has resided in the United States for fourteen years) to the Vice President.

THIRTEENTH AMENDMENT (1865)

WHAT IT SAYS

Section 1. Neither slavery nor involuntary servitude, except as a punishment for crime whereof the party shall have been duly convicted, shall exist within the United States, or any place subject to their jurisdiction.

Section 2. Congress shall have power to enforce this article by appropriate legislation.

WHAT IT MEANS

In 1863, President Abraham Lincoln issued the Emancipation Proclamation based on his war powers. It freed the slaves held within the Southern states that were in rebellion against the United States. The proclamation did not address the issue of slaves held in the border states that remained within the Union. Following the end of the war, Congress passed a constitutional amendment to end slavery throughout the United States. Submitted to the states, it was speedily ratified.

Although the Supreme Court initially had doubts over whether the amendment covered anyone other than African

Africans who had been enslaved, it later held, in the Slaughterhouse Cases (1872), that it would apply to "Mexican peonage or the Chinese coolie labor system" or any other system of forced labor. The courts have also ruled that the Thirteenth amendment forbids "peonage", the practice of forcing people to work to pay off their debts against their will. But the Supreme Court has rejected claims t mandatory community service, taxation, and the military draft is involuntary servitude under the Thirteenth Amendment.

FOURTEENTH AMENDMENT (1868)

WHAT IT SAYS

Section 1. All persons born or naturalized in the United States and subject to the jurisdiction thereof, are citizens of the United states and of the State wherein they reside. No State shall make or enforce any law which shall abridge the privileges or immunities of citizens of the United States; nor shall any state deprive any person of life, liberty, or property, without due process of law; nor deny to any person within its jurisdiction the equal protection of the laws.

Section 2. Representatives shall be apportioned among the several States according to their respective members counting the whole number of persons in each State, excluding Indians not taxed. But when the right to vote at any election for the choice of electors for President and Vice-President of the United States, Representatives in Congress, the Executive and Judicial Officers of a State, or the members of the Legislature thereof, is denied to any of the male inhabitants of such State, being twenty-one years of age, and citizens of the United states, or in any way abridged, except for participation in rebellion, or other crime, the basis of representation therein shall be reduced in the proportion which the number of such male citizens shall bear to the whole number of male citizens twenty-one years of age in such State.

Section 3. No person shall be a Senator or Representative in Congress, or elector of President and Vice president, or hold any office, civil or military, under the United States, or under any State, who, having previously taken an oath, as a member of Congress, or as an officer of the United States, or as a member of any State legislature, or as an executive or judicial officer of any State, to support the Constitution of the United States, shall have engaged in insurrection or rebellion against the same, or given aid or comfort to the enemies thereof. But Congress may by a vote of two-thirds of each House, remove such disability.

Section 4. The validity of the public debt of the United States, authorized by law, including debts incurred for payment of pensions and bounties for services in suppressing insurrection or rebellion, shall not be questioned. But neither the United States nor any State shall assume or pay any debt or obligation incurred in aid of insurrection or rebellion against the United States, or any claim for the loss or emancipation of any slave; but all such debts, obligations and claims shall be held illegal and void.

Section 5. The Congress shall have power to enforce, by appropriate legislation, the provisions of this article.

WHAT IT MEANS

Although it was created primarily to deal with the civil rights issues that followed the abolition of slavery, the Fourteenth Amendment has affected a broad range of American life, from business regulation to civil liberties to the rights of criminal defendants. Over time, the Supreme Court has interpreted the amendment to apply most of the guarantees of the Bill of Rights to the states as well as the federal government. The amendment contained three new limitations on state power; states shall not violate citizen's privileges or immunities or deprive anyone of life, liberty, or property without due process of law, and must guarantee all persons equal protections by the law. The limitations on state power dramatically expanded the reach of the U.S. Constitution.

Fulfilling its original purpose, the Fourteenth Amendment made it clear that everyone born in the United States, including a former slave, was a citizen. This voided the Supreme Court's ruling in *Fred Scott v. Sanford* (1857), which had asserted that African Americans were not citizens, and therefore were not entitled to constitutional rights. Yet, for a century after the ratification of the Fourteenth Amendment, the Supreme Court believed that racial segregation did not violate the "equal protection of the laws" provision in the amendment as long as equal facilities were provided for all races. This attitude changed dramatically in 1954 when the justices concluded that the intent of the Fourteenth amendment made racially segregated schools unconstitutional. The Court has gradually adopted a much broader interpretation of the amendment that extends greater protection to women, minorities, and non-citizens

The Fourteenth Amendment also specified that all adults must be counted for purposes of apportioning the House of Representatives. Ironically, this provision increased the number of representatives for the former Confederate states when they reentered the Union. By the twentieth century, this provision also justified the Supreme Court's insistence that state legislative bodies and the U.S. House of Representatives be apportioned equally. The amendment also addressed concerns about the number of Confederates seeking to serve in Congress after the Civil War. Former Confederate federal and state officials and military personnel were required to take an oath of loyalty to the United States. The former Confederate states were also prohibited from repaying the Confederate debts or compensating former slave owners for the property they lost with the abolition of slavery.

Finally, the last section of the amendment gave Congress the power to enforce all the provisions within the whole amendment. Under this provision, Congress passed the Civil Rights act of 1964, the Voting Rights Act of 1965, sections of other civil rights legislation that protect women's rights, and the Americans with Disabilities Act, affording equal treatment for disabled people.

Over time, the Supreme Court has interpreted the Fourteenth Amendment's due process clause to incorporate (or apply) many of the guarantees of the Bill of Rights to the states, as well as to the federal government. The concept of incorporation has dealt mostly with such "fundamental" rights as freedom of speech, press, religion, assembly, and petition. Because the Court has not held the states subject to some of the other provisions of the Bill of Rights, such as the right to bear arms or the right to a trial by jury in civil cases, its approach has been called "partial incorporation".

FIFTEENTH AMENDMENT (1870)
WHAT IT SAYS

Section 1. The right of citizens of the United States to vote shall not be denied or abridged by the United States or by any State on account of race, color, or previous condition of servitude.

Section 2. The Congress shall have power to enforce this article by appropriate legislation.

WHAT IT MEANS

The Fifteenth Amendment prohibits the use of race in determining who can vote. The last of the three Reconstruction Era amendments, ratified shortly after the Civil War, the Fifteenth amendment sought to advance the civil rights and liberties of the freed slaves and other African Americans. Section 2 of the amendment gave Congress the power to enforce it, by establishing federal legislation that ensures racial equality in voting.

The ratification of the Fifteenth Amendment in 1870 initially resulted in African Americans voting and holding office in many southern states. Later in the nineteenth century, these states imposed poll taxes, literacy tests, and other tactics to keep African Americans from voting. The ratification of the Twenty-forth amendment in 1964, and the passage of the Voting Rights Act of 1965, along with a number of Supreme Court decisions, has once again guaranteed voting rights as the Fifteenth Amendment envisioned.

SIXTEENTH AMENDMENT (1913)

WHAT IT SAYS

The Congress shall have power to lay and collect taxes on incomes, from whatever source derived, without apportionment among the several States, and without regard to any census or enumeration.

WHAT IT MEANS

In Article 1, sections 2 and 9 the U.S. Constitution said that no direct taxes could be imposed unless made in proportion to the population, as measured by the census. This meant that rather than taxing individuals directly, Congress had to levy taxes in each state based on the stat's population.

During the Civil War, the federal government imposed an income tax to pay for the war's expense, but in *Pollock v. Farmer's Loan & Trust Co.* (1895), the Supreme Court later declared federal income taxes unconstitutional because they were direct taxes. This ruling limited Congress's power to tax a complicated formula that would be difficult to impose. Congress therefore sent to the states the Sixteenth Amendment, which specifically gives Congress the power to impose a direct income tax. This amendment greatly expanded the scope of federal taxing and spending and has been the basis for all subsequent federal income tax legislation.

SEVENTEENTH AMENDMENT (1913)

The Senate of the United States shall be composed of two Senators from each state, elected by the people thereof, for six years; and each Senator shall have one vote. The electors in each state shall have the qualifications requisite for electors of the most numerous branch of the State legislatures.

When vacancies happen in the representation of any State in the senate, the executive authority of such State shall issue writs of election to fill such vacancies: Provided, That the legislature of any state may empower the executive thereof to make temporary appointments until the people fill the vacancies by election as the legislature may direct.

This amendment shall not be so construed as to affect the election or term of any Senator chosen before it becomes valid as part of the constitution.

WHAT IT MEANS

Initially, the legislatures of each sate elected their U.S. senators. In a number of instances, disagreements between the two houses of a state legislature left Senate seats vacant for protracted periods. In addition, reformers accused special interests of corrupting the process of electing senators. The Seventeenth Amendment ought to solve these problems by having senators directly elected by the voters. This change left all the Senate's constitutional power in place, unlike reforms that took place at the same time in other parliamentary governments, such as Great Britain's , where the power of the House of Lords, or upper chamber, was curtailed. As a result, the U.S. senate retained equal authority over legislation with the House of Representatives.

EIGHTEENTH & TWENTY-FIRST AMENDMENTS (1919 & 1933)

WHAT IT SAYS

(Eighteenth Amendment) section 1. After one year from the ratification of this article the manufacture, sale, or transportation of intoxicating liquors within, the importation thereof into, or the exportation thereof from the United States and all territory subject to the jurisdiction thereof for beverage purposes is hereby prohibited.

Section 2. The Congress and the several States shall have concurrent power to enforce this article by appropriate legislation.

Section 3. This article shall be inoperative unless it shall have been ratified as an amendment to the Constitution by the legislature of the several States, as provided in the Constitution, within seven years from the date of the submission hereof to the States by the Congress.

(Twenty-first Amendment) section 1. The eighteenth article of amendment to the Constitution of the United States is hereby repealed.

Section 2. The transportation or importation into any State, Territory, or possession of the United States for delivery or use therein of intoxicating liquors, in violation of the laws thereof, is hereby prohibited.

Section 3. This article shall be inoperative unless it shall have been ratified as an amendment to the Constitution by conventions in the several States, as provided in the Constitution, within seven years from the date of the submission hereof to the States by the Congress.

WHAT IT MEANS

The Eighteenth Amendment resulted from a national effort to control the making, distribution, sale, and consumption of alcoholic beverages. Prohibition, called a "noble experiment" in a paraphrase of President Herbert Hoover's explanation of its goals, was an attempt to control reckless and destructive personal behavior. Its supporters argued that Prohibition would reduce crime, eliminate the need for poorhouses and prisons, and improve the health of all Americans.

When the Eighteenth Amendment was enacted, many of its supporters assumed that it covered only whiskeys and other hard liquors. But, when Congress passed the enforcement legislation, the Volstead Act, in 1919, it included beer and wine along with spirits. This sweeping provision made it difficult for the federal government to enforce Prohibition. Although arrests and hospitalizations related to alcoholism declined during the first years after the amendment went into effect, many negative consequences also became apparent. The amendment drove the lucrative alcohol business underground, giving rise to a large illegal market. Prohibition encouraged Americans to flout the law, resulting in a general disrespect for authority, and strengthened organized crime.

By 1932, many citizens recognized that Prohibition had failed, and organized a popular movement for its repeal. That year, the Democrats endorsed repeal, and their victory in the election demonstrated the public support for ending prohibition. Its supporters were in such a hurry to undo the amendment that they provided for ratification by state conventions. This gave the votes in each state a say, but also avoided waiting for the state legislatures to convene. The Twenty-first Amendment repealed national Prohibition, but left it to the states to devise their own laws and restrictions on intoxicating beverages.

NINETEENTH AMENDMENT (1920)

WHAT IT SAYS

Section 1. The right of citizens of the United States to vote shall no be denied or abridged by the United States or by any State on account of sex.

Section 2. Congress shall have power to enforce this article by appropriate legislation.

WHAT IT MEANS

Throughout the nineteenth century, most women were excluded from voting and holding elective office. Beginning in 1848, women organize a suffrage movement to win the right to vote. Some western sates grant women voting rights, and Montana elects a woman to the U.S. House of Representatives in 1916. After a century of women's petitions, parades, and protests, Congress responds with the nineteenth Amendment. Although the amendment gave Congress the authority to enact legislation to implement it, the states did not resist granting women the right to vote and hold office.

TWENTIETH AMENDMENT (1933)

WHAT IT SAYS

Section 1. The terms of the President and Vice-President shall end at noon on the 20th day of January, and the terms of Senators and Representatives at noon on the 3rd day of January, of the years in which such terms would have ended if his article had not been ratified; and the terms of their successors shall then begin.

Section 2. The Congress shall assemble at least once in every year, and such meeting shall begin at noon on the 3rd day of January, unless they shall by law appoint a different day.

Section 3. If, at the time fixed for the beginning of the term of the President, the President elect shall have died, the Vice-President elect shall become President. If a President shall not have been chosen before the time fixed for the beginning of his term, or if the President elect shall have failed to qualify, then the Vice-President elect shall act as President until a President shall have qualified; and the Congress may by law provide for the case wherein neither a President elect nor a Vice-President elect shall have qualified, declaring who shall then act as President, or the manner in which one who is to act shall be selected, and such person shall act accordingly until a President or Vice-President shall have qualified.

Section 4. The Congress may by law provide for the case of the oath of any of the persons from whom the House of Representatives may choose a President whenever the right of choice shall have devolved upon them, and for the case of the oath of any of the persons from whom the Senate may choose a Vice-President whenever the right of choice shall have devolved upon them.

Section 5. Sections 1 and 2 shall take effect on the 15th day of October following the ratification of this article.

Section 6. This article shall be inoperative unless it shall have been ratified as an amendment to the Constitution by the legislatures of three-fourths of the several States within seven years from the date of its submission.

WHAT IT MEANS

March 4 was initially chosen as the date a new President, Vice President, and Congress took office, because there needed to be time to travel to the capital and for the new representatives and senators to settle their affairs at home before sitting as a Congress. As transportation and communications improved, this meant that the departing Congress and President remained in office for an unnecessarily long time. By moving the beginning of the new term from march 4 to January 20 (and in the case of Congress to January 3) proponents of the Twentieth Amendment hoped to put an end to the "lame duck" syndrome. Lame ducks, incumbents who had been defeated or had not stood for reelection, were perceived to be able to accomplish little of value, and Congress and these Presidents were less likely to support each other's initiatives.

This shortened interval between the election and the convening of a new Congress on January 3 and the Presidential inauguration on January 20 allows the outgoing President time to consider the outgoing Congress's legislation for signature or veto while enabling the government to be passed swiftly to the new administration.

The Twentieth Amendment also provides for succession plans if the newly elected President or Vice President is unable to assume his or her position. If the President is not able to hold office, either because of death or failure to qualify, the Vice President will act as President. If the Vice President is also not able to carry out the Presidential duties, Congress may select someone to act as President.

TWENTY-SECOND AMENDMENT (1951)

WHAT IT SAYS

Section 1. No person shall be elected to the office of the President more than twice, and no person who has held the office of President, or acted as President, for more than two years of a term to which some other person was elected President shall be elected to the office of the President more than once. But this Article shall not apply to any person holding the office of President, when this Article was proposed by the Congress, and shall not prevent any person who may be holding the office of President, or acting as President during the remainder of such term.

Section 2. This article shall be inoperative unless it shall have been ratified as an amendment to the Constitution by the legislatures of three-fourths of the several States within seven years from the date of its submission to the States by the Congress.

WHAT IT MEANS

Nothing in the original Constitution limited the number of terms that a President could serve, but the nation's first President, George Washington, set a precedent by declining to run for a third term, suggesting that two four-year terms were enough for any President. Washington's precedent survived until 1940, when Franklin D. Roosevelt, a Democrat who had steered the nation through the Great Depression, ran for a third term on the eve of the second world War. Roosevelt won a third term in 1940 and a fourth term in 1944.

Following Roosevelt's death in April 1945, just months into hi fourth term, Republicans in Congress took the lead in proposing a limit of two terms for future presidents. The amendment specified that if a Vice President took over for a President but served less than two years of the former President's term, the new president could serve for two full four-year terms. If more than two years of the presidential term remain when the Vice President assumes office, the new President may serve only one additional term.

TWENTY-THIRD AMENDMENT (1961)
WHAT IT SAYS

Section 1. The District constituting the seat of Government of the United States shall appoint in such manner as the Congress may direct:

A number of electors of President and Vice President equal to the whole number of Senators and Representatives in Congress to which the District would be entitled if it were a State, but in no event more than the least populous State; they shall be in addition to those appointed by the States, but they shall be considered, for the purposes of the election of President and Vice President, to be electors appointed by a State; and they shall meet in the District and perform such duties as provided by the twelfth article of amendment.

Section 2. The Congress shall have power to enforce this article by appropriate legislation.

WHAT IT MEANS

The Constitution allowed Congress to select an area ten miles square to serve as the permanent seat of the federal government. Since 1800, the government has operated out of the District of Columbia. There were few permanent residents of the district at first, but by 1960 its population exceeded three-quarters of a million people. As a federal district, the capital has neither an elected local governor nor the right to vote in national elections. At the same time, District residents had all the responsibilities of citizenship.

The Twenty-third Amendment did not make Washington, D.C., a state, but did grant its citizens the right to vote in Presidential elections and it allotted the District the number of electors it would have had if it were a state. The amendment did not provide the District with representation in Congress, but subsequently the District gained a nonvoting delegate in the House of Representatives and an elected local government.

TWENTY-FOURTH AMENDMENT (1964)

WHAT IT SAYS

Section 1. The right of citizens of the United States to vote in any primary or other election for President or Vice President for electors for President or Vice President, or for Senator or Representative in Congress, shall not be denied or abridged by the United States or any State by reason of failure to pay any poll tax or other tax.

Section 2. The Congress shall have power to enforce this article by appropriate legislation.

WHAT IT MEANS

Although the Fifteenth Amendment prohibited voting discrimination on account of race, many southern states enacted laws to make it difficult for African Americans to vote. The Twenty-fourth Amendment was designed to address one particular injustice, the poll tax. The requirement to pay a fee in order to vote kept low-income citizens, both white and black, from taking part in elections. The Twenty-fourth Amendment made it illegal to charge any voter for the right to cast a ballot in any federal election.

TWENTY-FIFTH AMENDMENT (1965)
WHAT IT SAYS

Section 1. In case of the removal of the President from office or of his death or resignation, the Vice President shall become President.

Section 2. Whenever there is a vacancy in the office of the Vice President, the President shall nominate a Vice President who shall take office upon confirmation by a majority vote of both Houses of Congress.

Section 3. Whenever the president transmits to the President pro tempore of the Senate and the Speaker of the House of Representatives his written declaration that he is unable to discharge the powers and duties of his office, and until he transmits to them a written declaration to the contrary, such powers and duties shall be discharged by the Vice President as Acting President.

Section 4. Whenever the Vice President and a majority of either the principal officers of the executive departments or of such other body as Congress may by law provide, transmit to the President pro tempore of the Senate and the Speaker of the House of Representatives their written declaration that the President is unable to discharge the powers and duties of his office, the Vice President shall immediately assume the powers and duties of his office, the Vice President shall immediately assume the powers and duties of the office as Acting President.

Thereafter, when the president transmits to the President pro tempore of the Senate and the speaker of the

House of Representatives his written declaration that no inability exists, he shall resume the powers and duties of his office unless the Vice president and a majority of either the principal officers of the executive department or of such other body as Congress may by law provide, transmit within four days to the president pro tempore of the Senate and the speaker of the House of Representatives their written declaration that the president is unable to discharge the powers and duties of his office. Thereupon Congress shall decide the issue, assembling within forty-eight hours for that purpose if not in session. If the Congress, within twenty-one days after receipt of the latter written declaration, or, if Congress is not in session, within twenty-one days after Congress is required to assemble, determines by two-thirds vote of both Houses that the president is unable to discharge the powers and duties of his office, the Vice President shall continue to discharge the same as Acting President; otherwise, the President shall resume the powers and duties of his office.

WHAT IT MEANS

Following the assassination of president John F. Kennedy in November 1963, Vice President Lyndon B. Johnson became President, and the office of Vice President sat vacant for more that a year until the next election. The Twenty-fifth Amendment was then passed to allow the President to appoint a Vice President if that office becomes vacant, subject to a vote of approval by the House and Senate. The Twenty-fifth Amendment also clarifies what happens upon the death, resignation, or temporary incapacity to the President.

The Twenty-fifth Amendment went into effect in 1967 and was first applied in 1973 upon the resignation of Vice President Spiro Agnew, who was facing charges of bribery and corruption. President Richard Nixon then appointed House Republican minority leader Gerald R. Ford as the new Vice President. Less than a year later, Nixon resigned the Presidency as a result of the Watergate scandal. Ford became President and appointed former New York governor Nelson Rockefeller as Vice President. Ford and Rockefeller thus became the nation's first unelected team of President and Vice President.

If a President should fall seriously ill or for some other reason must temporarily step down, the amendment provides that the President give notice of the disability to the president pro tempore of the Senate (the presiding officer of the senate) and the speaker of the House. The Vice President is then authorized to serve as acing President to carry on the president's duties. The President can resume the duties of office upon giving appropriate notice to the congressional leadership. The Vice president and the cabinet can ask for a vote of Congress should they doubt the President's fitness to resume office. A vote of two-thirds of each house is required to prevent a President's return.

The "acting President" provision of the Twenty-fifth Amendment was first invoked on July 13, 1985, when President Ronald Reagan underwent cancer surgery. He issued a letter transferring power to Vice President George H. W. Bush and sent another letter to the Speaker of the House and president pro tempore of the Senate, as the amendment required. Following his surgery, Reagan notified them that he was fit to resume his Presidential duties. In 2002, President George W. Bush signed similar letters to transfer power temporarily to Vice President Dick Cheney, while bush was sedated briefly during a medical procedure know as a colonoscopy.

TWENTY-SIXTH AMENDMENT (1971

WHAT IT SAYS

Section 1. The right of citizens of the United States, who are eighteen years of age or older, to vote shall not be denied or abridged by the United States or by any State on account of age.

Section 2. The Congress shall have power to enforce this article by appropriate legislation.

WHAT IT MEANS

The unpopularity of the military draft during the Vietnam War raised questions about why young men between eighteen and twenty-one should be qualified to fight for their country but no to vote for the leaders who made decisions about war and peace. The Twenty-sixth Amendment lowered the voting age to eighteen. It was a continuation of a movement toward democratization that began with efforts to remove property qualifications for voting, and expanded to include African Americans and women. Along the way other obstacles such as poll taxes, literary tests, and residency requirements also fell to constitutional challenges and change.

TWENTY-SEVENTH AMENDMENT (1992)

WHAT IT SAYS

No law varying the compensation for the services of the Senators and Representatives shall take effect, until an election or Representatives shall have intervened.

WHAT IT MEANS

The Twenty-seventh Amendment prevents any congressional pay raise from going into effect until after the voters have been able to cast ballots in the next election, registering their approval or disapproval. With the voters in mind, legislators were likely to be more cautious about increasing their own salaries. James Madison introduced the Amendment in 1789 and it was sent to the states with the Bill of rights. An insufficient number of states ratified it and the amendment lay dormant until 1982, when public outrage over a large boost in congressional salaries encouraged the states to revive the amendment. Unlike modern amendments, the Twenty-seventh had no time limit for ratification, so that some state legislatures ratified it more than two hundred years apart. In 1992, the Michigan state legislature passed the amendment, and it was finally ratified.

APPENDIX OR INDEX

DEFINITIONS:

Amendment- An act of making better or the condition of being made better.

Preamble- A short section of preliminary remarks: forward, induction, introduction, lead-in, overture, preface, and prelude.

Ratify- To accept officially: adopt, affirm, approve, confirm, pass, sanction. Ratification- The act of confirming officially.

Bibliography:

"Our Constitution" by Donald Al Ritchie & Justice Learning.org. A Project of the Annenberg Foundation Trust at Sunny lands; c 2006; Trustees of the University of Pennsylvania, Published by Oxford University Press, Inc.,

198 Madison Ave., New York, New York 10016, www.oup.com

THE BILL OF RIGHTS

We Ran across an interesting article which contrasts *"what the Bill of Rights actually says"* with the current, Politically-correct meaning as decided by the politicians, lawyers/judges and Civil Service bureaucrats.

AMENDMENT 1:

Congress shall make no law respecting an establishment of religion, or prohibiting the free exercise thereof, or abridging the freedom of speech, or of the press; or the right of the people peaceably to assemble, and to petition the government for a redress of grievances.

Congress shall make no law establishing religion, but shall act as if it did; and shall make no laws abridging the freedom of speech, unless such speech can be construed as "commercial speech" or "irresponsible speech" or "offensive speech;" or shall [not] abridge the right of the people to peaceably assemble where and when permitted; or shall [not] abridge the right to petition the government for a redress of grievances, under proper procedures.

AMENDMENT 11;

A well regulated Militia, being necessary to the security of a Free State, the right of the people to keep and bear arms, shall not be infringed.

A-well regulated military force shall be maintained under the control of the President, and no entity within the United States shall maintain a military force beyond

Presidential control. Any Amendment to this Constitution barring involuntary servitude shall not be applied to conscription by the military. The right of the people to keep and bear arms shall be determined by the congress and the States and the Cities and the Counties and the Towns and someone named Fred.

AMENDMENT 111:

No Soldier, shall in time of peace, be quartered in any house, without the consent of the Owner, nor in time of war, but in a manner to be prescribed by law. No Soldier shall, in time of peace, be quartered in any house, without the consent of the owner, unless such house is believed to have been used, or believed may be used, for some purpose contrary to law or public policy.

No Soldier shall, in time of peace, be quartered in any house without the consent of the owner, unless such house is believed to have been used, or believed may be used, for some purpose contrary to law or public policy.

AMENDMENT IV

The right of the people to be secure in their persons, houses, papers, and effects, against unreasonable searches and seizures, shall not be violated, and no Warrants shall issue, but upon probable cause, supported by Oath or affirmation, and particularly describing the place to be searched, and the persons or things to be seized.

The right of the people to be secure in their persons, houses, papers, and effects against unreasonable searches and seizures may not be suspended except to protect public welfare [as defined by the political class].

Any place or conveyance shall be subject to search by law enforcement forces of any political division, and such places or conveyances, or any property within them, may be confiscated without judicial proceeding if suspected of being used in a manner contrary to law.

AMENDMENT V:

No person shall be held to answer for a capital, or otherwise infamous crime, unless on a presentment or indictment of a Grand Jury, except in cases arising in the land or naval forces, or in the Militia, when in actual service in time of War or public danger, nor shall any person be subject for the same offence to be twice put in jeopardy of life or limb; nor shall be compelled in any criminal case to be a witness against himself, nor be deprived of life, liberty, or property without due process of law; nor shall private property be taken for public use, without just compensation.

Any person may be held to answer for a crime of any kind, or for utterance interpretable as planning or encouraging one, upon just suspicion; and may be put in jeopardy of life and liberty by the state courts and by the federal judiciary, and of jeopardy of life while incarcerated; and may be compelled to be a witness against himself by the submission of his body or any portion thereof when so ordered by empowered authority, or by testimony in proceedings excluding criminal trial. Private property forfeited or confiscated under judicial authority shall become the property of the governments of competent jurisdiction and shall be immune from seizure by injured parties.

AMENDMENT VI:

In all criminal prosecutions, the accused shall enjoy the right to a speedy and public trial, by an impartial jury of the State and district wherein the crime shall have been committed, which district shall have been previously ascertained by law, and to be informed of the nature and cause of the accusation; to be confronted with the witnesses against him; to have compulsory process for obtaining witnesses in his favor, and to have the Assistance of Counsel for his defense.

In all criminal prosecutions, the accused shall enjoy the right to avoid prosecution by exhausting the legal process and its practitioners. Failure to succeed shall result in speedy plea-bargaining. Convicted persons shall be entitled to appeal until sentence is completed. It shall be unlawful to bar or deter an incompetent person, but encouraged to bar a fully informed person, from service on a jury.

AMENDMENT VII:

In suits at common law, where the value in controversy shall exceed twenty dollars, the right of trial by jury shall be preserved, and no fact tried by a jury, shall be otherwise reexamined in any court of the United States, than according to the rules of the common law.

In civil suits, where a contesting party is a person whose private life may interest the public, the right of trial in the Press shall not be abridged.

AMENDMENT VIII:

Excessive bail shall not be required, nor excessive fines imposed, nor cruel and unusual punishments inflicted.

Sufficient bail may be required to ensure that dangerous persons remain in custody pending trial. There shall be no right of the public to be afforded protection from dangerous persons, and such protection shall be dependent upon incarceration facilities available.

AMENDMENT IX:

The enumeration in the Constitution, of certain rights, shall not be construed to deny or disparage others retained by the people.

The enumeration in The Constitution of certain rights shall be construed to deny or discourage others which may from time to time be extended by the branches of Federal, State or Local government, unless such rights shall themselves become enacted by Amendment.

AMENDMENT X:

The powers not delegated to the United States by the Constitution, nor prohibited by it to the States, are reserved to the State respectively, or to the people.

The powers not delegated to the United States by the Constitution shall be deemed to be powers residing in persons holding appointment therein though the Civil Service, and may be delegated to the States and local Governments as determined by the public interest. The public interest shall be determined by the Civil Service.

THE DECLARATION OF INDEPENDENCE OF THE THIRTEEN STATES IN AMERICA

IN CONGRESS, JULY 4, 1776

When in the Course of human events it becomes necessary for one people to dissolve the political bands which have connected them with another and to assume among the powers of the earth, the separate and equal station to which the Laws of Nature and of Nature's God entitle them, a decent respect to the opinions of mankind requires that they should declare the causes which impel them to the separation.

We hold these truths to be self-evident, that all men are created equal, that they are endowed by their Creator with certain unalienable Rights, that among these are Life, Liberty and the pursuit of Happiness. ------- That to secure these rights, Governments are instituted among Men, deriving their just powers from the consent of the governed,---- That whenever any Form of Government becomes destructive of these ends, it is the Right of the People to alter or to abolish it, and to institute new Government, laying its foundation on such principles and organizing its powers in such form, as to them shall seem most likely to effect their Safety and Happiness. Prudence, indeed, will dictate that Governments long established should not be changed for light and transient causes; and accordingly all experience hath shown that mankind are more disposed to suffer, while evils are sufferable than to right themselves by abolishing the forms to which they are accustomed. But when a long train of abuses and usurpations, pursuing invariably the same Object evinces a design to reduce them under absolute Despotism, it is their right, it is their duty, to throw off such Government, and to provide new Guards for their future security. ------ Such has been the patient sufferance of these Colonies; and such is now the necessity which constrains them to alter their former Systems of Government. The history of the present King of Great Britain is a history of repeated injuries and usurpations, all having in direct object the establishment of an absolute Tyranny over these States. To prove this, let Facts be submitted to a candid world.

He has refused his Assent to Laws, the most wholesome and necessary for the public good.

He has forbidden his Governors to pass Laws of immediate and pressing importance, unless suspended in their operation till his Assent should be obtained; and when so suspended, he has utterly neglected, to attend to them.

He has refused to pass other Laws for the accommodation of large districts of people, unless those people would relinquish the right of Representation in the Legislature, a right inestimable to them and formidable to tyrants only.

He has called together legislative bodies at places unusual, uncomfortable, and distant from the depository of their Public Records, for the sole purpose of fatiguing them into compliance with his measures.

He has dissolved Representative Houses repeatedly, for opposing with manly firmness his invasions on the rights of the people.

He has refused for a long time, after such dissolutions, to cause others to be elected, whereby the Legislative Powers, incapable of Annihilation, have returned to the People at large for their exercise; the State remaining in the mean time exposed to all the dangers of invasion from without, and convulsions within.

He has endeavored to prevent the population of these States; for that purpose obstructing the Laws for

Naturalization of Foreigners; refusing to pass others to encourage their migrations hither, and raising the conditions of new Appropriations of Lands.

He has obstructed the Administration of Justice by refusing his Assent to Laws for establishing Judiciary Powers.

He has made Judges dependent on his Will alone for the tenure of their offices, and the amount and payment of their salaries.

He has erected a multitude of New Offices, and sent hither swarms of Officers to harass our people and eat out their substance.

He has kept among us, in times of peace, Standing Armies without the Consent of our legislatures.

He has affected to render the Military independent of and superior to the Civil Power.

He has combined with others to subject us to a jurisdiction foreign to our constitution, and unacknowledged by our laws; giving his Assent to their Acts of pretended Legislation: For quartering large bodies of armed troops among us.

For protecting them, by a mock Trial from punishment for any Murders which they should commit on the Inhabitants of these States:

For cutting off our Trade with all parts of the world:

For imposing Taxes on us without our Consent:

For depriving us in many cases, of the benefit of Trial by Jury:

For transporting us beyond Seas to be tried for pretended offences:

For abolishing the free System of English Laws in a neighboring Province, establishing therein an Arbitrary government, and enlarging its Boundaries so as to render it at once an example and fit instrument for introducing the same absolute rule into these Colonies.

For taking away our Charters, abolishing our most valuable Laws and altering fundamentally the Forms of our Governments:

For suspending our own Legislatures and declaring themselves invested with power to legislate for us in all cases whatsoever.

He has abdicated Government here, by declaring us out of his Protection and Waging War against us.

He has plundered our seas, ravaged our coasts, burnt our towns, and destroyed the lives of our people.

He is at this time transporting large Armies of foreign Mercenaries to complete the works of death, desolation, and tyranny, already begun with circumstances of Cruelty & Perfidy scarcely paralleled in the most barbarous ages, and totally unworthy the Head of a civilized nation.

He has constrained our fellow Citizens taken Captive on the high Seas to bear Arms against their Country, to become the executioners of their friends and Brethren, or to fall themselves by their Hands.

He has excited domestic insurrections amongst us, and has endeavored to bring on the inhabitants of our frontiers, the merciless Indian Savages whose known rule of warfare is an undistinguished destruction of all ages, sexes and conditions.

In every stage of these Oppressions, we have petitioned for Redress in the most humble terms: Our repeated Petitions have been answered only by repeated injury. A Prince, whose character is thus marked by every act which may define a Tyrant, is unfit to be the ruler of a free people.

Nor have we been wanting in attentions to our British brethren. We have warned them from time to time of attempts by their legislature to extend an unwarrantable jurisdiction over us. We have reminded them of the circumstances of our emigration and settlement here. We have appealed to their native justice and magnanimity, and we have conjured them by the ties of our common kindred. to disavow these usurpations, which would inevitably interrupt our connections and correspondence. They too have been deaf to the voice of consanguinity. We must, therefore, acquiesce in the necessity, which denounces our Separation, and hold them, as we hold the rest of mankind, Enemies in War, in Peace Friends.

We, therefore, the Representatives of the United States of America, in General Congress, Assembled, appealing to the Supreme Judge of the world for the rectitude of our intentions, do, in the Name, and by Authority of the good People of these Colonies, solemnly publish and declare, That these United Colonies are, and of Right ought to be Free and Independent States, that they are Absolved from all Allegiance to the British Crown, and that all political connection between them and the State of Great Britain, is and ought to be totally dissolved; and that as Free and Independent States, they have full Power to levy War, conclude Peace contract Alliances, establish Commerce, and to do all other Acts and Things which Independent States may of right do. ------ And for the support of this Declaration, with a firm reliance on the protection of Divine Providence, we mutually pledge to each other our Lives, our Fortunes and our sacred Honor.

------ John Hancock

New Hampshire: Josiah Bartlett, William Whipple, Matthew Thornton

Massachusetts: John Hancock, Samuel Adams, John Adams, Robert Treat Paine, Elbridge Gerry

Rhode Island: Stephen Hopkins, William Ellery

Connecticut: Roger Sherman, Samuel Huntington, William Williams, Oliver Wolcott

New York: William Floyd, Philip Livingston, Francis Lewis, Lewis Morris

New Jersey: Richard Stockton, John Witherspoon, Francis Hopkinson, John Hart, Abraham Clark

Pennsylvania: Robert Morris, Benjamin Rush, Benjamin, Franklin, John Morton, George Clymer, James Smith, George Taylor, James Wilson, George Ross

Delaware: Caesar Rodney, George Read, Thomas McKean

Maryland: Samuel Chase, William Paca, Thomas Stone, Charles Carroll of Carrollton

Virginia: George Wythe, Richard Henry Lee, Thomas Jefferson, Benjamin Harrison, Thomas Nelsen, Jr., Francis Lightfoot Lee, Carter Braxton

North Carolina: William Hooper, Joseph Hewes, John Penn

South Carolina: Edward Rutledge, Thomas Heyward, Jr., Thomas Lynch, Jr., Arthur Middleton

Georgia: Button Gwinnett, Lyman Hall, George Walton

CHAPTER 3: **Inspired by God**

The principals of this country were founded on a strong belief in God and every decision made was prayed about as well as our Leaders. God used the power of the Holy Spirit to move in the lives of these courageous men who laid down the laws of the land. Being that we are a democracy, the Godly principals follow the principles God set for us in the Bible. The Old Testament was being saved by keeping the law. The New Testament was salvation by grace. The two most important commandments were Love the Lord your God with your whole heart and love your neighbor as you love yourself. The laws of the land are set up the same way. We are to put God first and then our neighbor.

George Washington

There was a question some were asking, "Was George Washington a Christian?"

This is a question often asked today, and it arises from the efforts of those who seek to impeach Washington's character by portraying him as irreligious. Interestingly, Washington's own contemporaries did not question his Christianity but were thoroughly convinced of his devout faith- - a fact made evident in the first-ever compilation (collection) of the "The Writings of George Washington", published in the 1830's.

In volume X11 of the writings of Jared Sparks (*The Dictionary of American Biography)* delved into the religious character of George Washington, and included numerous letters written by the friends, associates, and family of Washington which testified of his religious character. Based on that extensive evidence, Sparks concluded:

To say that he (George Washington) was not a Christian would be to impeach his sincerity and honesty. Of all men in the world, Washington was certainly the last whom any one would charge with dissimulation or indirectness (hypocrisies and evasiveness); and if he was so scrupulous in avoiding even a shadow of these faults in every known act of his life, (regardless of) however unimportant, is it likely, is it credible, that in a matter of the highest and most serious importance (his religious faith, that) he should practice through a long series of years a deliberate deception upon his friends and the public? It is neither credible nor possible.

To know Washington, we ought to understand that he was more than our first President and the Father of our Country, but also a man of profound Christian faith. Don't take our word for it read his own words. Washington kept a prayer journal. This is one of several entries.

"Direct my thoughts, words and work. Wash away my sins in the immaculate blood of the lamb, and purge my heart by thy Holy Spirit, from the dross of my natural corruption, that I may with more freedom of mind and liberty of will serve thee, the ever lasting God, in righteousness and holiness this day, and all the days of my life."

"Increase my faith in the sweet promises of the Gospel. Give me repentance from dead works. Pardon my wanderings, and direct my thoughts unto thyself, the God of my salvation. Teach me how to live in thy fear, labor in thy service, and ever to run in the way of thy commandments. Make me always watchful over my heart, that neither the terrors of conscience, the loathing of holy duties, the love of sin, nor an unwillingness to depart this life, may cast me into a spiritual slumber. But daily frame me more and more into the likeness of thy son Jesus Christ, that living in thy fear, and dying in thy favor, I may in thy appointed time attain the resurrection of the just unto eternal life. Bless my family, friends and kindred unite us all in praising and glorifying thee in all our works

begun, continued, and ended, when we shall come to make our last account before thee blessed Saviour, who hath taught us thus to pray, our Father."

These next words were spoken by George Washington as he resigned his commission as general of the Continental Army on December 23, 1783,

"I consider it an indispensable duty to close this last solemn act of my official life by commending the interests of our dearest country to the protection of Almighty God and those who have the superintendence of them into His holy keeping."

Alexander Hamilton

Hamilton, who regularly led his house hold in prayer, also wrote about the connection between Christianity and political freedom. He helped to form the Christian Constitutional Society. In an 1802 letter to co-founder James Bayard, he said:

"I not offer you the outline of the plan they have suggested. Let an association be formed to be denominated "The Christian Constitutional Society," its object to be first: The support of the Christian religion. Second: The support of the United States."

"I have carefully examined the evidences of the Christian religion, and if I was sitting as a juror upon its authenticity I would unhesitatingly give my verdict in its favor. I can prove its truth as clearly as any proposition ever submitted to the mind of man."

He was fatally shot in a duel with Burr in July of 1804. His last words were:

"I have a tender reliance on the mercy of the Almighty, through the merits of the Lord Jesus Christ. I am a sinner. I look to Him for mercy; pray for me.

Abraham Lincoln

In 1823, when Abraham was 14, his parents joined the Pigeon Creek Baptist Church. There was bitter rivalry among Baptists, Methodists, Presbyterians, and other denominations. This may help explain why Lincoln never joined any church, and why he never attended church regularly. Yet he became a man of deep religious feelings. He came to know the Bible thoroughly. Biblical references and quotations enriched his later writings and speeches. As President, he kept a Bible on his desk and often opened it for comfort and guidance.

"In regards to this great Book (the Bible), I have but to say it is the best gift God has given to man. All the good the Saviour gave to the world was communicated through this Book. But for it we could not know right from wrong. All things most desirable for man's welfare, here and hereafter, are found portrayed in it."

--Abraham Lincoln

"I believe I am an humble servant in the hands of our Heavenly Father; I desire that all my words and acts may be according to His will."

--Abraham Lincoln

Proclamation Appointing a National Fast Day

Washington, D.C.

March 30, 1863

By the President of the United States of America.

A Proclamation.

Whereas, the Senate of the United States, devoutly recognizing the Supreme Authority and just Government of Almighty God, in all the affairs of men and of nations, has, by a resolution, requested the President to designate and set apart a day for National prayer and humiliation.

And whereas it is the duty of nations as well as of men, to own their dependence upon the overruling power of God, to confess their sins and transgressions, in humble sorrow, yet with assured hope that *genuine repentance will lead to mercy and pardon; and to recognize the sublime truth, announced in the Holy Scriptures and proven by all history, that those nations only are blessed whose God is the Lord.*

And, insomuch as we know that, by His divine law, nations like individuals are subjected to punishments and chastisements in this world, may we not justly fear that the awful calamity of civil war, which now desolates the land, may be but a punishment, inflicted upon us, for our presumptuous sins, to the needful end of our national reformation as a whole People? We have been the recipients of the choicest bounties of Heaven. We have been preserved, there many years, in peace and prosperity. We have grown in numbers, wealth and power, as no other nation has ever grown. *But we have forgotten God.* We have forgotten the gracious hand which preserved us in peace, and multiplied and enriched and strengthened us; and we have vainly imagined, in the deceitfulness of our hearts, that all these blessings were produced by some superior wisdom and virtue of our own. **Intoxicated with unbroken success, we have become too self-sufficient to feel the necessity of redeeming and preserving grace, too proud to pray to the God that made us!**

It behooves us then, to humble ourselves before the offended Power, to confess our national sins, and to pray for clemency and forgiveness.

Now therefore, in compliance with the request and fully concurring in the views of the Senate, I do, by this my proclamation, designate and set apart Thursday, the 30th day of April, 1863, as a day of national humiliation, fasting and prayer. And I do hereby request all the People to abstain, on the day, from their ordinary secular pursuits, and to unite, at their several places of public worship and their respective homes, in keeping the day holy to the Lord, and devoted to the humble discharge of the religious duties proper to the solemn occasion.

All this being done, in sincerity and truth, let us then rest humbly in the hope authorized by the Divine teachings, that the united cry of the Nation will be heard on high, and answered with blessings, no less than the pardon of our national sins, and the restoration of our now divided and suffering Country, to its former happy condition of unity and peace.

In witness whereof, I have hereto set my hand and caused the seal of the United States to be affixed.

Done at the City of Washington, this thirtieth day of March, in the year of our Lord one thousand eight hundred and sixty-three, and of the Independence of the United States the eighty seventh.

By the President: Abraham Lincoln

William H. Seward, Secretary of State.

(© 2005 EadsHome Ministries)

John Adams

"The general principles upon which the Fathers achieved independence were the general principles of Christianity...I will avow that I believed and now believe that those general principles of Christianity are as eternal and immutable as the existence and the attributes of God." *(June 28,1813: Letter to Thomas Jefferson)*

We recognize no Sovereignty but God, and no King but Jesus!" *(April 18 1775, on the eve of the Revolutionary War after a British major ordered John Adams, John Hancock, and those with them to disperse in "the name of George the Sovereign King of England.")*

(July 4th) ought to be commemorated as the day of deliverance by solemn acts of devotion to God Almighty." *(Letter written to Abigail on the day the Declaration was approved by Congress).*

"We have o government armed with power capable of contending with human passions unbridled by morality and religion. Avarice, ambition, revenge, or gallantry, would break the strongest cords of our Constitution as a whale goes through a net. **Our Constitution was made only for a moral and religious people. It is wholly inadequate to the government of any other."** *–October 11, 1798*

"I have examined all religions, as well as my narrow sphere, my straightened means, and my busy life, would allow; and the result is that the Bible is the best Book the world. It contains more philosophy that all the libraries I have seen." *--December 25, 1813 letter to Thomas Jefferson*

© 2005 EadsHome Ministries

John Hancock

On April 15, 1775, four days before the "Shot Heard "Round the World,"

"In circumstances dark as these, it becomes us, as Men and Christians, to reflect that, whilst every prudent Measure should be taken to ward off the impending judgment...

"All confidence must be withheld from the Means we use; and reposed only on the GOD who rules in the

Armies of Heaven, and without whose Blessing the best human Counsels are but Foolishness—and all created power Vanity.

"It is the happiness of his Church that, when the Powers of Earth and Hell combine against it...that the Throne of Grace is of the easiest access—and its Appeal thither is graciously invited by the Father of Mercies, who has assured it, that when his Children ask Bread he will not give them a Stone...

"RESOLVED, that it be, and hereby is recommended to the good People of this Colony of all Denominations, that THURSDAY the Eleventh Day of May net be set apart as a Day of Public Transgression...and a blessing on the Husbandry, Manufactures, and other lawful Employments of this People; and especially that the union of the American Colonies in Defense of their Rights (for hitherto we desire to thank Almighty God) may be preserved and confirmed...And that AMERICA may soon behold a gracious Interposition of Heaven, "By Order of the (Massachusetts) Provincial Congress, John Hancock, President."

Roger Sherman

As a theologian, he wrote a personal creed which was adopted by his church:

"I believe that there is one only living and true God, existing in three

Thomas Jefferson

The Virginia Act for Establishing Religious Freedom
By Thomas Jefferson, 1786

Well aware that Almighty God hath created the mind free; that all attempts to influence it by temporal punishments or burdens, or by civil incapacitations, tend only to beget habits of hypocrisy and meanness, and are a departure from the plan of the Holy Author of our religion, who being Lord both of body and mind, yet chose not to propagate it by coercions on either, as was in his Almighty power to do; that the impious presumption of legislators and rulers, civil as well as ecclesiastical, who, being themselves but fallible and uninspired men, have assumed dominion over the faith of others, setting up their own opinions and modes of thinking as the only true and infallible, and as such endeavoring to impose them on others, hath established and maintained false religions over the greatest part of the world, and through all time; that to compel a man to furnish contributions of money for the propagation of opinions which he disbelieves, is sinful and tyrannical; that even the forcing him to support this or that teacher of his own religious persuasion, is depriving him of the comfortable liberty of giving his contributions to the particular pastor whose morals he would make his pattern, and whose powers he feels most persuasive to righteousness, and is withdrawing from the ministry those temporal rewards, which proceeding from an approbation of their personal conduct, are an additional incitement to earnest and unremitting labors for the instruction of mankind; that our civil rights have no dependence on our religious opinions, more than our opinions in physics or geometry; that, therefore, the proscribing any citizen as unworthy the public confidence by laying upon him an incapacity of being called to the offices of trust and emolument, unless he profess or renounce this or that religious opinion, is depriving him injuriously of those privileges and advantages to which in common with his fellow citizens he has a natural right; that it tends also to corrupt the principles of that very religion it is meant to encourage, by bribing, with a monopoly of worldly honors and emoluments, those who will externally profess and conform to it; that though indeed these are criminal who do not withstand such temptation, yet neither are those innocent who lay the bait in their way; that to suffer the civil magistrate to intrude his powers into the field of opinion and to restrain the procession or propagation of principles, on the supposition of their ill tendency, is a dangerous fallacy, which at once destroys all religious liberty, because he being of course judge of that tendency, will make his opinions the rule of judgment, and approve or condemn the sentiments of others only as they shall square with or differ from his own; that it is time enough for the rightful purposes of civil government, for its officers to interfere when principles break out into overt acts against peace and good order; and finally, that truth is great and will prevail if left to herself, that she is the proper and sufficient antagonist to error, and ha s nothing to fear from the conflict, unless by human interposition disarmed of her natural weapons, free argument and debate, errors ceasing to be dangerous when it is permitted freely to contradict them.

Be it therefore enacted by the General Assembly, That no man shall be compelled to frequent or support any religious worship, place, or ministry whatsoever, nor shall be enforced, restrained, molested, or burdened in his body or goods, nor shall otherwise suffer on account of his religious opinions belief; but that all men shall be free to profess, and by argument to maintain, their opinions in matters of religion, and that the same shall in nowise diminish, enlarge, or affect their civil capacities.

And though we well know this Assembly, elected by the people for the ordinary purposes of legislation only, have no powers equal to our own and that therefore to declare this act irrevocable would be of no effect in law, yet we are free to declare, and do declare, that the right thereby asserted are of the natural rights of mankind, and that if any acct shall be hereafter passed to repeal the present or to narrow its operation, such act will be an infringement of natural right.

Benjamin Franklin

The Constitutional Convention met at Philadelphia in the hot summer of 1787 to rewrite the articles of Confederation which had been so ineffective. The quarrels between the States were deep and divisive; each state lowered or raised its own tariffs and coined its own money. There was no Union. The delegates began to realize that they needed to do something more than patch up the Articles of Confederation. It was a stormy convention. The debate over representation grew more bitter and hopelessly deadlocked. The strength of George Washington's personality was the glue that had held them together, and his power was waning. At one point, Ben Franklin, 81 years of age, rose and spoke quietly:

"In the beginning of the contest with Britain, when we were sensible of danger, we had daily prayers in this room for Divine protection. Our prayers, Sir, were heard, and they were answered. All of us who were engaged in the struggle have observed frequent instances of superintending Providence in our favor...And have we now forgotten this powerful Friend? Or, do we imagine we no longer need His assistance?

I have lived, Sir, a long time, and the longer I life, the more convincing I see of this truth: 'that God governs in the affairs of man. And if a sparrow cannot fall to the ground without His notice, is it probable that an empire can rise without his Aid?'

We have been assured, Sir, in the Sacred Writings that except the Lord build the house, they labor in vain that build it. I firmly believe this. I also believe that, without his concurring aid, we shall succeed in this political building no better than the builders of Babel; we shall be divided by our little, partial local interests; our projects will be confounded; and we shall become a reproach and a byword to future ages. And what is worse, mankind may hereafter, from this unfortunate instance, despair of establishing government by human wisdom and leave it to chance, war, or conquest.

I therefore beg to move that, henceforth, prayers imploring the assistance of Heaven and it's blessing on our deliberation be held in this assembly every morning before we proceed to business."

Benjamin Rush (1744-1813)

Benjamin Rush, a signer of the Declaration of Independence, was considered by his peers to be one of the most prominent of the Founding Fathers, alongside Ben Franklin, George Washington, John Adams, and Thomas Jefferson. Today, for the most part, he is unknown by most Americans. Read the incredible accomplishments of this very important founding father.

As a physician he had no equal and was called the "Father of American Medicine" because of his numerous medical discoveries. He was also called the "Father of American Psychiatry, a statement found on his gave to the day.

Benjamin Rush was also called the **"Father of Public Schools Under the Constitution"** because he was the first to advance the idea of free public schools, and also a pioneer in the opportunity for women's education. He helped Abigail Adam's (John Adam's wife) dream become a reality by establishing the *Young Ladies Academy of Philadelphia*, one of America's first educational institutions for women.

He wrote textbooks, formed curriculum plans, crafted educational policies, and helped establish fine universities and colleges. As the founder of public education in America, listen to his definition of what education should contain:

"The only foundation for a useful education in a republic is to be laid in religion. Without this there can be no virtue, and without virtue there can be no liberty--- "

On March 28, 1787 when Dr. Benjamin Rush proposed his plan for public education in America her wrote:

"Let the children who are sent to those schools be taught to read and write---(and a)bove all, let both sexes be carefully instructed in the principles and obligations of the Christian religion. This is the most essential part of education— "

In another educational proposal he wrote:

"It will be necessary to connect all these (academic) branches of education with regular instruction in the Christian religion."

Benjamin Rush was a founder of the Pennsylvania Society for Promoting the Abolition of Slaver and served as its president.

His activities in the Christian faith included being the founder and vice-president of the Philadelphia Bible Society, which was the beginning of Sunday Schools across America. Francis Scott Key, the author of *The Star Spangled Banner* later became the Vice-President for the American Sunday School Union.

In 1791Dr. Rush wrote a lengthy pamphlet entitled "A Defense of the Use of the Bible as a Schoolbook". Here is how that writing began:

"It is now several months since I promised to give you my reasons for preferring the Bible as a schoolbook to all other compositions. Before I state my argument, I shall assume the five following propositions:

1. That Christianity is the only true and perfect religion; and that in proportion as mankind adopts its principles and obeys its precepts they will be wide and happy.
2. That a better knowledge of this religion is to be acquired by reading the Bible than in any other way.
3. That the Bible contains more knowledge necessary to man in his present state than any other book in the world.
4. That knowledge is most durable and religious instruction most useful, when imparted in early life.
5. That the Bible, when not read I schools, is seldom read in any subsequent period of life.

Love God

In order to be a successful leader you have to love God. If you believe you are above Him and do not need Him, you will be doing everything on your own. Your own self-interests and agenda with raise its ugly head through and your followers will see through you.

Wisdom in the truest sense can only come from God. Godly wisdom is not man's wisdom. There is contradiction and the two cannot be as one. You will make the right choices that are needed if you seek God for guidance and direction.

Power has a way of making a man or woman feel they can do anything, even at the expense of others. They can feel they are above the law and what they want is law. Dictatorship is a ruling power where one man feels he is God. He generally rules with an iron fist and death can be the price for disobedience. Removing him from power usually comes with his own death. His successor could be family or someone groomed for very young.

A democracy is the best form of government because officials are elected by the people. There are elections every four years. There are laws that determine the behavior of the President and a House and Senate that make up Congress. All are bound by the laws of their elected position. Removing from office is possible and necessary at times.

Without the love of God on our side, doing anything is reckless and dangerous. We need to be humble and have faith to believe that someone bigger than us is in control. We have to surrender control to Him so we can do and be what He wants of us. We have to love God to run this country because if we do not we will be turning this world over to Satan and it will be the demise of this world.

Love your Neighbor

We have to love our neighbor in order to be what God wants this world to be. Total disregard for your neighbor, his home, his family, his life is our responsibility. There are the laws in place to protect your neighbor. When life and possessions of another become so secondary to someone without any consciencousness of his rights, we have a world in chaos. We then have to monitor with local police to defend the victim.

Someone thinking he has a right to do this to his or her neighbor has been raised without a consciences knowing that these things are not for the taking, regardless of the consequences. Apathy and indifference are so dangerous because it is too easy to cross the line. Someone else's pain has no effect on the one taking. The need to have or possess is stronger than the thoughts and feelings of your neighbor.

Most victims are a result of someone older, bigger, stronger, so they can get what they want. Truly a coward at heart, they choose the weak and the helpless. To be that callous to disregard the victim is painful in the heart of God. We are to help those that need help not hurt them. Thank God there are those who love their neighbor and will reach out to them. God is please as you give your heart a chance to do good for someone because you want to. God will bless you for that.

CHAPTER 4: **Our Foundation: The Bible and Godly Principals**

Our foundation or the laws of the land, we compiled through the Constitution, the Bill of Rights, and the Declaration of Independence. We need truth to lay a foundation of what is right and wrong. Our fore fathers were wise and Godly because they had a relationship with God in prayer and in their lives. They knew where their strength was from. The Bible was their text book and in the beginning as with Abraham Lincoln and many others, the Bible was taught in Public School.

The basis of truth to us is the documents our fore fathers drew up so we would have a reference to go to generation after generation. They knew it would be necessary. Before reading and writing it was handed down verbally from family to family. Formal education was relatively new.

Changing the laws is very difficult. We have a few Constitutional amendments but it is extremely hard to make a change. That is why laws are so complicated. They try to cover every situation and person to the full extend of the law.

The ruling of the Supreme Court is almost set in cement. It is a law when determined a law. The seat as a Supreme Court Judge is a lifetime commitment. We have to seek God for the wisdom to know who or what we will need in the future.

I do not believe that it is a coincidence that all governmental gatherings are started out with prayer. If we cease to do this, again, we are turning our Country over to the enemy. We have a Chaplain always in attendance at times like this. No matter what your political beliefs, you have to recognize our need for God to run this country.

Some Things Should Be Off Limits

With the Bill of Rights came freedom for all. This is wonderful because God did create everyone equal. We may have different attributes, economic achievements and a wonderful family or not a family at all. There is an imbalance in these areas of life. The equality God speaks about is an equal opportunity to achieve heaven for eternity. Also, every human being has equal rights under the law. Some are favored or use money to elevate themselves, but when it comes to judgment by the court of law, it is to be the same for everyone.

One problem I do have is that some of the laws are used in a destructive manner. Some feel that freedom of speech means you can say or do anything that you want. There has to be boundaries if it harms or hurts someone else. There can be such a fine line between the rights of one at the expense of another. I do not believe we have been able to establish that line which should not be crossed.

We are visual people and our eyes can deceive us. We can have everlasting images stay in our mind, especially if we did not want it there. Movies and television is a perfect example. I resent watching something that I believe will not cross my line I have set for myself. All of the sudden it could be language, inappropriate dress, or seeing something I do not want to see. Especially seeing child exposed to things they are not mature enough to process. Then mom and dad have the uncomfortable questions before they are ready.

We have come to a place where we have chosen one persons right over another. We are being desensitized to what we believed was morally wrong. One explanation I give is that they run the camera just 15 minutes too long. They used to set up a situation and we could imagine if we wanted to. But now they show what is behind close doors. Personally I do not want to see what is going on. There has to be a drawn line to what we used to call privacy. Each person has their own story to think or tell. I do not want to be told by the producer's opinion. Sex is sexier with the clothes on and the "I wonder?" to let the imagination flow.

The Flag

There are few things in this world that I really get angry about. The Burning of the American Flag in the name of freedom of speech by some who protest this country is wrong. This should not be allowed. Some things should be off limits. If you protest this country and do not like something, just leave. The wonder and appeal of this country is that you can burn the flag without consequences. It is hurtful to those of us who have embrace this country, died for this country, and would defend this country no matter what.

Those who disagree should challenge themselves to do something for this country to elevate the standard we have set. Exercise some love for your country and give something of yourself to contribute. The peace corps is a wonderful place to put your loyalties and your neighbor will benefit. Chances are that if you are protesting you have never given yourself to any cause except destruction.

The **flag of the United States of America** consists of 13 equal horizontal stripes of red (top and bottom) alternating with white, with a blue rectangle in the canton bearing 50 small, white, five-pointed stars arranged in nine offset horizontal rows of six stars (top and bottom) alternating with rows of five stars. The 50 stars on the flag represent the 50 U.S. states and the 13 stripes represent the original Thirteen Colonies that rebelled against the British crown and became the first states in the Union. Nicknames for the flag included "the **Stars and Stripes**" and "**Old Glory**," with the latter nickname coined by Captain William Driver, a nineteenth century shipmaster.

Because of its symbolism, the stared blur canton is called the "union." This part of the national flag can stand alone as a maritime flag called **the Union Jack** which served as the U.S. jack on warships from 1777 until 2002. It continues to be used as a jack by various federally–owned vessels, including those of the Coast Guard, Military Sealift Command, and National Oceanic and Atmospheric Administration.

The Symbolism of the United States flag is among the nation's most widely recognized and used symbols. Within the U.S. it is frequently displayed, not only on public buildings, but on private residences, as well as iconically in forms such as decals for car windows, and clothing ornaments such as badges and lapel pins. Throughout the world it is used in public discourse to refer to the U.S., both as a nation state, government, and set of policies, but also as an ideology and set of ideals.

Many understand the flag to represent the freedoms and rights guaranteed in the U.S. Constitution and its Bill of Rights and perhaps most of all to be a symbol of individual and personal liberty as set forth in the Declaration of Independence. Through the Pledge of Allegiance and other political uses the flag has also come to be associated with U.S. nationalism, patriotism, and even militarism. The flag is a complex and contentious symbol, around which emotions run high.

In terms of the symbolism of the design itself, a book about the flag published by the Congress in 1977 states: "The star is a symbol of the heavens and the divine goal to which man has aspired from time immemorial; the stripe is symbolic of the rays f light emanating from the sun." George

Washington is credited for saying; "We take the stars from Heaven, the red from our mother country, separating it by white stripes, thus showing that we have separated from her, and the white stripes shall go down to posterity representing Liberty.

Many people also take the red and white to stand for the blood of hose who gave their lives for freedom, and the presumed purity of the freedom ideal, respectively.

Our American flag has so much meaning for us and the history of this country. It is only cloth but put together with the colors and designs to represent this great country. Every country has a flag which seem by others, knows that this flag represent another country. There is no power in the flag, just power in the people and what we believe. For someone to feel they can disregard or flag and destroy it, should have to do something positive to elevate this country.

Your name is only a name until it identifies a person. You then become your name. If your name is desecrated, you are desecrated. If your name is drawn through the mud, then you are drawn through the mud. This is defiling me because my name is mine.

The flag is a symbol of what we stand for. Many have died believing in this flag and its symbolism. Reverence is so necessary to have respect for us and our country.

Disagreeing with Leaders

With freedom again come our rights to do certain things in the name of freedom of speech. We are so fortunate that our fore fathers knew how important this was and is. We have a need to speak our mind and disagree if we feel the need.

The area I feel we have stepped over the line is being disrespectful to someone in authority who has earned or been voted in by the people. There are social graces that need to be put into play when expressing our opinion. We can disagree with the point of view but this does not mean we can put down the person. Today it seems that the alternative to running against someone in political office or another type of position, their character and personal issues are targeted to show the dark side of someone who does not need the world to know. It has nothing to do with the issue. Making someone look bad or tear them down is wrong. This is dirty fighting and it does not love your neighbor. Disagree about the politics but do not demean the person.

We are to pray for our leaders in office. We are to respect their position even if you do not agree. They have been voted in that office by a majority ruling and that settles it. We have got to get back to defending our leaders instead of letting people put unwarranted discussion about someone instead of the thing they stand for. Respect is lost because our children are not seeing it in the adult world, especially at home. Our actions do speak louder than words.

Trust in ourselves

Trust is a word that is used often but is not implemented as it should be. Those around us tell us to trust them and then they are not trust worthy. Lying seems to be the course of action chosen instead of telling the truth. Lying is not taken seriously enough so that the foundation of this world can get back to trusting your neighbor.

With all of the Homeland Security we have to implement, it is a daily reminder that we cannot really trust any stranger. Everyone seems to have an agenda and afraid to reach out to help someone. It has become a world where we cannot let our children out of our sight. Our children make mistakes which can be devastating but they are just kids. They are in a world where they are looked at as victim and are preyed upon. The weak and the innocent are vulnerable to the adult world that wants to take what they want or need.

The world is becoming a place that we tend to withdraw and stay close to home. That has even become a place that someone wants to take what you have. All the security you plan on and surprise is usually the element that takes over. Disbelief that this is happening is the paralyzing factor. Also, anyone stronger than you definitely has the advantage. Without any ability to fight you have become the victim and it affects your life forever.

Believe in ourselves

In order to trust in yourself, you have to believe in yourself. If you do not have the confidence to do that, then your efforts could be in vain. You need the courage and conviction of God to know that you can do and be anything you desire.

Learning to trust is a work in progress. How you handle yourself in times of difficulty is an indication of how you feel about yourself. If you are having a battle over sin or sorrow, you have to believe that you will do the right thing. It takes strength and courage to do what is right, the confidence to do that, then your efforts could be in vain. You need the courage and conviction of God to know that you can do and be anything you desire.

If your battle is in the area of sin of the flesh, you need to take account of your ability to resist. If you are weak in this area, give yourself time to be able to withstand. You will learn that the more you say no, the easier it will be. Take one step at a time.

If you know the Word of God, then you can trust yourself to do what God wants you to do. Believe that all things are possible to those who are in Christ Jesus. Experience after experience will give you the maturity needed to truly "trust in yourself and believe in yourself".

Believe

Most everyone wants someone or something to believe in. In the earlier part of the book, I bring out the basis of our fore fathers religion and it was a strong belief in God; knowing it has to be God that the foundation of this country needed to be built on. They were spiritual men seeking the laws and rights of this country. They believed in someone greater than themselves to make the decision they had to make. They sought God for answers and prayer before meeting. They were church attending men that felt that the Bible should be taught in school. Look how far we have moved away from that philosophy.

If you only believe in yourself, your job, your money then you will be empty. We need God in our lives and love Him; we need to love in our lives to love our neighbor. We cannot live as an island and think only of ourselves. We have to believe that this world exists for a reason and it is better than us. I believe it is for the salvation of my soul, learning of Jesus, committing my life to Him, and knowing that heaven is my home for eternity. If I thought all there is to life is what I know of it right now, I would have nothing to live for. I need something bigger than myself to work to and for.

Those that do not believe in anything it shows in how they live their lives. They try to fill up their life with things, people, places; never being satisfied. This is an empty life and without belief in God, an empty life and eternal condemnation.

Having Faith and Believing

Actually, God asks very little of us if you really think about it. We just have to have enough faith and believe everything is going to be okay. God is God, and anyone who says different is a liar. If we believe this, than serving God should be simple.

Simplicity does not always meant easy in this sense of the word. If we are good, we are rewarded. If we are bad, we are punished. God does not have a grey area. He is absolute.

Human beings are the only creatures that try to negotiate life to fit their comfort zone. Animals do what is expected, and react accordingly. They do not have the consciousness to do otherwise. Man was given the free will, and we see what that has gotten us. Sin is the result of choice and a bad one at that.

Seek for a deeper faith than you have. We should have enough faith that we can walk on water. If God said it, it is true. This is the absolute of God, and believing in His Word, is the result of faith that can move mountains.

Have Faith and Believe

Faith is a gift
From high above,
Believing in what you can't see
But know it is real.

Faith can move mountains
God tells in His Word,
It can begin as a mustard seed
And grow as a tree, so big.

Faith is he tool God gives us
To walk in the path set forth,
You know that all is true
Because belief is in your heart.

Faith is believing
Because God said it was so,
You know His character
So to question is not a choice.

Faith is walking on water
When life tells you "no",
You will not sink
If enough faith will come.

Faith is healing the sick
The lame, and the blind,
It is knowing in your heart
You have the Spirit kind.

Faith is seeing past what you know
Believing the results are different,
What you see seems impossible
But faith will carry to the other side.

Faith is believing what we can't see
Hold on to faith, like a lost child,
It will open heaven your home to be
God is waiting, your reward is free.

(Excerpt from "Christian Struggles Poems" by Anita DeMeulenaere)

CHAPTER 5: **The American Way**

During a years time millions of immigrants from all over the world gain access to the United States. Most of them are led here by their undying dreams and great expectations of the land of the free. They have a high desire to better their lives and become one of those that people write about. Unforeseen problems usually are what this small majority of success seekers end up with. Their lack of comprehending the English language seems to be what holds them back from progressing in our society. They do desire citizenship.
(Anomoymous)

Citizenship

All persons born or naturalized in the United States, and subject to the jurisdiction thereof, are citizens of the United States and of the state wherein they reside. No state shall make or enforce any law which shall abridge the privileges or immunities of citizens of the United States; nor shall any state deprive any person of life, liberty, or property, without due process of law; nor deny to any person within its jurisdiction the equal protection of the laws – X1V Amendment to the U.S. Constitution.

Citizenship is one of the most coveted gifts that the U.S. government can bestow, and the most important immigration benefit that USCIS can grant. Most people become U.S. citizens in one of two ways:

- By birth, either within the territory of the United States or to U.S. citizen parents, or
- By Naturalization.

In addition, in 2000, Congress passed the Child Citizenship Act (CCA), which allows any child under the age of 18 who is adopted by a U.S. citizen and immigrates to the United States to acquire immediate citizenship.

Constitutional citizenship will tell you that if you are going to be involved in government in the United States, citizenship is a must. To be a Senator or Representative, you must be a citizen of the United States. To be President, not only must you be a citizen, but you must also be natural-born. Aside from participation in government, citizenship is an honor bestowed upon people by the citizenry of the United States when a non-citizen passes the required tests and submits to an oath.

A Natural-born citizen is defined by the 14th Amendment this way: "All persons born or naturalized in the United States, and subject to the jurisdiction thereof, are citizens of the United States and of the State wherein they reside." But even this does not get specific enough. As usual, the Constitution provides the framework for the law, but it is the law that fills in the gaps.

Currently, Title 8 of the U.S. Code fills in those gaps. Section 1401 defines the following as people who are "citizens of the United States at birth:"

- Anyone born inside the United States
- Any Indian or Eskimo born in the United stated, provided being a citizen of the U.S. does not impair the person's status as a citizen of the tribe
- Any one born outside the United States, both of whose parents are citizens of the U.S., as long as one parent has lived in the U.S.
- Any one born outside the United States, if one parent is a citizen and lived in the U.S. for at least one year and the other parent is a U.S. national
- Any one born in a U.S. possession, if one parent is a citizen and lived in the U.S. for at least one year

- Any one found in the U.S. under the age of five, whose parentage cannot be determined, as long as proof of non-citizenship is not provided by age 21
- Any one born outside the United Stated, if one parent is an alien and as long as the other parent is a citizen of the U.S. who lived in the U.S. for at least five years (with military and diplomatic service included in this time)
- A final, historical condition: a person born before 5/24/1934 of an alien father and a U.S. citizen mother who has lived in the U.S.

Anyone falling into these categories is considered natural-born, and is eligible to run for President or Vice president.

Independence Day4th of July

In the United States, Independence Day (commonly know as "the Fourth of July" or "July Fourth") is a federal holiday celebrating the adoption of the Declaration of Independence on July 4, 1776, declaring independence from the Kingdom of Great Britain.

Independence Day is commonly associated with parades, barbecues, beer, picnics, baseball games, and various other public and private events celebrating the history, government, and traditions of the United States. Fireworks have been associated with the fourth of July since 1777.

Independence Day fireworks are often accompanied by a pops orchestra playing patriotic songs such as "The Star-spangled banner", "God Bless America", "America the Beautiful", "My Country, Tis of Thee", "This Land Is Your Land", and "Stars and Stripes Forever". Some of the lyrics recall images of the Revolutionary War or the War of 1812. While the "1812 Overture" refers to Russia's defeat of

Napoleon, it has been traditionally used by the Boston Pops and broadcast nationwide on PBS, so many Americans also associate this musical work wit the July 4th fireworks.

"The Star-Spangled Banner", the USA's national anthem, commemorates the United States flag that was visible by the light of the *rockets' red glare, the bombs bursting in air*. This view of the flag through a night of bomb bursts inspired the captive Francis Scott Key during the War of 1812, and provided hope for the United States as it defended Fort McHenry.

Firework shows are held in many states, and many fireworks are sold for personal use or as an alternative to a public show. Safety concerns have led some states to ban fireworks or limit the sizes and types allowed. Illicit traffic transfers many firecrackers from less restrictive states, showing that the American people have nevertheless found a way to celebrate "with pomp and parade, with shows, games, sports, guns, bells, bonfires, and illuminations."

Most fireworks shows in the United States end in an intense finale, with a volley of fireworks launched almost simultaneously. Major displays are held in New York and Boston harbors and on the National Mall in Washington, DC. Detroit, Michigan and Windsor, Ontario also host one of the largest fireworks displays in the world over the Detroit River each year to celebrate both American Independence Day and Canada Day during the Windsor-Detroit International Freedom Festival.

CHAPTER 6: **Patriotism**

Patriotism denotes positive and supportive attitudes to a "fatherland" by individuals and groups. The "fatherland" (or motherland) can be a region or a city, but patriotism usually applies to a nation and/or a nation-state. Patriotism covers such attitudes as: pride in its achievements and culture, the desire to preserve its character and the basis of the culture, and identification with other members of the nation. Patriotism is closely associated with nationalism, and is often used as a synonym for it. Strictly speaking, nationalism is an ideology – but it often promotes patriotic attitudes as desirable and appropriate. (Both nationalist political movements, and patriotic expression, may be negative towards other people's fatherland).

Patriotism has ethical connotations: it implies that the "fatherland" (however defined) is a moral standard or moral value in itself. The expression *my county right or wrong* – perhaps a misquotation of the American naval officer Stephen Decatur, but also attributed to Carl Schurz – is the extreme form of this belief Patriotism also implies that the individual should place the interests of the nation above their personal and group interests. In wartime, the sacrifice may extend to their own life. Death in battle for the fatherland is the archetype of extreme patriotism.

Types of Patriotism

Patriotism relies heavily on **symbolic** acts, such as displaying the flag, singing the national anthem, participating in a mass rally, placing a patriotic bumper sticker on one's vehicle, or any other way of publicly proclaiming allegiance to the state. Symbolic patriotism in wartime is intended to raise morale, in turn contributing to the war effort. Peacetime patriotism cannot be so easily linked to a measurable gain for the state, but the patriot does not see it as inferior.

Loyalty for the Country

Bear true faith and allegiance to the U.S. constitution, the Army, your unit, and other soldiers.

("Army Values")

"Loyalty is the big thing, the greatest battle asset of all. But no man ever wins the loyalty of troops by preaching loyalty. It is given to him as he proves his possession of the other virtues." *(Brigadier General S. L. A. Marshal - Men Against Fire)*

Since before the founding of the republic, America's Army has respected its subordination to its civilian political leaders. This subordination is fundamental to preserving the liberty of all Americans. You began your Army career by swearing allegiance to the Constitution, the basis of our government and laws. Pay particular attention to Article 1, Section 8, which outlines Congressional responsibilities regarding the armed forces, and Article 11, Section 2, which designates the president as commander in chief. Beyond or allegiance to the Constitution, you have an obligation to be faithful to the Army, the institution and its people, and to your unit or organization. Few examples illustrate loyalty to country and institution as well as the example of Gen. George Washington in 1782.

Gen. George Washington at Newburg

Following its victory at Yorktown in 1781, the Continental Army set up camp at Newburgh, New York, to wait for peace with Great Britain. The central government formed under the Articles of Confederation proved weak and unwilling to supply the Army properly or even pay the soldiers who had won the war for independence. After months of waiting many officers, angry and impatient, suggested that the army marches on the seat of government in Philadelphia, Pennsylvania, and force Congress to meet the Army's demands. One colonel even suggested that Gen. Washington become King George 1.

Upon hearing this, Gen. Washington assembled his officers and publicly and emphatically rejected the suggestion. He believed that seizing power by force would have destroyed everything for which the Revolutionary War had been fought. By this action, Gen. Washington firmly established an enduring precedent: America's armed forces are subordinate to civilian authority and serve the democratic principles that are now enshrined in the Constitution. Gen. Washington's action demonstrated the loyalty to country that America's Army must maintain in order to protect the freedom enjoyed by all Americans.

Gen. Washington's example shows how the obligation to subordinates and peers fits in the context of loyalty to the chain of command and the institution at large. As commander of the Continental Army, Gen. Washington was obligated to see that his soldiers were taken care of. However, he also was obligated to ensure that the new nation remained secure and that the continental Army remained able to fight if necessary. If the Continental Army had marched on the seat of government, it may well have destroyed the nation by undermining the law that held it together. It also would have destroyed the Army as an institution by undermining the law that held it together. It also would have destroyed the Army as an institution by destroying the basis for the authority under which it served. Gen. Washington realized these things and acted based on his knowledge. Had he done noting else, this single act would have been enough to establish Gen. George Washington as the father of his country.

Loyalty is a two-way street: you should not expect loyalty without being prepared to give it as well. Leaders can neither demand loyalty nor win it from their people by talking about it. The loyalty of your people is a gift they give you when and only when, you deserve it - when you train them well, treat them fairly, and live by the concepts you talked about. Leaders who are loyal to their subordinates never let them be misused.

Soldiers fight for each other, loyalty is commitment. Some of you will encounter the most important way of earning this loyalty: leading your soldiers well in combat. There's no loyalty fiercer than that of soldiers who trust their leader to take them through the dangers of combat. However, loyalty extends to all members of an organization, to your superiors and subordinates, as well as your peers.

Loyalty extends to all members of the Total Force. The reserve components, Army National Guard and Army Reserve, play an increasingly active role in the Total Force's mission. Most DA civilians will not be called upon to serve in combat theaters, but their contributions to mission accomplishment are nonetheless vital. As an Army leader, you'll serve throughout your career with soldiers of the active and reserve components as well as DA civilians. All are members of he same team, loyal to one another.

Loyalty Day, 2003
By the President of the United States of America

A Proclamation

To be an American is not a matter of blood or birth. Our citizens are bound by ideals that represent the hope of all mankind: that all men are created equal, endowed with unalienable rights to life, liberty, and the pursuit of happiness. On Loyalty Day, we reaffirm our allegiance to our country and resolve to uphold the vision of our Forefather.

Our founding principles have endured, guiding our Nation toward progress and prosperity and allowing the United States to be a leader among nations of the world. Throughout our history, honorable men and women have demonstrated their loyalty to America by making remarkable sacrifices to preserve and protect these values.

Today, America's men and women in uniform are protecting our Nation, defending the peace of the world, and advancing the cause of liberty. The world has seen again the fine character of our Nation through our military as they fought to protect the innocent and liberate the oppressed in Operation Iraqi Freedom. We are honored by the service of foreign nationals in our Armed Services whose willingness to risk their lives for a country they cannot yet call their own is proof of the loyalty this country inspires. Their

service and sacrifice and a testament to their love for America, and our soldiers' honor on and off the battlefield reaffirms or Nation's most deeply held belief: that every life counts, and that all humans have an unalienable right to live as free people.

These values must be imparted to each new generation. Our children need to know that our Nation is a force for good in the world, extending hope and freedom to others. By learning about America's history, achievements ideas, and heroes, our young citizens will come to understand even more why freedom is worth protecting.

Last September, I announced several initiatives that will help improve students' knowledge of American history, increase their civic involvement, and deepen their love for our great county. The We the People initiative will encourage the teaching of American history and civic education by providing grants for curriculum development and training seminars. The Our Documents initiative will use the Internet to bring information about and the text of 100 of America's most important documents from the national Archives to classrooms and com-munities across the country. These initiatives are important, for it is only when our children have an understanding of our past that they will be able to lead the future.

This Loyalty Day, as we express allegiance to our Nation and its founding ideals, we resolve to ensure that the blessings of liberty endure and extend for generations to come.

The Congress, by Public Law 85-529, as amended, has designated May 1 of each year as "Loyalty Day," and I ask all Americans to join me in this day of celebration and in reaffirming our allegiance to our Nation.

NOW, THEREFORE, I GEORGE W. BUSH, President of the United States of America, do herby proclaim May 1, 2003, as Loyalty Day. I call upon all the people of the United States to join in support of this national observance. I also call upon government officials to display the flag of he United States on all government buildings on Loyalty Day.

IN WITNESS WHEREOF, I have hereunto set my hand this thirtieth day of April, in the year of our Lord two thousand three, and of the Independence of the United states of America the two hundred and twenty-seventy.

-George W. Bush

(http://www.whitehouse.gov/news/releases/2003/04)

The Soldier' Creed

- I am an American Soldier.
- I am a warrior and a member of a team. I serve the people of the United States and live the Army values.
- I will always place the mission first.
- I will never accept defeat.
- I will never quit.
- I will never leave a fallen comrade.
- I am disciplined, physically and mentally tough, trained and proficient in my warrior tasks and drills, always maintain my arms, my equipment and myself.
- I am an expert and I am a professional.
- I stand ready to deploy, engage, and destroy the enemies of the United States of America in close combat.
- I am a guardian of freedom and the American way of life.
- I am an American Soldier.
- I will never quit.

The Soldier's Faith

Oliver Wendell Holmes, Jr.

(An address Delivered on Memorial Day, May 30, 1895, at a Meeting Called by the Graduating Class of Harvard University. President Theodore Roosevelt's admiration for this speech was a factor in Holmes' nomination to the U.S. Supreme Court. The most quoted line of this speech if "We have shared the incommunicable experience of war; we have felt, we still feel, the passion of life to its top.")

Any day in Washington Street (in Boston), when the throng is greatest and busiest, you may see a blind man playing a flute. I suppose that some one hears him. Perhaps also my pipe may reach the heart of some passer in the crowd.

I once heard a man say, "Where Vanderbilt sits, there is the head of the table. I teach my son to be rich." He said what many think. For although the generation born about 1840 and now governing the world, has fought two at least of the greatest wars in history, and has witnessed others, war is out of fashion, and the man who commands attention of his fellows is the man of wealth. Commerce is the great power. The aspirations of the world are those of commerce. Moralists and philosophers, following its lead, declare that war is wicked, foolish, and soon to disappear.

The society for which many philanthropists, labor reformers, and men of fashion unite in longing is one in which they may be comfortable and may shine without much trouble or any danger. The unfortunately growing hatred of the poor for the rich seems to me to rest on the belief that money is the main thing (a belief in which the poor have been encouraged by the rich), more than on any other grievance. Most of my hearers would rather that their daughters or their sisters should marry a son of one of the great rich families than a regular army officer, were he a beautiful, brave, and gifted as Sir William Napier. I have heard the question asked whether our war was worth fighting, after all. There are many, poor and rich, who think that love of country is an old wives tale, to be replaced by interest in a labor union, or, under the name of cosmopolitanism, by a rootless self-seeking search for a place where the most enjoyment may be had at the least cost.

Meantime we have learned the doctrine that evil means pain, and the revolt against pain in all its forms has grown more and more marked. From societies for the prevention of cruelty to animals up to socialism, we express in numberless ways the notion that suffering is a wrong which can be and ought to be prevented, and a whole literature of sympathy has sprung into being which points out in story and in verse how hard it is to be wounded in the battle of life, how terrible, how unjust it is that any one should fail.

Even science has had its part in the tendencies which we observe. It has shaken established religion in the minds of very many. It has pursued analysis until at last this thrilling world of colors and passions and sounds has seemed fatally to resolve itself into one vast network of vibrations endlessly weaving an aimless web, and the rainbow flush of cathedral windows, which once to enraptured eyes appeared the very smile of God, fades slowly out into the pale irony of the void.

And yet from vast orchestras still comes the music of mighty symphonies. Our painters even now are spreading along the walls of our Library glowing symbols of mysteries still real, and the hardly silenced cannon of the East proclaim once more that combat and pain still is the portion of man. For my own part, I believe that the struggle for life is the order of the world, at which it is vain to repine. I can imagine the burden changed in the way it is to be born, but I cannot imagine that it ever will be lifted from men's backs. I can imagine a future in which science shall have passed from the combative to the dogmatic state, and shall have gained such catholic acceptance that it shall take control of life, and condemn at once with instant execution what now is left for nature to destroy. But we are far from such a future, and we cannot stop to amuse or to terrify ourselves with dreams. Now, at least, and perhaps as long as man dwells upon the globe, his destiny is battle, and he has to take the chances of war. If it is our business to fight, the book for the army is a war-song, not a hospital-sketch. It is not well for soldiers to think much about wounds. Sooner or later we shall fall; but meantime it is for us to fix our eyes upon the point to be stormed, and to get there if we can.

Behind every scheme to make the world over, lies the question, What kind of world do you want? The ideals of the past for men have been drawn from war, as those for women have been drawn from motherhood. For all our prophecies, I doubt if we are ready to give up our inheritance. Who is there who would not like to be thought a gentleman? Yet what has that name been built on but the soldier's choice of honor rather than life? To be a soldier or descended from soldiers, in time of peace to be ready to give one's life rather than suffer disgrace, that is what the word has meant; and if we try to claim it at less cost that a splendid carelessness for life, we are trying to steal the good will without the responsibilities of the place. We will not dispute about tastes. The man of the future may want something different. But who of us could endure a world, although cut up into five-acre lots, and having no man upon it who was not well fed and well housed, without the divine folly of honor, without the senseless passion for knowledge outreaching the flaming bounds of the possible, without ideals the essence of which is that they can never be achieved? I do not know what is true. I do not know the meaning of the universe. But in the midst of doubt, in the collapse of creeds, there is one thing I do not doubt, that no man who lives in the same world with most of us can doubt, and that is that the faith is true and adorable which leads a soldier to throw away his life in obedience to a blindly accepted duty, in a course which he little understands, in a plan of campaign of which he has little notion, under tactics of which he does not see the use.

Most men who know battle know the cynic force with which the thoughts of common sense will assail them in times of stress; but they know that in their greatest moments faith has trampled those thoughts under foot. If you wait in line, suppose on Tremont Street Mall, ordered simply to wait and do nothing, and have watched the enemy bring their guns to bear upon you down a gently slope like that of Bacon Street, have seen the puff of the firing, have felt the burst of the spherical case-shot as it came toward you, have heard and seen the shrieking fragment go tearing through your company, and have known the next or the next shot carries your fate; if you have advanced in line and have seen ahead of you the spot you must pass where the rifle bullets are striking; if you have ridden at night at a walk toward the blue line of fire at the dead angle of Spottsylvania, where for twenty-four hours the soldiers were fighting on the two sides of an earthwork, and in the morning the dead and dying lay piled in a row six deep, and as you rode you herd the bullets splashing in the mud and earth about you; if you have been in the picket-line at night in a black and unknown wood, have heard the splat of bullets trees upon the trees, and as you moved have felt your foot slip upon a dead man's body; if you have had a blind fierce gallop against the enemy, with your blood up and a pace that left no time for fear—if, in short, as some, I hope many, who hear me, have know, you have known the vicissitudes (vibrations) of terror and triumph in war; you know that there is such a thing as the faith I spoke of. You know your own weakness and are modest; but you know that man has in him that unspeakable somewhat which makes him capable of miracle, able to lift himself by the might of his own soul, unaided, able to face annihilation for a blind belief.

From the beginning, to us, children of the North, life has seemed a place hung about by dark mists, our of which comes the pale shine of dragon's scales and the cry of fighting men, and the sound of swords. Beowolf, Milton, Durer, Rembrandt, Schopenhauer, Turner, Tennyson, from the first war song of the race to the stall-fed poetry of modern English drawing rooms, all have had the same vision, and all have had a glimpse of a light to be followed. "The end of worldly life awaits us all. Let him who may, gain honor ere death. That is best for a warrior when he is dead." So spoke Beowolf a thousand years ago.

Not of the sunlight,
Not of the moonlight,
Not of the starlight!
O Young Mariner,
Down to the haven.
Call your companions,
Launch your vessel,
And crowd your canvas.
And, ere it vanishes
Over the margin,
After it, follow it,
Follow the Gleam.

So sang Tennyson in the voice of the dying Merlin.

When I went to the war I thought that soldiers were old men. I remembered a picture of the revolutionary soldier which some of you may have seen, representing a white-haired man with his flintlock slung across his back. I remembered one or two examples of revolutionary soldiers whom I have met, and I took no account of the lapse of time. It was not long after, in winter quarters, as I was listening to some of the sentimental songs in vogue, such as—

Farewell, Mother, you may never

See your darling boy again,

That it came over me that the army was made up of what I should now call very young men. I dare say that my illusion has been shared by some of those now present, as they have looked at us upon whose heads the white shadows have begun to fall. But the truth is that war is the business of youth and early middle age. You who called this assemblage together, not we, would be the soldiers of another war, if we should have one, and we speak to you as the dying Merlin did in the verse which I have just quoted. Would that the blind man's pipe might be transformed by Merlin's magic, to make you hear the bugles as once we heard them beneath the morning stars! For you it is that now is sung the Song of the Sword:--

The War-Thing, the Comrade,

Father of Honor,

And Giver of kingship,

The fame-smith, the song master.

Priest (saith the Lord)

Of his marriage with victory

●●●

Clear singing, clean slicing;

Sweet spoken, soft finishing;

Making death beautiful

Life but a coin

To be staked in a pastime

whose playing is more

Than the transfer of being;

Arch-anarch, chief builder,

Prince and evangelist,

I am the Will of God:

I am the Sword.

War, when you are at it, is horrible and dull. It is only when time has passed that you see that its message was divine. I hope it may be long before we are called again to sit at that master's feet. But some teacher of the kind we all need. In this snug, over-safe corner of the world we need it, that we may realize that our comfortable routine is no eternal necessity of things, but merely a little space of calm in the midst of the tempestuous untamed streaming of the world, and in order that we may be ready for danger. We need it in this time of individualist negations, with its literature of French and American humor, revolting as discipline, loving flesh-pots, and denying that anything is worthy of reverence—in order that we may remember all that buffoons forget. We need it everywhere and at all times. For high and dangerous action teaches us to believe as right beyond dispute things for which our doubting minds are slow to find words of proof. Out of heroism grows faith in the worth of heroism. The proof comes later, and even may never come. Therefore I rejoice at every dangerous sport which I see pursued. The students a Heidelberg, with their sword-slashed faces, inspire me with sincere respect. I gaze with delight upon our polo players. If once in a while in our rough riding a neck is broken, I regard it, not as a waste, but as a price well paid for the breeding of a race fit for headship and command.

We do not save our traditions, in our country. The regiments whose battle-flags were not large enough to hold the names of the battles they had fought vanished with the surrender of Lee, although their memories inherited would have made heroes for a century. It is the more necessary to learn the lesson afresh from perils newly sought, and perhaps it is not vain for us to tell the new generation what we learned in our day, and what we still believe. That the joy of life is living, is to put out all ones powers as far as they will go; that the measure of power is obstacles overcome; to ride boldly at what is in front of you, be it fence or enemy; to pray, not for comfort, but for combat; to keep the soldier's faith against the doubts of civil life, more besetting and harder to overcome than all the misgivings of the battlefield, and to remember that duty is not to be proved in the evil day, but then to be obeyed unquestioning; to love glory more that the temptations of wallowing ease, but to know that one's final judge and only rival is oneself: with all our failures in act and thought, these things we learned from noble enemies in Virginia or Georgia or on the Mississippi, thirty years ago' these things we believe to be true. "Life is not lost", said she, "for which is bought Endless renown."

We learned also, and we still believe, that love of country is not yet an idle name.

Dear country! O how dearly dear

Ought thy remembrance, and perpetual band

Be to thy foster child, that from thy hand

Did common breath and nurtured receive!

How brutish is it not to understand

How much to her we owe, that all us gave;

That gave unto us all, whatever good we have!

As for us, our days of combat are over. Our swords are rust. Our guns will thunder no more. The vultures that once wheeled over our heads must be buried with their prey. Whatever of glory must be won in the council or the closet, never again in the field. I do not repine. We have shared the incommunicable experience of war; we have felt, we still feel, the passion of life to its top.

Three years ago died the old colonel of my regiment, Col. William Raymond Lee. He gave the regiment its soul. No man could falter who heard his "Forward, Twentieth!" I went to his funeral. From a side door of the church a body of little choir-boys came in alike a flight of careless doves. At the same time the doors opened at the front, and up the main aisle advanced his coffin, followed by the few grey heads who stood for the men of the Twentieth, the rank and file whom he had loved, and whom he led for the last time. The church was empty. No one remembered the old man whom we were burying, no one save those next to him, and us. And I said to myself, The Twentieth has shrunk to a skeleton, a ghost, a memory, a forgotten name which we other old men alone keep in our hearts. And then I thought: It is right. It is as the colonel would have it. This also is part of the soldier's faith: Having known great things, to be content with silence. Just then there fell into my hands a little song sung by a warlike people on the Danube, which seemed to me fit for a soldier's last word, another song of the sword, but a song of the sword in its scabbard, a song of oblivion and peace.

A soldier has been buried on the battlefield.

And when the wind in the tree-tops roared,

The soldier asked from the deep dark grave;

"Did the banner flutter then?"

"Not so, my hero," the wind replied.

"The fight is done, but the banner won,

Thy comrades of old have born it hence,

Have born it in triumph hence."

Then the soldier spoke from the deep dark grave:

"I am content."

Then he hear the lovers laughing pass,

And the soldier asks once more:

"Are these not the voices of them that love,

That love—and remember me?"

"Not so, my hero," the lovers say,

"We are those that remember not;

For the spring has come and the earth has smiled,

And the dead must be forgot."

Then the soldier spoke from the deep dark grave;

"I am content."

(Source: Posner, Richard "*The Essential Holmes: Selections From the Letters, Speeches, Judicial Opinions, and other Writings of Oliver Wendell Holmes, Jr.*", {University of Chicago Pres, 1992} © 1998 by Bob Dame.

A Soldier's Faith

To have faith is to believe without seeing

Not knowing what is going to happen,

But in the heart of a soldier there is

Faith believing in the defense of our country.

This faith has the ability to put their life on the line

Not thinking of themselves but all mankind,

Those of this country we love so much

To protect the democracy we cherish and such.

To be called to give your life for this cause
Is greater than the understanding of the average,
It comes from a place that believes their life
Is valuable to surrender for a greater reason.

To protect what is ours to possess goes back
When man had to defend his home and family,
Whether it was from animals or starvation
His determination was worth his own life.

As a soldier I look to heaven above
Where God resides with His son Jesus,
I may be seeing you in a short while or so
The reason is worth dying for my country.

Anita DeMeulenaere 2007

Tomb of the Unknowns

The **Tomb of the Unknowns** (also known as the **Tomb of the Unknown Soldier,** although it has never been officially named) is a monument in Arlington National Cemetery, United States dedicated to the American soldiers who have died without their remains being identified.

In late 1920 the United Kingdom had buried one of their unknown warriors in Westminster Abbey. France soon followed with their Tomb of the Unknown Soldier beneath the Arc de Triomjphe, and on March 4, 1921, the United Stated Congress approved the burial of an unidentified American soldier from World War 1 in the plaza of the new Memorial Amphitheater. The tomb's design was selected in a competition won by architect Lorimer Rich.

The white marble sarcophagus has a flat-faced form and is relieved at the corners and along the sides by neo-classic pilasters, or columns, set into the surface. The stone was quarried in Marble, Colorado. Sculpted into the east panel which faces Washington, D.C., are three Greek figures representing Peace, Victory, and Valor, Inscribed on the western panel of the Tomb are the words:

HERE RESTS IN
HONORED GLORY
AN AMERICANSOLDIER
KNOWN BUT TO GOD

The six wreaths carved into the north and south of the tomb represent six major battles of World War 1.

The Tomb sarcophagus was placed above the grave of the Unknown Soldier of World War 1. West of the World War 1 Unknown are the crypts of unknowns from World War 11 (north) and Korea (south). Between the two lies a crypt which once contained an unknown from Vietnam (middle). His remains were identified in 1998 as First Lieutenant Michael Blassie and removed. Those three graves are marked with white marble slabs flush with the plaza.

The Tomb Guards are considered one of the highest honors to serve as a sentinel for the graves of the Unknown Soldiers. Over 80% of soldiers who try out for this duty do not make it. The sentinels do not wear rank insignia on their uniforms, so they do not out rank the Unknowns, whatever their rank may have been. Soldiers serving in other roles, like Relief Commander and Assistant Relief Commander, do wear insignia of their rank.

Walking the Mat is a meticulous ritual the guard follows when watching over the graves:

- The soldier walks twenty one steps across the Tomb. This alludes to the 21-gun salute, which is the highest honor given to any military or foreign dignitary. His or her weapon is always on the shoulder opposite the Tomb (i.e., on the side of the gallery watching he ritual).
- On the 21st step, the soldier turns and faces the Tomb for 21 seconds.
- The soldier then turns to face the other way across the Tomb and changes his or her weapon to the outside shoulder.
- After 21 seconds, the first step is repeated.

This is repeated until the soldier is relieved of duty at the Changing of the Guard.

The mat is replaced once per year. The guards have special metal plates built into their shoes to allow for a more rugged sole and to give the signature click of the heel during maneuvers. The guards are issued sunglasses, due to the bright reflection from the marble surrounding the tomb and the amphitheater.

Changing of the Guard during the day in summer months, from March 15 to September 30, the guard is changed every half hour. During the winter months, from October 1 to March 14, the guard is changed every hour. After the cemetery closes to the public (7 p.m. to 8 a.m. during the winter), the guard is changed every two hours until the cemetery reopens.

The Soldier Poem

There is a special breed of person
Who sees their life bigger than they are,
A commitment stronger than we can imagine
Willing to give their life in the name of freedom.

What makes this special person choose to do this
To fight for their country willing to die?
A greater sense of self and pride within
To protect the values the country provides.

The value taken in the desire to protect
Is about a life willing to give,
To his brothers and sisters who belong
To this wonderful country we sing a song.

The soldier puts on a uniform and protection
To help them to be safe no matter what direction,
Unfortunately we cannot always prevent harm coming
Which can result in a life quiet, not returning.

As this soldier stands before God in this new form
Jesus tells him, "Well done my faithful servant",
You were willing to die for mankind because you love
As I was willing to die for mankind for their salvation.

No Greater Love

There is no greater love from a soldier
Than to lay down their life for their country,
This commitment has to run so deep
It s a part of who they are in their soul.

The shedding of blood is so significant
There is no greater power to behold,
There is life in the blood of a person
How well we all know.

What makes a man or woman do this
To believe this is their calling in life?
To fight for the rights that freedom gives
And protect what we hold so dear.

It has to be a love greater than we can understand
We question whether we could do this?
Thankfully we do not have to answer the call
Our time is past but our children do know.

There was one person, Jesus, 2000 years ago
That loved mankind beyond comprehension,
He chose to give His life as a sacrifice on the cross
Shedding His blood, so now heaven will be our home.

CHAPTER 7: **Sand Castles / America**

*"The lives of our ancestors are like **<u>Sandcastles,</u>** scattered in history. By remembering our past, the good grains of sand become the building material of future generations." (Ewing Family History Pages <u>www.google</u> research "Sandcastles")*

The definition of a Sandcastle is a type of sand sculpture which resembles a miniature building, often a castle. The two basic building ingredients, sand and water, are available in abundance on a sandy beach, so most sand play occurs there or in a sandpit.

Sand castles are typically made by children, simply for the fun of making them. However, adults sometimes engage in contests making sand sculptures, in which the goal is to create structures which don't appear to be constructed just from sand; they can become large and complex. Other vulnerable media are ice and snow, leading to ice sculptures and snow sculptures.

Adults may find sand castle construction to be almost "Zen-like" in its ability to create total focus and relaxation. Whether an hour or a day, alone or with a group of friends or family, sand castle play is increasingly seen as adult leisure time activity for beach vacationers.

Possibly we relate to our life as it is, liken to a sandcastle. We are absorbed in its coming together with an accumulation of small pieces. Bringing them into uniformity will be the beginning of our castle. Our life begins to take on meaning, so we continue to build. Our family increases and our masterpiece takes on shape. Our goal is to have a complete family as a unit to make what we are working for or looking at our future for the security we seek as human beings. Family is everything from the past to the future.

The Construction

The sand must be fine, or the wetted grains will not stick together. Dry land is loose, wet sand adherent, except when it is too wet. Sand used in the construction may dry or get wetter, changing the integrity of the structure; "landslides" are common.

The main tools for construction are a shovel, although using the hands alone is common, and a bucket or other container to bring water from the sea to the construction site. Also, pieces of wood, etc. can be used to reinforce structures.

Sand sculpting has been around for many decades and has become very popular more recently with hundreds of competitions held all over the world every year. It has become quite sophisticated and can be found in *Guinness World Records*, as well as in many commercial and promotional applications.

The construction is as important as the dream you are following. If that dream wants us to go to the top first, then there is no strong foundation. Our dreams and desires have to follow strong principals and values. Getting to the top before we have reinforced our life on Godly principles;, putting God first and then our neighbor. Trying to excel at the expense of someone else is wrong. This country is founded on the equal rights of others and hard work is the way to the top.

Some families have been constructed to where success is handed down from one generation to another. Some may think this is a blessing but it can be a curse. This sense of entitlement without working for it does not have the character building qualities as the average person. We know our limitations. Inheritance can have the curse of having no boundaries. As a person you have to have a strong foundation to build your life on or it will crumble.

Completion

Once you have completed your sandcastle, you can stand in awe at how it looks. You are proud of what you have down. You are bursting with pride at what possibility you have achieved. You are King of your Castle and you have arrived. You have that sense that you have done it all by yourself. You are an entity of just one. How wonderful you are because you did this all by yourself.

Is this really true? You could not have done anything without the creative mind God has given you. You could not have come to this place if your family had not given you their blessing. The weather had to be perfect, the sand to be able to construct and the time to do it. All these elements come into play even before you got here. No one stands alone without many people in your life that have given you the foundation you need to even be here. Instead of thinking yourself so wonderful, you should be thanking God for all those people in your life that He has given to you. If you were in any other country but America, you may not even been able to come to the beach.

When we forget our past and the sacrifice those who have gone before us, we make a terrible mistake of forgetting the blood, sweat and tears this country was built on. We have the privilege of living the dream they had in their heart. They believed in this country so much that they even chose to die for it so we can live in freedom. We look at the sandcastle WE built and take pride in what we have done. We forget that no man is an island, he does not stand alone.

We have forgotten gratefulness because we are selfish and self-seeking. We are impatient and we want what we want right now. We have become a nation of quick fixes, easy meals, and easy money. Most of us cannot even imagine being and doing without as some have had to endure. We need to get back to the history of this country and remember what we are made of and who brought us to this place now.

The Tide Comes In

Your perfect sandcastle is completed, you feel the pride of having built this, and then you reach the part of your life you knew was coming but how did it get here so fast? You built this castle for your future and then the tide comes in. You forgot that when you built your castle too close to the waters edge, the tide would come in and wash it away.

As the water comes closer, you try to stop it. You have nothing in your own power to change what is happening. The tide has been coming in and going out as long as the world was created. We know that but somehow we think we will be prepared.

The water has found its way to your castle and instead of a gradual disintegration, it seems to tumble all at once. You want to stop the water but you do not have the power to do so. You are in the hands of the water; all you can do is watch it tumble and become a part of the beach you built it on. In such a short time, all is gone. It happened so fast even though you knew it was going to come.

Our lives are like that. We go along day by day, knowing so many things can happen but really not preparing for it. Something's you cannot prepare for because you did not know it was going to happen. Accidents happen all the time and we know that. We cannot do anything about the things we cannot control.

What about the things we can do something about. As early as we can remember or comprehend, we know there will be a time of retirement. As early as your first paycheck, you are paying for Social Security (FICA). We start our life in the direction we want it to go, and we achieve the goals we have set or changed many times. Life is good, the family is healthy, and life is moving comfortably in the direction that is set.

Through you lifetime of family, work, achieving, building you know retirement is coming but it seems so far away. You hear about preparing for your future, but tomorrow is better than today. I will get to it but first...and the "get to it" never comes. You do invest in you future but not enough to make a difference. Then what you have done, is taken away by your company. You are out the loss.

There are ups and downs but nothing drastic. Suddenly there is the forced retirement you are facing. You do not panic too much because "I can get another job!" This is admirable but not what happens. You cannot get another job and you did not make education a priority. You depended upon the now instead of realizing that you may have to change professions. You are in the "its too late" phase wondering what happened.

You heard that you should have your hours paid for before retirement. You agree but you were intent on getting that bigger, better house, higher payment and another long term mortgage. That' all right, I will add to it later. You never make enough with the cost of living to be able to increase the principal on your mortgage.

You are now forced into retirement, you have debt, you have a mortgage, you have a car payment and your wife has also retired. The social security you have together is less than half of what you are used to live on. Your debt level is covered by the social security but what are you going to live on. You are in a desperate situation.

The tide has come in and washed away all the plans you had for your future. The trouble was that, as with the sandcastle, you built your life too close to the water. You did not prepare for your future the way it would have been wise. Your life is washed away as you knew it and you are facing the possibility of bankruptcy and foreclosure on your home. This was not supposed to happen like this but it has. For me, God is the only answer and I know because this is my story.

You have to simplify your life, get your priorities and change the way you live. We have adopted this sense of entitlement because we deserve it. You have got to learn to be the keeper of your own life and not be selling it to you creditors. Debt is the destruction of life as we know it. Buy now and pay later is self gratification at its worst. By the time you pay for it, you have more needs and then debt accumulates until you are held hostage to your debt.

CHAPTER 8: **The Great American Lie**

The Downfall of America

We have been raised in the greatest country in the world. There is not another in the world that can compare with America. We are a democracy founded by a few men that held to the principles I believe God wanted established for us. When we put God first, then we know it is right.

What happens when we stray from our Christian heritage and start making decision which is pleasing to the people? Human beings by nature are selfish so we can surmise that if we make decisions to please the people and do not stand on Godly principles that have gone before; we create a world that is not pleasing to God.

I do not know where you are in this world with the life you are living. Are you setting goals to a future which will fulfill the American dream or has life robbed you of your expectations? What has gone wrong and who is to blame?

In my opinion, in very simple terms it has been the credit card. We have fallen into the trap that we need to have one to exist. If you look at the world around you, it has evolved to where we are dependent on borrowing other people money. You can have now and pay later. This is true but before you pay the later, more needs occur and you are paying for what you already have. It is a vicious cycle that has made our lives held hostage by a bank the profits from you mistake. You did not think it was a mistake because this is how you have been functioning. Believe it or not there was a C.O.D. plan where you will pay when delivered. All the companies you order from by catalog or on-line, it is a credit card. I find my salvation in the debit card. I can still function in this world the way it is setup but if I do not have the money in my account, I cannot use the debit card. Even your checkout is so much easier with a debit card. You do not even have to sign your name. The transaction goes right to your bank. If you do not have the money, there is no purchase.

Let us explore the events in history that brought us to this place where we have sold our soul to money and the purchase of things. The mortgage of a home was not into existence; people used to by homes and cars with cash. When, how and why did this all change.

How many times have you said I am not going to do this or that? How many times have you said I am not going to be this or that? One morning you wake up and you have become that very person.

What the world has become is a result of greed and have now, pay later. I want, I get, I will pay. You have not learned to save for what you need, you have not learned to save for what you need and the "wanter is greater than the supplier" so you start borrowing and you are now trapped into the lie that you can have now. We pass this mentality down from one generation to the next. You see it on campuses where students have cards for their needs but usually it pays for their wants.

My grandchildren have cell phones, credit cards and all have abused the privilege. They are just not mature enough to be responsibility. They want and the world is giving it to them. Now the destruction begins.

Where Did It All Begin?

The **Barter System** is a type of trade that doesn't use any medium of exchange, in which goods or services are exchanged for other goods and/or services. It can be bilateral or multilateral as trade.

Barter and money have different means of balancing an economic exchange. Barter is used in societies where no monetary system exists. When there is one, it is also used, especially in economies suffering from a very unstable currency (as when hyperinflation hits).

In **Transaction Issues** Barter is possible when coincidence of wants of economic factors enables an exchange cycle between their bids. Before any transaction can be undertaken, each party must be able to supply something another party desires.

- Some communities develop a system of intermediaries who can store, trade, and warehouse commodities, but who may suffer economic risk.
- Others develop a system with a virtual value unit ("barter dollars," for example) to measure and balance exchanges, very similar to a monetary system.
- Multilateral barter is more complex to settle but allows trades that would not be possible with bilateral barter. This complexity can e reduced by *open barter* software.
- On the west coast of the United States the Beyond Barter organization extends the concept to a system based on free sharing of services. Although there's no attempt to balance contributions in individual transactions, controls ensure that members are not overburdened.

In the **History of Barter** to organize production and to distribute goods and services among their populations, many pre-capitalist or pre-market economies relied on tradition, top-down command, or community democracy instead of market exchange organized using barter. Relations of reciprocity and/or redistribution substituted for market exchange. Trade and barter were primarily reserved for trade between communities or countries. It is also used when the monetary system failed to measure the economic value of goods.

Barter becomes more ad more difficult as people become dispossessed of the means of production of widely-needed goods. For example, if money were to be severely devalued in the United States, most people would have little of value to trade for food (since the farmer can only use so many cars, etc.).

It is used on important transactions between firms or countries to exchange economic values, when monetary constraints are too expensive for the economic factors.

The History of Banking

The **history of banking** is closely related to the history of money. As monetary payments became important, people looked for ways to safely store their money. As trade grew, merchants looked for ways of borrowing money to fund expeditions.

The **first banks** were probably the religious temples of the ancient world

In them was stored gold in the form of easy-to-carry compressed plates. Their owners justly felt that temples were the safest places to store their gold as they were constantly attended and well built and were sacred, thus deterring would-be thieves. There are extent records of loans from the 18th century BC in Babylon that were made by temple priests to merchants.

The **history of western banking** is usually traced back to the coffee houses of London. The London Royal Exchange was established in 1565. At that time moneychangers were already called bankers, though the term "bank" usually referred to their offices, and did not carry the meaning it does today. There was also a hierarchical order among professionals; at the top were the bankers who did business with heads of state, next were the city exchanges, and at the bottom were the pawn shops or "Lombard's". Most European cities today have a Lombard street where the pawn shop was located.

Capitalism began around the time of Adam Smith (1776) there was a massive growth in the banking industry. Within the new system of ownership and investment, money holders were able to reduce the State's intervention in economic affairs, remove barriers to competition, and, in general, allow anyone willing to work hard enough – and who also has access to capital – to become a capitalist. It wasn't until over 100 years after Adam Smith, however, that US companies began to apply his policies in large scale and shift the financial power from England to America.

The growth of commercial banking began to emerge as a world financial center by the early 1900's in New York. Companies and individuals acquired large investments in (other) companies in the US and Europe, resulting in the first true market integration. This comparatively high level of market integration proved especially beneficial when World War 1 came – both sides in the conflict sought funds from the United States, by issuing new securities and selling existing holdings, though the Allied Powers raised by far the larger amounts. Being a lender to the world resulted in the largest growth of a financial economy to that point.

The stock market crash in 1929 was a global event – markets crashed everywhere, all at the same time, and the volume of foreign selling orders was high The Great Depression followed, and the banks were blamed for it, although the evidence has never been strong to connect the speculative activities of the banks during the 1920's with either the crash or the subsequent depression of the 1930's. Nonetheless, there were three prominent results from these events that had great effect on American banking.

- The first was the passage of the Banking Act of 1933 that provided for the Federal Deposit Insurance system and the Glass-Steagall provisions that completely separated commercial banking and securities activities.
- Second was the depression itself, which led in the end to World Warr 11 and a 30-year period in which banking as confined to basic, slow-growing deposit taking and loan making within a limited local market only.
- And third was the rising importance of the government in deciding financial matters, especially during the post-war recovery period. As a consequence, there was comparatively little for banks or securities firms to do from the early 1930's until the early 1960's.

In the 1970's, a number of smaller crashes tied to the policies put in place following the depression, resulted in deregulation and privatization of government-owned enterprises in the 1980's, indication that governments of industrial countries around the world found private-sector solutions to problems of economic growth and development preferable to state-operated, semi-socialist programs. This spurred a trend that was already prevalent in the business sector, large companies becoming global and dealing with customers, suppliers, manufacturing, and information centers all over the world.

Global banking and capital market services proliferated during the 1980's and 1990's as a result of a great increase in demand from companies, governments, and financial institution, but also because financial market conditions were buoyant and, on the whole, bullish. Interest rates in the United States declined from about 15% for two-year U.S. Treasury notes to about 5% during the 20-year period, and financial assets grew then at a rate approximately twice the rate of the world economy. Such growth rate would have been lower, in the last twenty years, were it not for the profound effects of the internationalization of financial markets especially U.S. Foreign investments, particularly from Japan, who not only provided the funds to corporations in the U.S., but also helped finance the federal government; thus, transforming the U.S. stock market by far into the largest in the world.

Nevertheless, in recent years, the dominance of U.S. financial markets has been disappearing and there has been an increasing interest in foreign stocks. The extraordinary growth of foreign financial markets results from both large increases in the pool of savings in foreign countries, such as Japan, and, especially, the deregulation of foreign financial markets, which has enabled them to expand their activities. Thus, American corporations and banks have started seeking investment opportunities abroad, prompting the development in the U.S. of mutual finds specializing in trading in foreign stock markets.

Such growing internationalization and opportunity in financial services has entirely changed the competitive landscape, as now many banks have demonstrated a preference for the "universal banking" model so prevalent in Europe. Universal banks are free to engage in all forms of financial services. Make investments in client companies, and function as much as possible as a "one-stop" supplier of both retail and wholesale financial services.

Many such possible alignments could be accomplished only by large acquisitions, and there were many of them. By the end of 2000, a year in which a record level of financial services transactions with a market value of $10.5 trillion occurred, the tip ten banks commanded a market share of more that 80% and the tip five, 55%. Of the top ten banks ranked by market share, seven were large universal-type banks (three American and four European), and the remaining three were large U.S. investment banks who between them accounted for a 33% market share.

This growth and opportunity also led to an unexpected outcome; entrance into the market of other financial intermediaries: non-banks. Large corporate players were beginning to find their way into the financial service community, offering competition to established banks. The main services offered included insurances, pension, mutual, money market and hedge funds, loans and credits and securities. Indeed, by the end of 2001 the market capitalization of the world's 15 largest financial services providers included four non-banks.

In recent years, the process of financial innovation has advanced enormously increasing the importance and profitability of non-bank finance. Such profitability priory restricted to the non-banking industry, has prompted the Office of the Comptroller of the Currency (OCC) to encourage banks to explore other financial instruments, diversifying banks' business as well as improving banking economic health. Hence, as the distinct financial instruments are being explored and adopted by the banking and non-banking industries, the distinction between different financial institutions is gradually vanishing.

A recent innovation in 2005 was the creation of prosper.com, a financial institution based on the idea of a person-to-person (P2P) system. Prosper.com allows individuals and groups to bid on interest rates for loans as either borrowers or lenders, effectively making each individual person a banking institution. The system is protected by credit ratings and identity verification.

Taxes

The **History of Taxation Levels** was first known in Ancient Egypt around 3000 BC – 2800 BC in the first dynasty of the Old Kingdom. Records from the time document that the Pharaoh would conduct a biennial tour of the kingdom, collecting tax revenues from the people. Early taxation is also described in the Bible. In Genesis 47:24 (NIV) it states, *"But when the crop comes in, give a fifth of it to Pharaoh. The other four-fifths you may keep as seed for the fields and as food for yourselves and your households and your children."* Joseph was telling the people of Egypt how to divide their crop, providing a portion to the Pharaoh. A share (20%) of the crop was the tax. While not money, the idea is the same.

Quite a few records of the government tax collection in Europe since at least the 17th century is still available today. But the taxation levels are hard to compare to the size and flow of the economy since production numbers are not as readily available.

Taxes are most often levied as a percentage, called the **tax rate.** An important distinction when talking about tax rates is to distinguish between the marginal rate and the effective (average) rate. The effective rate is the total tax paid divided by the total amount the tax is paid on, while the marginal rate is the rate paid on the next dollar of income earned.

An **ad valorem tax** is one where the tax base is the value of a good, service, or property. Sales taxes, tariffs, property taxes, inheritance taxes, and value added taxes are different types of as valorem tax. An ad valorem tax is typically imposed at the time of a transaction (sales tax or value added tax (VAT) but it may be imposed on an annual basis (property tax) or in connection with another significant event (inheritance tax or tariffs). An alternative to ad valorem taxation is an excise tax, where the tax base is the quantity of something, regardless of its price.

Saving Money

Saving money is the solution to balancing life as we live it. We make money, have to spend money and we need to save money. We have to stay within our budget (the amount of money we take in and live on). Saving money should be a part of our budget. A good financial advisor who I admire once told me of a simple solution to your budget is: 10% for your tithes to the Lord, 10% in your saving which is paying you, and live on the 80% that is left. This simple formula really tells it all. If we would start out life like this, the foundation would be formed to stick by and teach your children. Now we are teaching them to by now and pay later. Tithing and saving money are not a part of our budget but should be. Our actions do speak louder that our words to our children.

It was said, the simplest way to save money is to spend little and spend it sensibly: to be thrifty. You can also save your money by keeping it in a safe place. A third way is to 'invest' your money wisely: to spend it on something with a dependable value.

Why save? Money is itself a convenient means of saving wealth. Other things of value, such as food or animals, cannot be kept for ever, but coins will last for long periods without deteriorating. This is shown by the thousands of ancient coins dug up every year.

But money does need to be looked after. It might fall into the wrong hands, or the temptation to spend it unwisely may be too great to resist. More simply, it might lose its value.

What to save? Money is not necessarily the most sensible material to save. Its value seems fixed, but the same sum of money may not always buy the same amount. There is little point in saving if it will buy less as time passes.

It may be better to save up what you will need, or some other durable commodity whose value in money (or, better still, in other commodities) will increase.

Where should you put the money you save? You could just hide it. Or, to be safe, you could give it to a bank to look after. But neither choice would take account of the money's tendency to lose is value.

The way around this is invest your money: to exchange it for something whose value will last or increase, or lend it at interest, so that you get back more than you lent.

The Basic Principles of Investing is to start investing now. Do not procrastinate. Begin now because an early start can make all the difference. An early start provides a long time horizon for compounding to show its true benefit for the investor.

Know yourself and your current situation: what is your current net worth, monthly income and expenses? Where can your reduce your expenses? How much debt are you carrying? At what rate of interest? How much are you saving? How are you investing it? What are your returns?

Your Financial Goals: What are they? How much will you need to achieve them? Are you on the right track?

Risk Tolerance level: How much risk are you willing and able to accept? Risk tolerance is determined by your personality, age, job security, health, net worth, emergency fund, and the length of your investing horizon.

Sort out your finances before you even think about investing; know where your money goes each month. Track your spending habits. If you're carrying debt at a high rate of interest, especially credit card debt, you should unburden yourself before you begin investing. Save enough to cover three to six months of expensed for emergencies. Never invest in anything you don't understand.

Invest long term and do not be influenced by short-term fluctuations. These are inevitable as all economies as well as business experience the boom and bust cycle. Don't try to time the market. Get in and stay in. Review your plan periodically, and whenever your needs or circumstances change. If you are not confident that your plan makes sense, talk to an investment advisor or someone you trust.

Investing in Stocks and Mutual Funds which are a long term view to help you safely invest in the 'riskier' investments, such as stocks, which the market rewards in general. This requires patience and discipline, but it increases returns. This approach reduces your choices to two: stocks and stock mutual finds. In the long run, they're the winners. The additional risk is worth it due to the power of compounding. 10% a year for 20 years if 570%, but 7% a year for 20 years is only 280%.

Arm yourself with knowledge and always do your homework. Knowledge is power. Understand personal finance matters that could affect you. Understand your current investments and the risks associated with them. Be cautious when evaluating the advice of anyone with a vested interest.

If you're going to invest in stocks, research companies until you understand them. Consider joining an investment club. Examine historical data or participate in a stock market simulation. If you don't have the time, consider mutual finds, especially index finds.

Get help if you need it because the do-it-yourself approach may not be suitable for everyone. If you try it and it's not working, or you're afraid to try it at all, or you don't have the time or desire, then you should seek professional assistance. If you want others to handle your financial affairs for you, remain involved to some degree, to make sure your money is being spent wisely.

Social Security in the United States currently refers to the Federal Old-Age, Survivors, and Disability Insurance (OASDI) program.

The original Social Security Act and the current version of the Act, as amended encompass several social welfare or social insurance programs.

Social Security in the United States is a social insurance program funded through dedicated payroll taxes called FICA (Federal Insurance Contributions Act). Tax deposits are formally entrusted to Federal Old-Age and Survivor Insurance Trust Fund, or Federal Disability Insurance Trust Fund, Federal hospital Insurance Trust Fund or the Federal Supplementary Medical Insurance Trust Fund. The main part of the program is sometimes abbreviated (OASDI), in reference to its three beneficiaries (OA for retirement, S for widows and survivors income, D for the disabled, and I for insurance). When initially signed into law by President Franklin D. Roosevelt in 1935, the term *Social security* covered unemployment insurance as well. The term, in everyday speech, is used only to refer to the benefits for retirement, disability, survivorship, and death, which are the four main benefits provided by traditional private-sector pension plans. In 2004, the U.S. Social Security system paid out almost $500 billion in benefits. By dollars paid, the U.S. Social Security program is the largest government program in the world.

Social Security is set up that at the age of 65, which is changing with added months depending on your age, you are entitled to benefits that have accumulated in your working years. It is not meant to be your entire retirement income. The Medicare Medical portion of the program will not completely cover your medical needs. You need a supplemental program as well.

The cost of living deteriorates your fixed income so that what you thought would be enough to retire on, will not cover all your needs. If you do not have your house paid for, you should not consider retiring unless there is not mortgage. The taxes and insurance with be enough to have to pay for.

Investing for your retirement has to be a priority and it will come sooner than later. If you are disabled and cannot work, you must plan for this. If you carry debt it will drown your finances and hold you in bondage so that the income you have will go to paying off your debt or put you home into fore closure.

You cannot plan for everything but wise decisions are a must. Thinking past today so that tomorrow will be possible when it arrives.

The Answer: Borrowing Money

I would imagine the first place to find the answer to your financial situation is to borrow money. We generally go to our family as the first means to our dilemma. As children, mom and dad are the answer. We continue with this mentality unless mom and dad cut off the apron strings. The hardest thing in the world may be having to say "no" to your children but it has to be done. The parent's financial future is in jeopardy if they take what they have accumulated and start bailing out their children's financial problems.

A situation where it is very common in families is with immigrants settling in another country and helping to support the family until they can reciprocate and return the money as they can. Often it becomes a situation they the rest of the family can follow and migrate to that country also.

We seem to borrow money for all sorts of things. Education would be a priority because you are investing in your future. Most parents plan on helping with their children's higher education or help in them getting a scholarship or a loan. When a child takes responsibility to do well in school, it takes such a burden off the parents and the child has tremendous pride in him. This is the ideal scenario.

Financing – Mortgages, Cars, Loans, etc

With borrowing money usually it has to be paid back some how. An interest is charged on the money borrowed with the promise that the debt will be paid in full. If you finance from a lending institution, such as a bank, credit union, or a credit company you will pay interest on that money and they will keep track of your credit account payments which give you a credit rating. This responsibility is the beginning of your financial history.

The purchase of your first house will have to be financed by a mortgage company. They will charge you interest on the money borrowed. This is probably the longest investment and the most expensive you will ever have.

To purchase your first car it will come from the financing of the car company, band or credit union. This is not as long but at the end of the contract, your car is not worth much in terms of getting back on your investment. The good thing is that you have been able to drive the car before it is paid for. Car insurance is also a monthly investment on your car and necessary or you do not drive or get your license for the car. Even if you pay cash for the car, maintenance and insurance is continually part of owning a car.

The Credit Card

We are now introduced to the credit card. This is the gold mine that you think will save your life. You can buy now and pay later; anything you want or need. The economy is so saturated with credit card they are plaguing college students with financial independence. Students do not have the maturity and self control just like most of us. This should be illegal but it is not. Too many parents feel it is a good idea if their child needs something but they use it on unnecessary things. It is too easy to draw a line between a want and a need.

With my credit card experience, I always planned on paying off the balance. What I did not take into account is that I have more needs in a month and by the time the bill comes, I cannot pay off the debt. So then I carry a balance and then next month I will pay off the balance. Then another need next month and the cycle continues.

What happened to me was the fact that everything started costing too much. The clothes for the kids, the doctor appointments, the broken washing machine; you name it and it all cost more than I could afford. Our income could not keep up with our needs. Times of unemployment were the worst. The interruption of income always sets you back. Our debt finally put us into bankruptcy and fore closure of our home because of a force retirement before we were ready to embrace that time in our life. You never know so all you can do is your best at what you have. My weapon of warfare was prayer and to me it was the best. God carried us through and made a way where we thought it could not be possible.

You have to get back to a cash and carry mentality. If you do not have the money, you do not buy. You would be surprised at how it will feel if you do wait until you have the money. An emergency is one thing you cannot control. A debit card will do everything a credit card will do except it will take the money out of your checking account. The only thing you have to do is deduct the amount from the balance in your check book. It is the same as paying your bills on-line. The money is withdrawn from your account. You are being a responsible person with your finances.

The Credit Card Poem

This little piece of plastic all shiny
I am told it is my security,
If I have a problem I need some money
It will rescue me without any questions.

I feel secure and it is so nice to have
Even if I need something I can use,
What a wonderful friend to have
At my beckon call as I demand.

I can spend, spend, spend as I desire
All I have to do is pay back some,
This is great then I can have more
To fill me up with much galore.

At month's end I see the results
My first month relationship with my card,
I open up the envelop and it is revealed
I spent so much I cannot not believe.

I was going to pay it all back
But once I got started I could not stop,
I did not think I spent so much
Now I owe and the interest is theirs.

The Result: Debt

Debt is that monster than holds us in Bondage. Spending money is therapeutic and the result is that we have obtained something. It can be good or bad; it has satisfied the flesh for the moment until we want again.

Desire is a strong emotion that needs a lot of discipline. Keeping our wants and needs separate is difficult in a world that makes you believe you can have anything you want. With the accessibility of money through credit, and making good money, we can have anything now and pay later. It used to be saving for what you want and then buy. Often by the time you save the money, the urge has passed and you have not fallen into the category "wants" instead of "needs". We are told there are so many things that we need or have to have. Even the smallest of children who watch TV see a want to get the parent to buy.

Most marriages fall into the maze of financial ruin because both do not agree. Entitlement seems to be a part of our vocabulary. Men and women do not see wants and needs the same. Both should have access to finances so that they can both supply what they feel is necessary. Large decisions or ones that need financing have to be negotiated and agreed upon. If you agree with your partner do not come back later with regret. If you agree, let it go. If you cannot agree, let it go possibly until a better time. Thinking things over often look different another day.

Debt is one of those blind parts of life that are there but we tend to over look what it is doing to us. It is almost like a lie, hidden so no one sees but you know it is there. In reality it is a lie because you are saying you own something and yet you are still paying for it. The façade presented to your family and neighbors looks good but inside there is deterioration. It is almost like putting clean clothes on a dirty body. You appear to be clean because of the clean clothes but your body is dirty and no one can see that. This is a lie because you are saying one thing and doing another.

The bondage of debt will control your life. You will get to the point where you cannot get out and you keep going deeper. You have to either make more money or change your way of living. Often with inflation, a second job is necessary for the husband or the wife has to go to work. Being wise in your finances early in your life is such an asset. Hopefully your parents were a good role model in the role of finances and running their home. If the pattern was good and you saw positive reinforcements, then you should continue to do the same. If you had poor role models, seek help to break habit you were used to seeing. You can change and you can make a difference.

Debt Poem

Debt is never meant to be in our life
We thought we knew we should save,
But things happen so our needs increase
Then the demand is greater than the supply.

Just this once I will get help
I shall repay as soon as I can,
Another problems does arise
Now I have two instead of one.

Do not panic I can take care of the first
But along comes three and we are torn,
Do I deal with what I should
Or do I borrow more to pay off one?

Now the interest is accumulating daily
If I did not have a balance it would disappear,
But because I could not do what I want
My debt is accumulating one on top of the other.

This ugly word which should be innocent
But this world is made up of wants and needs,
Have I satisfied only my needs to be free
Or have I purchased my wants along with these?

The Bondage Poem

The shackles are invisible
But hold as if they are real,
You are in bondage of something
That God wants you to be free.

We are not meant to be held
In a state that controls our lives,
We are a Child of God born of Him
Revealed in the Spirit of our hearts.

We must determine to loose the chains
That tie us to this wrong,
The need to release ourselves is so strong
But your will does not have the strength.

God does not want us to live
In this state that controls our lives,
Freedom is the key to release the bondage
Determined by your own will.

Faith in God to deliver the healing
Is the medicine needed for your pain,
Believe He is there every minute
To carry you through what remains.

CHAPTER 9: **The Conclusion of Human Rights**

Human Rights refer to universal rights of human beings regardless of jurisdiction or other factors, such s ethnicity, nationality, religion, or sex.

The ideas of human rights descended from the philosophical idea of natural rights; some recognize no difference between the two and regard both as label for the same thing while others choose to keep the terms separate to eliminate association with some features traditionally associated with natural rights.

As is evident in the United Nations Universal Declaration of Human Rights, human rights, at least in the post-war period, are conceptualized as based on inherent human dignity, retaining their universal character.

The existence, validity and the content of human rights continue to be the subject to debate in philosophy and political science and many other forms. Legally, human rights are defined in international law and covenants, and further, in the domestic laws of many states. However, for many people the doctrine of human rights goes beyond law and forms a fundamental moral basis for regulating the contemporary geo-political order. For them, they are democratic ideals. (Wikipedia, the free encyclopedia www.google.com)

I am sitting in the Library and I am looking at all the books pertaining to American History. I see The Constitution, The Bill of Rights, and The Declaration of Independence in particular. As I am starring at these wonderful books the record our history, I have a vision that is very real to me.

All the books are standing upright like soldiers standing in a row. Then I see in the center of this vision scorching paper and then fire burning a hole in the center and the paper folding back. What I see revealed now are the books fallen down on their side as would be wounded soldiers. The firm standing, upright books have now fallen off their foundation; they are still on the self but not securely in place where they were put.

The Vision

This is how I evaluate this vision. We are still living as our forefathers believed but we have fallen off our foundation. We have strayed too far to the left, veering away from the Godly Documents our forefathers established for this country. This country was founded on the Godly principals that they believed and they knew we needed to hold to those beliefs. They believed in the Bible as the Word of God and I believe God inspired them to write these documents through His eyes. I believed they prayed over every word written and every word meant just what it says. If they started to steer away from course, they came back on track. They knew the human rights of all mankind were a Godly principal. We are a Christian nation and they wanted this country to stay that way. They knew Freedom for all in their beliefs and the right of all to life, liberty and property is what God taught in the Bible. We are not to be any respecter of anyone.

Back on course

We need to get back on course. It is not too late but as long as we put money and power ahead of people we are definitely in trouble. The politicians have been controlled by "special interests" people who want their own agenda put ahead of the needs of the people. We probably spend more to please these people than we give to those in need. I do not understand why every election it is the same old thing. We need health care for all people, education should be number one because this is power for our country, and affordable living with expenses for the retired and those in need.

Medicine is so outrageous. The aspirin was discovered as a pain reliever and it has stood the hands of time. Penicillin was discovered and it changed history. These are simple solutions that we have come to complicate. Most all remedies are an extension of these and they cost next to nothing in the large scope of things. How did we get to this place?

I love my country but now that I am in my sixties, I see a larger picture over many years. I was six when we got our first TV, my parents had Studebaker's (that is a car in the 1940's-50); we were post depression. My father was a Doctor at the Oakland County TB Sanitarium and as Medical Director a house was provided for him and his family. We received food from the hospital and the house was ours to live in.

When my father decided to go out on his own, he and my mother had to purchase a house, furniture, etc. They did go into debt because they were not able to save money while at the Sanitarium. His pay was more perks from the hospital than monetary compensation for the work he did. This was their downfall as most every American, the overwhelming necessity to borrow money so we can purchase what we need. The embracing of buy now and pay later made it possible for everyone to be equal.

This lie has been the demise of all Americans. We have sold our soul to the almighty dollar and are in bondage to debt. Our creditor owns us, our country controls us with the belief that we can and we can be anything we want if we try hard enough. This is true but we have to borrow money for our children to go to College and they graduate with massive debt. Our country has gotten out of financial balance that the parents cannot afford their own life let alone pay for the education of their children. We could not save the money because of our debt level. If we could have only stayed where we buy now when we have the money, our creditors would not own us and our paycheck. Could we ever in a million years thought we would pay this much for a house, a car, medical and education. No wonder our country is in trouble. The politicians have moved us to the left so far that we do not even trust our politicians and they are controlled by the party they represent.

I am sad because I love this country and we have sold out ourselves because of personal gain. Our affluence has us in a place now that other people want to destroy us in the name of their God and cleansing the wealth and prosperity of this country. They are a self-imposed cleansing unit determined to destroy us. They are letting Satan use them to destroy the God in this country. In fact, some Americans have been doing the same thing. They are not only denying God but they are letting those determined to take God out of this country in the name of evolution and equal rights, that they are helping the enemy. This country was founded on God and it is great because God has favored us. This will change if we do not stop the tyranny and destruction of the human spirit and get back to the basics that our forefathers designed in the U.S. Constitution. This is our Bible of the country, the Bill of Rights is the Ten Commandments of this country, and the Declaration of Independence is our determination to be free and be the democracy we embrace. *"Oh God, forgive us for taking our eyes off of you and onto ourselves. This selfishness for personal gain has gotten us to where we are today. We need to go back to where the rules were set by those that were here before us. You inspired them to set up the documents they presented to this country and they were meant to be the Bible people are to live by. Help us, O Lord, to go back to our roots, embrace the love we had for this country and be the citizen we were meant to be. Thank you Lord, in your name we pray. Amen.*

CHAPTER 10: **The "Y" factor**

To give this book an analogy, it would be to visualize the capital letter "Y". Two separate entities coming together as one. We have our life as humans in this world and we have a spiritual life. In order to be a complete person, you have to be complete with body, soul and spirit.

God has to be in all parts of our lives. We cannot have a true democratic society without God. He is our wisdom in matters of leading this awesome country in the principals of our fathers laid down for us. These rules were inspired by Godly men and they knew they had to have God in all aspects of the government to rule wisely. Man cannot receive the guidance they need to make honest and fair judgment. It has to have a basis of truth and that is the bible.

The bench mark for truth is in the bible for the country and for our spiritual growth. How to love God and to love your neighbor can only come from a source greater than that of human instincts. We often respond with what we think or feel instead of what is right or wrong. The bible will tell you exactly what God wants in any situation. It is bigger that anyone or us.

Tying the Two Together

As I thought on both parts of our lives, the two cannot successful stand on its own. We need God in both parts of our lives.

When government tries to take God out of the country and strays from the foundation that was set for us from our fore fathers, we are in trouble. There are those who have fought to separate Church and State. This does not mean we take God out of the country. Our fore fathers wanted the Bible taught as part of the curriculum in school. This is why the schools are in trouble. They are doing everything on their own. We need God back.

Even in churches, there are those who want to let your conscience be your guide. This is not of God either. The bible has to be your guide. Your conscience can be formed from your past, giving you a false sense of right and wrong. Truth has to be the deciding factor and that comes from God's word, the Bible.

There are those who call God by a name other than the God of Abraham, Isaac and Jacob. The God of the Holy Trinity, spoken of by Jesus and is weaved throughout the Old and New Testament. There is only one God and one God only. Jesus is the Christ, the Son of God and the Holy Spirit is the Spirit of God. All others are blasphemies.

God meant this world to be founded on Godly principles and to worship in churches everywhere. When we feel we do not need God or put something ahead of God, then there is failure. You will never be happy and eternity is out of your grasp.

God is specific in His Word telling us what He expects of us. We are to obey but the obedience is rewarded by eternity with Him. God never expects more from us than we are able or capable. He does expect us to follow Him after we learn of His ways.

The standing foundation for the two legs is God. Both need this foundation to exist with strength and conviction. Without God in our spiritual life and our human life, chaos and unhappiness exist. Something will always be missing. The foundation that God knows we need is Him. He has provided both in the documents made available to us. The constitution and the bible are the basis for truth. Anything that tries to change that or compromise the original meaning is wrong. This is what God gave us and He wants it to stand as it is. Do not change anything, even though generation after generation pass by the word of God remains strong.

Our Spiritual Rights

When we take the Christian side of the "Y", we see how important it is to the whole. God meant for this world to be established on Christ. As we saw in the Garden of Eden, sin was established. We had to come back to a relationship with God because sin separates us from God. Jesus made this possible with His death and resurrection. The journey from our birth is a work in process. We have to continually strive to be what God wants us to be.

Discipline is probably the one factor that is the hardest to defeat. The flesh is so strong; it takes strength of will power to overcome. We are challenged to see what we are made of. God gave His life for us. The least we can do is live for Him. We need to crucify the flesh so the spirit can grow.

Our Christian rights are weaved throughout the bible. If we follow the pattern God has set before us, our rights will remain strong. As a Christian, our rights are heaven. If we follow the rules that Jesus set down for us for redemption, live the way the bible tells us, than heaven will be our home.

Our Human Rights

The constitution is very specific about the rights of man. They too were put down by godly men who had a strong faith in God. Everyone is to be treated equally regardless of race, color, creed, financial status, political position, or innocent until proven guilty. Without God we cannot be fair and righteous because we will judge from our human thoughts and feeling. God judges from the heart and the principles laid down in the bible are the same principles laid down in the constitution and the bill of rights.

Our human rights are so important to the balance of this world. Everyone should be able to live their own life if they follow the rules. When we are forced to live and believe a different way than ours, than our human rights are now destroyed. Our fore fathers wanted to protect us from this.

Our human rights are the other leg of the "Y". You need both legs to make the "Y". Each is separate but come together like the joining of two rivers into a common flow of water. Each was separate but now become one.

Epilogue

My vision is complete as I have shared with you. God gave me this vision and I felt compelled to write to and for those who would listen.

Realize how far left we have come from what this country was founded on. When it comes to voting for our representatives, how many of them stand on the principles of God and country? Do they represent the country with the constitution and the laws made for man? Do they believe the bible is the inspired word of God?

It is getting harder to distinguish what they believe. You may have to dig deeper to find the answers. I pray for the guidance of the Holy Spirit to teach me what I need to know. I want God's man in office and I want God's man leading my church. Too often, the world compromises its values and stands to please others. You want someone that wants to please God.

-Anita DeMeulenaere

Acknowledgements:

My references have come from The Bible (NIV and the Open Bible KJV)

The research from the books of the World Book Encyclopedia.

Research from the computer www.yahoo.com; www.google.com; Wikipedia Free Encyclopedia

www.ingramcontent.com/pod-product-compliance
Lightning Source LLC
LaVergne TN
LVHW011216080426
835509LV00005B/161